D1429383

TWO DECADES OF IRISH WRITING

Douglas Dunn

TWO DECADES OF IRISH WRITING

– A Critical Survey –

A CARCANET PRESS PUBLICATION

SBN 85635 070 2

Acknowledgements are due to the editors of the following magazines, in which some of these essays have appeared: *The Lace Curtain* (for 'On Other Grounds: The Poetry of Brian Coffey' by Stan Smith), *The New Review* (for 'The Poetry of Patrick Kavanagh' by Seamus Heaney and 'Flann O'Brien' by Lorna Sage) and *Poetry Nation* (for 'The Prose of Samuel Beckett' by James Atlas and 'Austin Clarke and Padraic Fallon' by Donald Davie).

First published 1975
by Carcanet Press Limited
266 Councillor Lane
Cheadle Hulme, Cheadle,
Cheshire SK8 5PN

Printed in Great Britain
by Eyre & Spottiswoode Ltd., at Grosvenor Press,
Portsmouth.

Contents

Introduction

IRISH WRITING in the twentieth century has had its fair share of enthusiasts. Yeats, Joyce, and Beckett have attracted, inevitably, many clever and perceptive academic critics. One result has been the emergence of 'Irish literature' as a subject.

Younger Irish writers have both benefited and suffered from this level of concentration on their predecessors. While it might, on occasion, have the baleful side-effect of noticing new work simply on the grounds of its being Irish, another consequence that is less than helpful to Irish writers is that they stand to be for ever discussed in relation to what Yeats said on the same subject, or, as I see from a recent review of John MacGahern's novel, *The Leave-taking*, the extent to which a novelist might echo patterns found in Joyce.

Difficulties raised by the wide acceptance of Yeats by the Irish public have been kicked against at least since the 1930s. Pitiful as it is that Yeats's blend of melody, magic, politics and the spirit of Irishness should have become a burden on the creativity of his contemporaries and successors, there is no denying that his purchase on Irish expectations is as severe as ever. Thomas MacGreevy, Brian Coffey and Denis Devlin were, like Beckett, and like Austin Clarke, cramped by the almost embarrassing prominence of Yeats. These writers are duly acknowledged here, certainly with no intention of downgrading Yeats in the process. Both Brian Coffey, who is alive and well, though in London, and the recently deceased Austin Clarke, are discussed at length.

As a tactic to draw attention to Coffey, and to make way for younger poets such as Augustus Young, Michael Hartnett and Trevor Joyce (and himself), Michael Smith, in his article here, assigns Yeats to 'world literature'. Flattering to Ireland as that must be, it appears almost impertinently brisk. On the other hand, Mr Smith attempts to define a universal principle from the prevailing national attitude to poetry. Aware that Irishness in writing is a thoroughly exportable quality, Mr Smith is like most Irish critics in that he knows it can be exploited at a level lower than that of truth. A primary act of Irish criticism is therefore to discriminate between caricature and authenticity. Readers, and probably some contributors, will find an opportunity to argue with Mr Smith, however, not on the issue of 'caricature'. 'Authenticity', a different salad of shamrocks altogether, is a word which can be made to belong to almost any literary cause.

Beckett, in his essay 'Recent Irish Poetry' (1934), damned what he called the 'accredited theme' of time and place. The celebratory exposure of Irishness it tended to produce was the result, he said, of a 'happily obliterated self', a 'flight from self-awareness'. That this argument still continues will be clear enough from the essays taken together. Nationalism, for instance, is seen by some as little more than a restriction on the possibility of a more spacious literature.

Mr Deane, eloquently engaging the subject of 'Irish Nationalism and Irish Literature', adopts an historical perspective. Poets like John Montague, Derek Mahon and Seamus Deane himself, have been unable to ignore the subject of history, while a search for a comprehensive expression of time and place is peculiarly strong in Seamus Heaney. Few of the interesting Irish poets are untouched by Beckett's remarks, perhaps less as a result of direct influence, than of particular experience. They contain something of Yeats as well as the lesson of Beckett (and, in the North of Ireland, MacNeice). It seemed inevitable, then, that ideas such as 'nationalism', 'provincialism' and 'parochialism' should be re-examined in this collection, as they have been by Seamus Deane and Michael Allen. The opening of Ms Sage's essay on Flann O'Brien — 'That the past impoverishes the present is still, despite Yeats, the great burden of Irish writing' — is an idea they attempt to sophisticate. Mr Smith, for instance, might have said, had he written that, 'because of Yeats'; Mr Deane would shake his head, stand on his politics, and insist that history, or the past, simply cannot go away to leave the Irish writing in the serene state of not having to bother. Louis MacNeice, whose Irishness Michael Longley energetically exposes, wrote that:

> Pride in history is pride
> In living what your fathers died,

— two incisive lines, constituting a very Irish remark. Yet Mr Deane's intellect is not, I think, going to own up to being informed by pride.

What appears to be different in contemporary Irish writing, from, say, English writing, is that Irish writers are forced to make practical *decisions* about their perspectives on history, politics and literature. As a catalyst to talent, the thinking demanded of an Irish writer in that situation ought not to be discounted. There is a searching turbulence about John Montague's poems, for instance, or John MacGahern's novels, an absence of comfortable mannerisms and relaxations, which indicates not only seriousness of purpose, but a scrupulousness of forethought rare in contemporary English letters.

Having been consistently developed, history and locality are unavoidable themes (or a reaction against them is unavoidable for some).

They are themes not merely inherited, but real. 'Searching the Darkness', a phrase from Thomas Kinsella, and Ms Longley's title, indicates that if the subject of history can be unattractively sombre, it has the inevitability of night. Two distinguished books, for example, are reminiscent of Ms Longley's title — MacGahern's *The Dark*, and Heaney's *Door into the Dark*. In such a context an Irish writer's longing for the luxury of a little self-regarding domesticity might be a generous act of rebellion (as, for instance, in James Simmons's poems), though it might also be irresponsible. The drama implicit in this tension can be seen in some of Seamus Deane's poems in his book *Gradual Wars*, where a fine sense of aesthetic control manages both public and domestic themes.

An important point emerges from the essays as a whole. Local connection and experience can be importantly creative, something to hang on to, in both fluid or stagnantly established literary situations. There is a strong sense of this in Terence Brown's article on John Hewitt and W. R. Rodgers, D. E. S. Maxwell's survey of poetry in the North of Ireland, and, particularly, in Seamus Heaney's essay on Patrick Kavanagh.

Mr Garfitt's essay on Irish fiction persuades me that my selection of younger critics was right. An older critic — perhaps even any Irish critic in this case — would have been unlikely to attempt a cleansing of Francis Stuart's reputation. Tom Paulin's sometimes heated criticism of Brian Moore's novels is another example, showing an eagerness to condemn unsurprising or easily anticipated points of view on subjects where, if veracity is everything, then an artistic degree of invention must also be found. As a result, the novels of Maurice Leitch and Florence Mary McDowell, the latter little known outside Ireland, can be seen as more worthy of attention than might have been thought.

That there are other poets and novelists who could have been discussed is not unknown to me. There will, I hope, be other occasions, and *lacunae* are always filled in time, which, if it sounds oracular, is none the less true enough.

There has been no space for discussions of Irish drama. Such plays as Brian Friel's *The Freedom of the City*, or David Rudkin's play about Casement, are, I am prepared to admit, unworthy of being ignored.

I offer my gratitude to all the contributors. Their practices set me a standard to live up to, though this in no way involves them in whatever editorial shortcomings the book might be seen to have.

Both the publisher and I gratefully acknowledge the generous financial support of An Comhairle Ealaion and the Arts Council of Northern Ireland.

Douglas Dunn,
Hull, January 1975

Irish Poetry and
Irish Nationalism
by Seamus Deane

BETWEEN THE end of the Famine in 1848 and Sinn Fein's triumph in 1918, Ireland became a modern nation, even though its development was distorted by the heavy after-effects of its colonial heritage. These, allied with the prohibitive influences of political Catholicism in the South and political Protestantism in the North, retarded a process which was otherwise astonishingly quick to achieve maturity, even though it lost that maturity with comparable speed during the crises which were implicit in the state's violent origins.

The modern Irish literary movement was born during those years although the birth-date is inevitably uncertain – perhaps it was the day of publication of the last part of Standish O'Grady's *History of Ireland* (1878–80); perhaps the year 1893 when the Gaelic League was founded, when J. T. Grein's Independent Theatre in London produced George Moore's *Strike at Arlingford* and Yeats's *Land of Heart's Desire*; when Hyde published his *Love Songs of Connacht* and Stopford Brooke delivered the inaugural lecture to the Irish Literary Society in London on 'The Need and Use of Getting Irish Literature into the English Tongue'.

The Land League was, however, prior to these and first and most effective in mythologizing the past in order to validate its blueprint for the future. Poets and scholars followed suit, more naïvely in some ways, more subtly in others. A. E. Malone's description of O'Grady's book as 'the reconstruction by imaginative processes of the life led by our ancestors in this country' has a direct bearing on the work of Moore, Yeats, Synge and Joyce, the four major writers of the revival. It has also a direct bearing on the nature of Irish nationalism which during this period shared with Irish literature the ambition to transform — in fact, to transfigure — Ireland from an inefficiently and brutally administered British colony into a country of the imagination — whether that imagination be fired by the contemplation of history or of art or of both. Indeed, Irish nationalism made an art of history by making the ideology of separatism from England appear to be the natural culmination of seven hundred years of history. No one can dispute this view as a fact, for it is not a fact; it is a metaphor of triumph, a way of getting history on your side, just as the British have made a similar metaphor of liberty out of their 1688 Protestant revolution. (The exclusive nature of such metaphors is most emphasized these days by the Northern Irish Protestants who have converted it into a dogma.) It is a way, to adapt Namier's phrase, of remembering the future and forgetting the past. Ireland's capacity to do this in politics and in literature gave her a prominence in the political and literary sphere which to many people is still as inexplicable as it is remarkable.

The degree of prominence achieved was to some degree at least in proportion to the intensity of the problem experienced. Ireland, more than most countries, has suffered the contradiction of living politically as if it were one thing while culturally knowing itself to be another. Yet the United Kingdom of Great Britain and Ireland was a domineering political fact which, rather than blighting Irish selfconsciousness, finally led to its emergence in a more radical form than had ever previously existed. The Irish peasantry were politicized, both by economic pressure and by ideology, at roughly the same time as they were transmogrified both by literary men of genius and by propagandists; and riots like those which occurred in 1907 at the production of Synge's *Playboy* showed both processes in a noisy collision which was itself an inevitable product of their silent collusion. A newspaper report on the uproar said of Synge's play: 'It is as if we looked into a mirror for the first time, and found ourselves hideous. We fear to face the thing. We shrink at the word for it. We scream.' The word for 'it', overworked to be sure, was identity.

Such remarks bring to mind the story of the Mexican revolution in which the legendary Zapata's peasants were amazed, in taking over the the mansions of their aristocratic oppressors, to see themselves for the first time in mirrors. The long revolution in Irish society and letters is only slightly different from this. The Land League created its own mirror for the Irish peasantry; so did the I.R.B., so did W. B. Yeats. The Irish did not discover their lost identity in the course of their revolution. They discovered in their identity the course of their lost revolution.

The notion of a Gaelic and free Ireland was a dream of identity to the realization of which the course of revolution was directed. It failed, certainly, but not completely. It succeeded in exhibiting to the world the spectacle of a glittering political dream tested to the point of extinction by political reality and death, and yet gaining new energies just at that point by the very fact of death itself. This aspect of the Irish revolution is frequently dismissed now in the Republic as something which smacks of fascism and racism, even though it is the Orange ideology which makes of race not simply a fetish but also a crisis. Moreover, the Republic is willing to give up almost everything pertaining to its structure in order to retain on the surface a liberal and humane gloss. The unavoidable fact, however, remains; it is of the nature of revolution to be self-sacrificing, not out of a merely abstract passion, but out of the moral passion for self-discovery and of the political passion for self-government. As Carlos Fuentes has put it, in handily Yeatsian terms, a revolution is a battle for 'faces against masks'. The masks of subservience, of foreign power, of colonialism are stripped off the Irish psyche slowly. Still, the political impetus of the initial period of the Irish revolution was given added force by the capacity of the Irish writers to create for each mask its appropriate mirror, to give to nationalist history a physiognomy which betrayed in its changes the evolution of the face of truth. Red Hanrahan, Christy Mahon, Leopold Bloom, Stephen Daedalus, Father Moran are all, even to blatancy, representative Irish figures. Each incarnates an achievement in self-consciousness, a triumph of identity, which is closely meshed in with the democratic impulses which produced Sinn Fein — the meaning of which (Ourselves) is precise and significant. (It's easier to scoff at the name if it is mistranslated as Ourselves Alone.)

Going back to Mexico and Carlos Fuentes (for the last time) I quote the latter's report of the answer a Mexican peasant gave him when, lost in Zapata territory, he asked the name of a village; 'Garduno in times of peace; Zapata in times of war.'

Such an answer reveals an elementary emotion to which in Ireland there is by now a very complex response. The existence of a modern revolutionary tradition entails the existence of an ideological tradition; and an ideology devoted to a place, a specific area, surrounds that place in a shimmering aura of significance which intensifies its brilliance in a period of violence. Marshall McLuhan once remarked that one of the notable features of the modern movements in literature was the immense contribution of the technologically backward areas, like Ireland or the American Deep South. He refers for an explanation to the continued existence in these places of an organic way of life which could sustain important creative work in itself and attract to it the nostalgia of those in the advanced areas who had been divorced by technology from it. In a way, this is no more than a glamorous version of the inspirational Celtic and the utilitarian Anglo-Saxon opposition which was popular about eighty years ago (although it had existed in less focused form long before) and still remains vestigially present in many minds. McLuhan's version has a greater penetrative power than the early form because it describes to some degree a fact which Arnold did not have available to him — the fact of the Irish Revival and of the efflorescence of literature in the American South. Each gave in its way retrospective credence to a flimsy theory, and consequently the suggestion seems to be that the flimsiness of the theory could be remedied by taking it out of the loose and dangerous idiom of race and lending it the more fashionable (and exacting?) idiom of technological advancement. The flimsiness is in a way reduced, but it nevertheless persists. If, however, we also take into account the force of political selfconsciousness (which is what nationalism as a movement primarily involved in Ireland), its prehensile attitude to history, its mythological capacity and its intense view of the homeland as a sacred place, subject in times of violence to stereoscopic alterations, then we move closer to an understanding of writers as diverse as Yeats, William Faulkner and Joyce. Among other things, all three of them take advantage of a history of political defeat for the construction of a tradition of artistic triumph. One becomes transmuted into the other so powerfully that the art can no longer live without the history or the history without the art. Parnell and Joyce, Yeats and 1916, Faulkner and the American Civil War, are regional linkages that have a peculiar bearing on the more than regional range of *Portrait of the Artist, The Statues* and *Go Down Moses.*

So to summarize this sketch of large issues, we might say that there are two respects in which Irish nationalism and Irish literature are intimate with one another. The first is in their regional loyalty, the second is in the transformations to which that loyalty is imaginatively subject in times of violence. This is not, of course, a peculiarly Irish experience. If we look at the development of eighteenth-century 'local attachment' into the intense national feeling of the poetry and prose of the Romantic revival in Germany and in England under the pressure and threat of the French Revolution, then we can understand Ireland's role in this process as a belated if nevertheless surprisingly powerful one. The violence of modern politics and attachment to locality are two inter-twined elements of all modern west European literatures up to the Second World War at least. Ireland would have been extraordinary had it produced a literature less intimate with its political fate, especially as its one differentiating factor was its colonial status, and therefore its differentiating emotion the depth of its attachment to place and to violence simultaneously. England could treat with France politically speaking in 1802 and 1815; but Ireland could not treat with England until it was granted the very status by the denial of which England had initially provoked the revolt. Identity was more deeply and tragically embedded in the Irish political-literary situation than it could be in that of the great nation states. This gave the Irish treatment of that problem — one to become more insistent throughout the world in the coming century — an extraordinary importance. The importance was inevitably magnified by Ireland's position as a European country. Ireland became many things in times of war — Cathleen Ni Houlihan, Saorstat Eireann, Eire, the Republic. It has yet to enjoy a psychological identity belonging to times of peace.

Of course any attempt to discuss the identifiably Irish features of Irish culture and writing has to take into account the hoary problem of the Irish gift for language, with Dublin wit shining in the east and Western poesy shimmering in the west. The notion has its Pan-Celtic extensions; Dylan Thomas and Hugh MacDiarmid suffer from its depredations and deprecations too. A reputation for linguistic extravagance is dangerous, especially when given to small nations by a bigger one which dominates them. By means of it, Celts can stay quaint and stay put; extravagance is their essence and fact not their forte. There are variations on this boring debate — for example, the Scots are factual and mechanical only, the Irish fanciful and disorderly only. As usual, if you want to find a home where a discredited cliché has become an article of loyal belief, go to Northern Ireland. Nevertheless, since we are speaking of literature, we are also speaking of language, and therefore of a kind of language which (we like to hope) has developed its own semiology in which we can perceive the literariness of literature. In Ireland, the problem of language as used by Irish writers is not in the end separable from the problem of the Irish language. A place deprived of its speech is rendered deaf to its traditions. Yet, having experienced this, Ireland, in the course of two centuries, has attempted to master, not only a new language, but also the new traditions that go with it while still feeling, sometimes profoundly, sometimes with irritation, the necessity to keep some sort of formative contact with the 'Hidden Ireland' and its old language, the prints of which are still traceable on the green English sward in which the poems and novels of the Irish revival stand, like transplanted trees which have learned to grow in new conditions. This perhaps explains the fondness of Irish writers for translations, adaptations, renovated versions of some of the more famous Gaelic lyrics and epics. It also reminds us again that the movement towards identity in politics and literature was associated with a movement for the recovery of the old language. The recovery of Irish is part of the dream of total nationhood. In its inevitable imperfection Irish writers in English can never entirely overcome the language problem; Irish writers in Irish are equally hamstrung. One group has no specific tradition and a general audience; the other has only specific tradition and no general audience. But of course out of such anxieties writing may emerge, since they are peculiarly the anxieties of a writer while also being oddly the anxieties of a whole culture. Otherwise I believe that a good deal of the difference between 'Celtic' and 'Saxon' uses of language can be explained by the urban and scientific developments in England which were neither matched in nor transmitted in any substantial form to Ireland. The vivacity of Irish language is an aspect of Irish cultural, social and economic traditions and not the product of some racial gene. This is not to deny its existence or its importance; but it should not be thought of as a useful means of distinguishing Irish writers from others. It should also be said that the English who remarked on Burke's, Shaw's or O'Casey's extravagance of language were not merely pointing out something about the Irish use of words; they were also exposing something about the English notion of extravagance.

There is very little to be gained from directing the argument any further towards the sterile debating points about the writer and his relationship/duties/attitudes to society. That notion of relationship is itself a kind of Pavlovian reaction to the stimulus terms *writer* and *society*. But since I could define neither, I'll avoid using them in that fixed sense. Modern Irish literature has been first cousin to scholarship, to symbolism and to politics, and it is in the web of *those* actual relationships that its authors can be best understood. Because of them, it is a body of literature given to ideologies and theologies; the doctrinaire elements in Joyce, Yeats, Flann O'Brien, O'Casey and Beckett are strong and indigenous parts of their work, even though the force of commitment is in most cases devoted to 'art' or 'writing'. Except for O'Casey, the least developed of them, they all fuse the ethic with the aesthetic impulse. Their doctrinaire attitudes are absorbed into the various works by a style of personal heroism which is, in its essence, that of the artist-ideologue, of a man looking for and finding a language in which the phenomenon of power can be expressed in terms of a theology of the self.

To take one brief example — the remarkable feature about Flann O'Brien's novels seems to me their preoccupation with potential forces unrecognized by the ordinary individual but available to those whose personalities are not so much extra- as infra-ordinary. They are members of the cult of the commonplace haunted by the occult possibility of some transforming change in the commonplace — even destructive change. For O'Brien the state of hope is a dark utopia, or more precisely, a necessary limbo, in which the protagonist hovers, caught between the real and the surreal, and unsure which of them is heaven or hell. One gains from his books the sense of a normal society in which the hope of revolutionary change has become a surrealist neurosis. They infer a degree of political disillusion which is total. It leads in the end to the transfer of democracy from the world in which he lives to the art by which he lives more intensely than he can in the so-called 'real'.

Even in the thirties and forties of this century, Irish literature retained its links with scholarship, politics and symbolism, especially in the work of Austin Clarke and Denis Devlin. But a new energy was visited upon the scene by Patrick Kavanagh. He is so obviously a lesser poet than Yeats and yet he is also so obviously more influential in Ireland that one is hard put to define his attraction or his quality. I should say that Kavanagh marks the disappearance of two things which had marked the best literature of the revival — the link between it and classical antiquity and its convention of the relationship between author and protagonist. It is a new, perhaps slightly selfconsciously liberated voice which we hear in poems like 'Shancoduff', enjoying the provincialism of place because it is also, and perhaps because of that even, the voice of a citizen of the imagination. His black hills are his Alps, and even the vein of sentimentality twists into an ambiguous sarcasm in the final question — which is put, after all, directly to the reader (that's its sarcasm) as well as to Kavanagh himself (that's its sentimentality):

> The sleety winds fondle the rushy beards of Shancoduff
> While the cattle-drovers sheltering in the Featherna Bush
> Look up and say: 'Who owns them hungry hills
> That the water-hen and snipe must have forsaken?
> A poet? Then by heavens he must be poor'
> I hear and is my heart not badly shaken?

On balance, I should say that *No, it's not*. But the reader's heart may be. Kavanagh is a poet of very cunning simplicities.

The 'I' of his poetry — easy and yet insistent — marks its freshest quality. Through it emerges his presence as the protagonist-as-author, rather than the more involved author-as-protagonist stances we meet in Joyce and Yeats. Kavanagh does not, in other words, send the beam of his personality through the prism of a poem in order to analyse the spectrum of his possible selves. The poem is translucent. Kavanagh emerges as he entered, still insistently himself. He is a bare-faced poet. No masks. In this, he is revolutionary, and especially so when we recognize his other strange quality — his regionalism. Ireland has always had a number of local poets, to each of whom a townland or a some-what larger area belongs. Their major theme is exile and return, and their most pronounced vein is one of unabashed and exploitative sentiment, with a good salting of schoolteacherish pedantry. Kavanagh belongs to them and is their apotheosis. In this sense, he is Irish in a way Yeats is not. He can be understood internally in terms of the culture which produced him; Yeats has to be seen in a wider context. The clear and monochromatic quality of Kavanagh's poetry comes from its fidelity to the miracle of the actual. The local home-grown fact is borne in upon him more powerfully than all the eventful world beyond; and in his acceptance we find a welcome freedom from allusiveness, from antiquity, world politics and the Irish revival. The restricted and negative function of these things in his poetry contrasts strongly with their governing power in Yeats's work.

We find this simultaneous separation from the literary revival and from nationalism in Flann O'Brien. Only Denis Devlin in these decades attempts to make some reconciliation between poetry and politics in, for instance, his poem 'On the Tomb of Michael Collins' — and that is a sad failure. No one of these authors (nor Samuel Beckett either) escapes the disillusion which followed upon the collapse of the nationalism and poverty of the period between 1930 and 1955. Ireland ceased to be a mythological centre and became a provincial backwater.

The most striking change in this situation came in the North. Paisley was on the move in the late fifties, whipping up the sectarian hatreds which the whole structure of the partitioned area exploited and perpetuated in the name of Unionism and in the interests of Britain. Simultaneously, under Sean Lemass, the South began to undergo its first phase of consumer-capital development. In literature, John Montague and Thomas Kinsella were rather isolated figures, one a Northerner, the other a Southerner, but neither yet defined in any significant way by these epithets. The emergence of Seamus Heaney and Derek Mahon marked, however, a new development. For here was work that, whatever its own intrinsic merits, was initially offering itself as that of a school — the Northern Poets. At first, these two and Michael Longley formed the nucleus; but now there is a scattering of poets — Muldoon, Ormsby, Simmons, Ciaran Carson, Tom McGurk, Seamus Deane and others. For present purposes, I can only usefully concentrate on Montague, Heaney and Mahon. Thomas Kinsella would obviously merit lengthy treatment, but in a somewhat different context, because the aspect of Irish poetry with which I am immediately concerned is naturally more pertinent to Northerners than to others who belong more properly and exclusively to the Dublin literary scene.

Despite the Northern Poets tag, Heaney and Mahon have very little in common as poets. Behind Heaney, one senses Gerard Manley Hopkins, Ted Hughes, Patrick Kavanagh, perhaps Keats; behind Mahon, Louis MacNeice, Beckett, Cavafy and early Auden. In fact, MacNeice's poems like 'Valediction' and Section XVI of *Autumn Journal*, although they do not wear well as poetry, are important as statements of a kind of rejection-in-acceptance of Ireland which is typical of the Northern Protestant mind in one of its subtler manifestations. Mahon belongs here, although with more verve and point, as in a poem like 'Beyond Howth Head'. The ambition of many of his poems seems to be astringency; their achievement is more often wryness or irony, but an irony that carries within it a note of lamentation, a grief that almost always becomes exquisite just as it is on the point of becoming profound:

Recognizing,
As in a sunken city
Sea-changed at last, the surfaces
Of once familiar places.
With practice you might decipher the whole thing
Or enough to suffer the relief and the pity.

Mahon is evasive, not because he avoids feelings, but because he passes through them quickly. However saturated he may be in them, he is careful that whatever tear is squeezed out in a poem will have an ironic, deprecatory highlight glistening within it. He goes into dangerous areas, but in a fast car, not on foot. He visits his origins but never finds them satisfactory and seems to wish he had spent time so used out in the world instead — and then regrets having had that wish. For him, Belfast is a dark country, an archaeological site, bleak monuments of men, hard flints of feeling. But Dublin never counterposes as the alternative modern capital. It is, after all, like Belfast, wanting perhaps in the dignity of that ruin, and being merely a consumers' dump instead. Mahon is a poet who cannot conceive of history as anything other than something from which he should escape. It is remarkable how often the figure in his poems is that of a spectator; or in the love poems as a man brought in from the outside to share a basic warmth. His escape is into Marxism, socialism, perhaps — there are faint attitudinal hints of this — but is into himself and his poems more surely and more finally. If Ireland is his fate, the meaning of it is to be gained outside Ireland. Stylish, fluent and then staccato, Mahon is our true exile — the man who belongs but does not wish to believe so, or disbelieves that he must always. His country is his art, and his fear of being tied that of the cosmopolitan who is always walking in the shadow of his provincial self. His language is surprisingly polysyllabic, given the simple verse forms he favours; yet at his best he can achieve both density and elegance by the combination. In addition, the language seeks (and usually finds) a cool temperature, the climate of decorum, which is like wit, but sometimes settles down into a grim appropriateness that seems flat in comparison to his better moments when the poem draws sweetly on some very bitter experience.

Mahon in fact exercises a very severe form of restraint in his poems. His is a poetry of manoeuvrability, each poem having the appearance of an artefact originally conceived to hold more feeling than in fact it does. He seems to want a deeper source of feeling than any he has yet probed; he refuses to will it out, but when it comes it has an ancestral ring to it. Belfast is behind it.

The things that happen in the kitchen-houses
And echoing streets of this desperate city
Should engage more than my casual interest,
Exact more interest than my casual pity.

Yet Mahon suspects both ancestry and its absence. It is not enough either of or in itself; so, on that score, he remains at an oblique angle to the present troubles, wishing there were some other way to take them than the only way in which they offer themselves — so far, at least. He is an Irish writer whose Protestantism survives in his uncertainty about Ireland — whether he wishes to belong to it, or whether he would be allowed to belong if he so wished. In a marvellously elegant manner, with his young Belfast mandarin hesitation and ease, he encapsulates a whole phase of Irish and Protestant feeling; and then, of course, as poets do, he uses this in other forms of development and exploration which are peculiarly his own. But these I must for the moment avoid.

Heaney's case is entirely different. He belongs to Ireland with an ease that is sometimes cosy and sometimes exactly right, as though his body temperature, and that of the atmosphere in which he is steeped, coincided. Poem after poem is an act of recovery and then of hoarding. He collects perfect specimens of his origins in a fine net of language and then treasures them in its thick skeins. He can be simultaneously precise and lush. The lushness is not at all a sign of ease; its depth is a measure of his demands upon the language and upon himself to attain resonance without losing realism. If he is compared to the fine Scottish poet, Norman MacCaig, in this respect, one would see, I think, the degree to which Heaney pledges himself, not merely to exact and evocative description, but to emotions (most of them the emotions of lostness) of which the description is the defining outline. Here he contrasts with Mahon, in that his poems always have a feeling proportionate to their form and the nature of their language. Sometimes the feeling is safe, the form is minor; but the balance remains.

A poem as important as 'Death of a Naturalist' reveals a certain luxuriance in lostness. Never was innocence so rewardingly lost. We feel he carried away a poem from the flax dam rather than a shock which later became a poem. The pain of loss is in some ways remarkably absent from a body of work so concerned with pastness. Yet in his latest book, *Wintering Out*, Heaney throws a good deal of what he had previously done into a more illuminated perspective. The sense of indulgence vanishes. Instead, with that haunting resurrection motif, the personal element is broadened to include the historical and pain flashes its signal more insistently as the poet comes more fully to grips, not with the past, but with its recovery and incorporation into the present — the present of his marriage, of the Northern crisis, of the living moment. The bogs swallow and preserve, and then allow to erupt the bridal queens and the slaughtered innocents of the Irish past. Queens and innocents, murder and violence, remind us in this volume of the degree to which in his previous work Heaney's wealth of language acted narcotically on the linkage between sexuality and violence.

Salmon, pumps, streams, guns, have all a sexual implication which branches and ramifies into the delicate twig-tracery of his sensory impressions; but the implied violence shadows it, giving to the delicacy of impression a voluptuous undertone and to the rhythm a slowly measured capacity, spondaic at times in its solemnity, to survive its own repetitiousness — the capacity, in other words, of an incantatory poetry which shifts itself out of realism towards allegory without ever definitively belonging to one or the other.

The separate achievements of Heaney and Mahon have been vulgarized by the 'Northern Poets' aspect of their reputations. This is to some degree no more than a newspaper phenomenon; but it has substance to it as well. The odd fact about the Northern Poets is that their appearance now seems both belated and inevitable, because a good deal of what they represent has had no previous existence in Irish literature at all. For a group that belongs to the North they are remarkably without political conviction. No reader of *The Honest Ulsterman* could find there a politics, an aesthetic; but he could find a good deal of laughter at the thought of having one or the other. This is fair enough, except that the laughter is itself borrowed; it involves the kind of 'free spirit' attitude you got in Berkeley in the early sixties. And that looks rather precious in the North at the moment — although preciosity is not a sin to which Northerners think themselves prone, largely because they think it means the opposite of crudeness. Nevertheless, the salient fact remains — Northern Ireland is in political crisis and Northern Poets seem more remote from it than any other group, even when they are not writing poetry — which in some cases is seldom.

No encompassing criticism is intended here. What bothers is the lack of a perspective in which the Northern Poets phenomenon can be understood and its importance credited. They supply the perspective to some extent by their a-political stance. I would suggest that John Montague completes it by his political commitment. Between 1966 and 1973 enough has happened in Northern Ireland and in the Republic to explain politically what has begun to happen to Irish nationalism and, in literary terms, how Irish poetry has registered the evolution that took place between the death of Kavanagh and the publication of Heaney's first book. In terms of this discussion the man who occupies the hiatus is Montague. He precedes Heaney and Mahon in time but he is in feeling contemporaneous with them. In him, more than in anyone else, we see the beginning of the Northern crisis develop, but we only see that after the fact because Mahon and Heaney had to write before Montague could be recognized. They gave a perspective on him; and he now gives a perspective on them and on the whole Northern Poets scene. Obviously Thomas Kinsella has a comparable stature in the

South; and is not entirely separable from what has happened in the North either. But his place in this situation would take up more space than I have at my disposal.

Montague has the conviction, deeper than it might at first appear, (although obvious in his book of stories *Death of a Chieftain*), of what being Irish, in terms of loss, means. And with that, he has the commensurate conviction of the importance of writing as a means to recover that loss both for himself and for the community he represents. Indeed, this is an important feature of his work, this consciousness of himself as the tongue of a community. He is fond of the conceit that he can give eloquence where dumbness reigned. As he can. Further, he has the desire to formulate this loss he feels so intensely in a work proportionate to such a theme. He sees a racial tragedy in the landscape of County Tyrone so complete that it has not found utterance; and to give it this, he peoples the landscape again with figures devoid of the sense of class but with a deep instinct for faction. We do not hear them speak; we hear Montague speak for them. The more ominously shadowed their presence, the more acutely sensitive his language to their silent background movements, epitomized so often in his liking for imagery of silhouette, contour, outline. Even his love poems make of silence a supreme and chaste virtue as in 'All Legendary Obstacles', one of the most beautiful. In a Montague lyric, silence rides on the words, we hear the mild thunder of their passage and then the silence comes again like an aftertaste. His poems have a stern, hermetic quality, even when they enter upon narrative (for example, 'Like Dolmens round My Childhood'). They somehow have an air of erudition, without being erudite. This comes, I think, from the fastidiousness of the language, each word chosen with the aplomb of a connoisseur. And yet, that is only one aspect of his work.

Montague has taken the risk of setting a poetry and a sensibility distinguished above all for their capacity to savour the quality of intimacies, against the brutalities of the present situation in the North. The risk is extreme, although in some ways inevitable. His dolmen figures in Tyrone are like his lovers in the love poems; symbols of a conspiracy to be intimate. But such conspiracies are private. The public pressure acts upon them like a lesion, tearing the light apart and dissipating the shadowy presences. After the publication of *The Rough Field* many of the facts of Irish poetry assumed shape and meaning; and the main fact is that the epic attempt in that poem marks the reuniting of the political and literary traditions which had previously been separated. It also marks the subjection of the poet to the demands of his time; and in that way it illuminates the choice of the Northern Poets to come at the crisis obliquely, hesitantly and not frontally, in case they should find their sensibilities so exposed as Montague's have been. In

Tides and in *The Rough Field* he is attempting the almost impossible task of inferring in a lyric sequence the existence of a whole civilization. I can think of no one since Baudelaire who has done this. Yet in attempting it, Montague has brought the regionalism of Kavanagh one step further and deeper. The border between his Tyrone and Kavanagh's Monaghan has a certain appropriateness now. It encloses Montague in history as much as it releases Kavanagh from it. Montague has a religious sense of the local and the past, Kavanagh of the local and the present. This is not a minor or merely verbal difference. It's the difference between the historical moment and the eternal moment. Moreover, the variations in that fidelity to place which is so characteristic of a culture impregnated by nationalism are nicely caught by the further comparison of Kavanagh and Montague on the one hand with Heaney and Mahon on the other. The first two have a genuinely religious sensibility in their response to the local area; the latter two have the sensibility of agnostics. Heaney and Mahon contemplate the phenomenon of belonging as an intermediate stage in a growth towards other things; Montague and Kavanagh regard it as a critical stage in which all other things are implicit and only waiting to be made explicit in terms of the local itself, not in those of any other experience which would run athwart it. But it is in Montague, with his historical concentration, that this fidelity assumes the shape of a political commitment, whereas in Heaney and Mahon one is more conscious of what in comparison looks like a disengagement from politics. Given what I have said, I think it should be by now allowable that Mahon could be damaged by such disengagement — but not necessarily; and that Heaney would have been damaged, but for the fact that commitment did take place, although in no frontal form, in *Wintering Out*, the best and most misunderstood of his books. Yet it remains true that Montague is more visibly surrendering more of himself as poet to the present crisis and is willing his own survival. Even if he is not successful, in terms of the poems he writes, he remains exemplary in terms of the risk he has taken.

We could put all this another way. There has been an evolutionary development in the relation of poetry to national feeling in Ireland throughout this century and it has had four main phases. The first, dominated by Yeats, is one of close affiliation, with strong doctrinaire overtones passing from the poetry to the politics and vice versa. The second, inhabited by Clarke, Devlin and Kinsella, is one of separation and disillusion, in which the right-wing tendencies of the first period are strongly criticized — largely because many of them had ceased to be tendencies and become facts. In both these phases, however, a favourite literary strategy is still that of placing Ireland and modern or antique Europe in strongly reverberative and satirical contrast to one another.

The third phase, comprising Kavanagh and Montague, is one of a deeper regionalism with a certain ambition now to formulate the whole culture in terms of the local part. European antiquity (*pace* Clarke) is now replaced by local antiquity as the sounding-board for ancestral feeling, although Montague evidently shares with Devlin and Kinsella the metropolitan sense which had previously been Joyce's and Moore's especial preserve. The fourth phase is that of the Northern poets, again in a state of separation from national feeling, more ambitious to redraft the emotional geography of the respective areas in terms, not of history and politics, but of the free personality. I should say that no one grouping excludes completely elements that belong to another group; but each is defined by the seniority it gives to certain kinds of pre-occupation. But all preoccupations are related to nationalism — the need to join with it or escape from it; with Ireland, and the need to create identity on its terms or to dictate identity on the poet's own. All through there is a fluctuation between open mythological possibilities and bitter provincial shutdown; between the sense of the self as definitively Irish and the sense of the self as free from any such category; between the sensibility of poets to whom sensory impression supplies a language for basic instinct, and those who seek instead in reading and reflection a language of the conscience; between country and town, geography and history, and, overriding all, the impulse to discover in the poem itself the eternal moment in which all such oppositions are reconciled.

Although Ireland has, like most places, settled for a predominantly lyric tradition in its poetry, the anxiety on the part of many poets to incorporate the fragments of memory, history and above all, the consciousness of having been subject to fragmentation, has led to a number of curious, sometimes brilliant, epic and narrative attempts. The epic bespeaks a culture which is whole; the lyric one which, while broken, is reconstituted in its fullness for the duration of the poem. It is an intensive art. If we look at epic attempts like Clarke's *The Vengeance of Fionn*, Devlin's *The Heavenly Foreigner*, Kavanagh's *The Great Hunger*, Kinsella's *Nightwalker*, Montague's *The Rough Field*, we are aware of their reliance of lyric passages rather than total structure for their effects. If this be conceded, then it leads to another point.

There are three subjects which between them have attracted the best efforts of Irish poets in this century — love, faith and growth. The remarkable absentee is politics. It is not absent *tout court*; but a political sensibility is not present in our best poetry. When it appears, it appears as commentary and gravitates towards satire. It has a sociological and an historical conscience, but only in Austin Clarke do we find any matching moral passion. This is a strange phenomenon in so self-consciously political a country, even if it be argued that the politics is largely symbolic and ritualized. (Although I can think of few places where this is not true.) One could cite many poets for whom politics was a mode of the imagination — Shelley, Hugo, Pound, Mayakovsky, MacDiarmid, Neruda. But to extend the list adds nothing to the point. Part of the explanation for the lack of this imaginative mode in Ireland is to be found, I believe, in the ways in which Irish nationalism developed as the major form of political consciousness. For it never lacked the moral passion; but after 1919 it lost much of its social and historical conscience, and while these remained undeveloped the moral passion became increasingly vapid, a cloud of feeling that never crossed a mountain range that would force it to shed the life-giving moisture it claimed to hold. Only recently has this mountain range loomed, in the North. But the lack of a comprehensive national political ideology has been in many ways the decisive factor in the failure of a political sensibility in the poets. Influenced by politics, they have not been modified by politics. Imaginatively they found themselves in a culture which could no longer connect its brilliantly re-created past to any conceivable future. No nationalist dream of the past has appeared until now to have the capacity to face and to change present facts, of which the North is the most recalcitrant. Now that it too has been forced to change, now that republicanism has taken on the ideology of social transformation, the fixed situation of past years has become fluid again. It is in this connection that the Northern poets, have their importance as a group. They are not articulating change. They are articulating what it is like to have been changed, to have undergone that process; and in such articulation, the existence and development of a political sensibility is inescapable. For many people, the future has already arrived. What politics is labouring to produce, poetry senses has already come.

The form of freedom promoted by a lyrical tradition is interior freedom. The traditional themes I have spoken of — love, faith and self-growth — were natural in a culture dominated by the inhibitions of its colonial-clerical heritage. Sexuality was one area where the inhibitions were particularly strong; religious faith was another; and self-growth had therefore been, from the beginning, the only form of liberty in a culture deeply deprived of it for so long in almost every other area. With these areas of concentration, lyric is inescapably the dominant form. It gives the fugitive moment of release permanence; it pits an infinite privacy against a finite convention; it gives form where form seemed absent. It reconstitutes unconscious shock as a moment of remembered beauty, and thus helps chart the evolution of a growth which had been only semi-conscious. It apprehends belief as an existential and not a merely institutional experience; and it understands privacy, in a puritanical culture, as the mark of true love. This is the sort of thing we find in Kinsella, Montague, Heaney and Mahon. But we also find in them a certain uneasy consciousness of the limitations in this form, one sign of which is their liking for lyric sequences (particularly in Montague and Kinsella) which can pass beyond the experience of interiority and enrich it by contact with other worlds. In the case of Heaney and Mahon, *Wintering Out* and *Lives* are, respectively, indications of a broadening from the sometimes luxuriant world of the self and its growth to the relation of that self to the blanker and more inscrutable worlds in which those selves are not yet central points of reference. This unease in them is matched by an unease in the culture, a move towards a greater openness and towards a crisis in which the private heroism of the free self begins to yield its pride of place to the spirit of a more communal (albeit more conscience-striken) consciousness. This is as far as one could at this moment go in defining the emergence of what could be called in these poets a political sensibility.

Montague's *The Rough Field* is, in this connection, a central document. It is a complicated mosaic in which various kinds of juxtaposition (for example, Sections II and III, 'The Leaping Fire' and 'The Bread God') are used for the sake, it would seem, of creating the shock of sudden perspective. It is precisely the shock of the world of privacy set against the public world; the language of the hustings of now and of long ago against the language of private association and growth, which belongs to now and to any time. The histories of the Montague family and of the clan O'Neill are interwoven with the past history of Ireland and its present crisis. All unite and then unravel again in the poet-protagonist's own consciousness with its own, faintly ironic and repeated lament, 'With all my circling a failure to return'. The poem is a quest for origins and origins are looked for in the hope that they might also become closures. The private tone of the poem has to keep itself apart from the public quotations which play like electricity around it, and one is conscious of the effort to preserve a certain objective rigour and purity without at the same time entirely sacrificing some of the more available and subjective lyrical effects. The pressure of the sequence tells upon each part of the poem and in one case — 'Hymn to the New Omagh Road' — causes it to collapse completely. Besides, the personal drama of the poem is too volatile to be held within the public frame. Irish history does not in the end have the same attraction for the poet as Montague's history. They do not synchronize as they are meant to. The politics has had exorcized from it all the ghosts of feeling save those of resignation and bitterness. Self-growth and the epic integration of the 'shards / Of a lost culture' are knit together by determination, not by inevitability. The poem's beauty is lyrical; the poem's ambition is epic. In it, two strands of the Irish poetic consciousness come together more clearly than ever before.

The voice itself has a strangeness — bred out of Gaelic craft and married to the cool idioms of modern American and French poetry. Hints of Richard Wilbur chase shadows of Yves Bonnefoy. Yet the tone is Montague's own: hesitant, nervous and then suddenly exact. It is the kind of poem in which the flaws are exposed by the presence of its perfections; and perhaps even more importantly it is the sort of poem in which we can see the forging, from a pure lyric steel, of the alloy of a political sensibility.

> Who knows
> the sound a wound makes?
> Scar tissue
> can rend, the old hurt
> tear open as
> the torso of the fiddle
> groans to
> carry the tune, to carry
> the pain of
> a lost (slow herds of cattle
> roving over
> soft meadow, dark bogland)
> pastoral rhythm.

The old hurt is an ancient wrong and it is an emotional scar; it is a cry of pain and the lament of the fiddle. The one absence I feel here is that of a more dictatorial tone, that of man possessing his culture and not possessed by it. But I'm not sure that this is a legitimate feeling on my part. It simply amounts to the wish that Montague would take a tougher line with loss. Yet to place such poignancy against the Ulster situation is a memorable risk.

Out of the context of Montague and the emergence of a political sensibility, we return to Heaney and Mahon. Anyone who has read 'Anahorish' (the re-plantation of Ulster by Gaelic vowels) or 'Summer Home' will appreciate the delicacy of Heaney's ear and its alertness to the small variations of sound and rhythm which can create large emotional effects. His poems tend to live off one another, sometimes in happy incest, sometimes in a sudden sea-change, by remaining alike and yet profoundly different, as though the genes of his inspiration had suddenly combined to create an extraordinary poem which nevertheless bears a strong family resemblance to its lesser brothers. In *Wintering Out* the difference in quality between the good and the best poems is more pronounced than in his earlier volumes where the quality was more even. Of all, 'The Tollund Man' seems to me the finest and it is also, happily, an example of the fusion of a political sensibility with the theme of self-growth. It has two arenas, Jutland and Ireland; two dimensions, the past and now; then two pasts, the distant and the recent; two voices, and therefore two present tenses, that of the opening stanza and that of the final lines. It is a quest, starting with a promise to go, 'Some day I will go to Aarhus' and ending 'at home'. The quest involves a number of interlocked journeys — the tumbril journey of the Aarhus man, the poet's car journey and the journey of the 'four young brothers, trailed / For miles along the lines'. This last is a reference to one of the many outrages committed by the B Specials on the minority community in the 1920s.

One of the voices in the poem speaks in sibilants in a whisper; the other speaks in fricatives, in a prayer. Each stanza combines the sensual touch of -s words like 'skins', 'seeds', 'stomach', 'noose', 'goddess', 'juices', 'saint's', 'reposes', with the harder -d endings, most of which are verbal, viz. 'pointed', 'caked', 'stand', 'tightened', 'opened', 'stained' and so on. Insinuated through this pattern is the dominant and tolling beat of the long vowelled words of which 'Some' is the first, 'home' the last, and 'bridegroom', 'honeycombed', 'stockinged', 'freedom', 'Tollund', other instances. It is by virtue of these delicate modulations that Heaney can translate from the private, memorializing realm with its violent sexual implications ('She tightened her torc on him / And opened her fen . . .') to the political realm of the 'man-killing parishes' of Ulster and Jutland where he is 'lost / Unhappy and at home'. The connections are not narcotic, or luxuriated upon, as was sometimes true of earlier poems. The experience of death underlies the poem in the shape of the Tollund Man and his bride, the soil, and the four young brothers (sleepers) murdered ritually at home. Here politics has become an aspect of growth. It is part of the poet's mode of imagination; and its presence has, if anything, heightened the delicacy of his musical effects and deepened the channel of feeling in which he moves. In this sense, Heaney too is shifting in his poetry from personal search to the incarnation of a communal experience which is specifically Irish and yet not at all limited by that fact; rather the reverse.

Mahon remarks on his status as poet *vis-à-vis* the violence, but in him the spectacle seems to provoke a wider, blanker kind of despair. Yet the almost metaphysical sense of absurdity which lives in him prohibits the despair becoming a tragic attitude. The notion that all this mess will, in any case, give out to a universal and blank silence, paradoxically turns the bitterness into a bleak comedy or sweetens it, as in W. S. Merwin, into a mystery. Beckett's presence in *Lives* is prominent; but so too is Mahon's deft and therefore not too blatant language for grief:

> What will remain after
> The twilight of metals,
> The flowers of fire,
>
> Will be the soft
> Vegetables where our
> Politics were conceived.

Such ultimates chasten commentary and remind us that what has here been called a political sensibility is capable of more extension than any analysis could predict or conceive.

Provincialism and Recent Irish Poetry:
The Importance of Patrick Kavanagh
by Michael Allen

PROVINCIALISM WAS a major European social and literary pre-occupation in the nineteenth century; but why does it still remain such a central concern in Ireland? Seamus Deane's suggestion (in the preceding essay) that Ireland was a provincial backwater between 1930 and 1955 is a variation on Daniel Corkery's general notion that Ireland is most provincial when most peaceful. One explanation of the continued Irish concern with this issue must obviously have to do with her relationship with England: the custom that lies upon her ' "heavy as frost and deep almost as life" ', Corkery says, is not her 'own custom, it is England's'. Louis MacNeice, in his book on Yeats, offers another explanation: that Ireland may sometimes be united against England, but is always divided against herself, characterized above all by an intensity of local feeling. 'A man from the next parish is a foreigner.' The example of Patrick Kavanagh, the most influential poet to have lived with Deane's twenty-five years of provincialism, shows that the preoccupation can be fruitful as well as debilitating; it lends support to both the above explanations which may thus be taken as complementary rather than contradictory.

As a nineteenth-century idea, the pejorative notion of provincialism, 'pertaining to a narrow and limited environment', appealed to that sense of superiority on grounds of mobility and wide acquaintance with the best people on which upper class people thrived socially. Their own presumably broad and expansive environment they could see as 'cosmopolitan' or 'metropolitan'; their way of life as 'urbane'. For intellectuals and artists these socially accepted, opposed or overlapping 'catchwords' (A. O. Lovejoy) offered the idea of the whole world as a structured hierarchical system of places. One's art, one's style, one's flow of thought, it was assumed, would profit from location in, or free access to, places high up in the hierarchy like Paris or London. Those doomed to places lower down could be pitied or patronized. Matthew Arnold snobbishly introduced this idea of provincialism to the English

literary journals in the course of popularizing the critical terminology
of Sainte-Beuve in 1864. The provincial note, he said, occurred in the
writer 'left too much to himself' with 'ignorance and platitude all round
him' too far from a 'supposed centre of correct information, correct
judgement, correct taste'. Writing produced in such circumstances
would, he said, exaggerate 'the value of its ideas' or rather 'give one idea
too much prominence at the expense of others'. This sense of 'provincial' was immediately taken up in the critical essays in Victorian
periodicals, the literary talk in London *salons*. But Arnold's very high
standards, his castigation of the whole of English culture as provincial
in comparison with that of France, tended to get lost when the
distinction was used by, say, Thackeray and his circle: they would use
it to dignify their own ethos and patronize a Charlotte Brontë or a
Thomas Hardy. It probably seemed no more than common sense to
assume that such provincial writers were inferior in cultural advantage
and could only profit by gaining mobility and access to superior circles.
George Eliot accepted her assimilation into the metropolitan melting
pot gratefully; Charlotte Brontë half accepted the benefits of her
London links. Even the young Hardy accepted the assumption
initially, deciding that, as a writer, he must have his headquarters in or
near London.

It seems clear to us now that for a writer whose art is uniquely
dependent on a native love of a particular terrain, an authentic sense of
a local society, such considerations might seem irrelevant (Faulkner
is the most obvious modern example). While Hardy conceded the value
of the metropolitan visits which continued after he had settled in
Dorchester, his confidence in his own gifts led him to repudiate the
basic premisses of urbane patronage. 'Arnold is wrong about provincialism', he wrote, 'if he means anything more than a provincialism of
style and manner ... A certain provincialism of feeling is invaluable. It is
of the essence of individuality and is largely made up of that crude enthusiasm without which no great thoughts are thought, no great deeds done.'
We can speculate that like Clym Yeobright he had originally renounced
the provinces for a metropolis where he thought customs and values
would be infinitely superior; but that he too found that he was putting
off 'one sort of life' for another that was 'not better than the one he
had known before. It was simply different.' He still recognized the
limitations of provincial society in terms which partially reflect Arnold's:
the scene of *The Woodlanders* for instance is 'a place where may usually
be found more meditation than action and more listlessness than
meditation; where reasoning proceeds on narrow premisses ...' But it is
important that he added 'and results in inferences wildly imaginative'.
The relationship between these inferences and his own 'provincialism
of feeling', 'individuality', 'enthusiasm' was to be established and

objectified through the creation of a self-contained fictional world. Genteel and cosmopolitan characters and scenes could be subordinated or excluded since 'there was quite enough human nature in Wessex for one man's literary purpose'. This conception of art rooted in the re-creation of an authentic self-contained regional world reached its height when Faulkner, an even more intransigent provincial, discovered what could be achieved by writing about his own little postage stamp of native soil, sublimating the actual into the apocryphal. These formulations are suggestive of the mode of Patrick Kavanagh's best work. What is more, the nineteenth-century 'debate' in which they germinated remains relevant in Ireland, where Yeats played Arnold's role and Kavanagh (I shall maintain) played Hardy's. In his book on the Southern writer, Cleanth Brooks argues that Hardy and Faulkner both gained great artistic strength from their identification with provincial cultures in a period when the intellectual and social values of the metropolitan commercial and cultural centres were defective. He is wrong, however, to place Yeats alongside these authors. Certainly Yeats was not a thoroughgoing cosmopolitan; he earned Joyce's rebuke ('a treacherous instinct of adaptability') in as much as he was not prepared to reject Irish literary circles for their 'temporising and poltroonery, their attitude of timid covert revolt on all issues not purely national' as Joyce did. But this was precisely because Dublin was as important to him as Sligo: he differs from the other writers referred to by Brooks in that he had no intimate and exclusive relationship with a rural traditional culture. In fact, in *Autobiographies* he described Irish culture in Arnoldian terms. He said that the incessant attempt to communicate with 'ignorant or still worse half-ignorant men' produced a 'sense of strain' for the writer; and because Ireland offered 'no ideas and ideals . . . no aesthetic culture or taste' wide reading frequently became mere pedantry. He resembled Arnold in his application of these strictures to a national culture he was finally, himself, committed to; Arnold's remedy for provincialism in England, an Academy on the French model, was one of Yeats's own most cherished Dublin projects; his only advice on the individual level was that talented young men should leave Ireland entirely between the ages of eighteen and twenty-five (the implication being that they should then return to Dublin to assist in the construction of a national metropolis). And though Yeats continued to regard the town as 'unmannerly' he did, as the century progressed, superintend the growth there of a recognizable literary establishment which accepted as credentials either a measure of genteel cosmopolitanism like his own or a 'genuine' peasant-pastoral *naïveté* which would be patronized.

Patrick Kavanagh was more like Hardy than like Yeats, though lacking in either's artistic stature. As the young Hardy thought it essential to

migrate to London to be a writer so the young Kavanagh set out for Dublin, believing it, he said later, to have been transformed into 'a literary metropolis' by Yeats, Lady Gregory and Synge. What he brought with him was an exact and authentic sense of his own region, a fresh and subversive verbal gift, a capacity to integrate these talents in original ways. And he too was to find that he was putting off 'one sort of life' for another that was 'not better than the one he had known before. It was simply different.' He was aware that his own genius was akin to Hardy's, that their similar cases could be summed up in such a phrase as 'roots in the soil'. What he tried to record as a difference between them ('Could any man be more remote from the simple elemental folk of Wessex than Hardy?') is not really a difference. Admittedly, Kavanagh was a small farmer while Hardy trained as an architect; but what made both men different from their 'folk' was their literary vocation, and their overwhelming need to justify themselves in the face of genteel metropolitan literary establishments to which they were outsiders.

Kavanagh's initial reception in Dublin literary circles was kindly enough; but in his view it was essentially patronizing, requiring that he should play the role of the unlettered peasant poet among the literati. He also discovered that the 'famed Dublin literary conversation' seemed to him 'tiresome drivel between journalists and civil servants'. In fact, what Kavanagh was offered by the genteel establishment when he came to Dublin was exactly what Hardy had been offered by the English establishment — a patronized role as a naïve peasant-pastoral writer. And like Hardy he refused to accept it. By what he said and what he wrote (The *Collected Pruse* with its anti-genteel title provides ample illustration as does Section IV of the *Collected Poems*) he alienated himself from the Dublin literary establishment; and in his alienation he wildly and erratically assumed either that he should have stayed at home or that Dublin lacked the advantages of London (an opinion which could only alienate him further). On the one hand, he repeatedly and mournfully doubted the distinction upon which his migration had been based, wondering if he had missed 'the big emotional gesture', wasted in malignant Dublin what could have been his four glorious years in Monaghan. On the other hand, he would suggest that what he was missing in Dublin were the intellectual life, inquiring minds, adventurous publishers, aristocratic belief in the importance of poets, which were available in London. In the latter mood, while he was exaggerating the cultural advantages of London, he did put his finger on the attraction which a major publishing centre is bound to have for writers, and the way this conditioned an envious hostility in Dublin: there was hardly a book published in Ireland, he said, that hadn't been rejected by every London publisher; and 'the provincial mentality' was 'to attack what it secretly worships'.

One can see that two overlapping social situations (one involving the relationship between London and Dublin, the other that between Dublin and Monaghan) prompted that obsessive preoccupation with provincialism which dominates the *Collected Pruse*. (The occasional interest in Joycean cosmopolitanism there and in Section IV of the *Poems* is more theoretical since it never corresponded to a real possibility for Kavanagh.) His contradictory feelings on the subject were only fully resolved in the poetry (as we shall see); he resolved them polemically however by concluding that there were only two mentalities informing poetry: that of the provincial, who has 'no mind of his own', and who 'does not trust what his eyes see until he has heard what the metropolis . . . has to say on any subject'; and the 'parochial' mentality, that of the writer who 'is never in any doubt about the social and artistic validity of his parish'. This position is based on antagonism to urbane gentility as patently as Hardy's was when he praised provincialism as 'the essence of individuality', characterized by the 'crude enthusiasm without which no great thoughts are thought, no great deeds done'. Kavanagh too wished to applaud a tendency outside metropolitan or cosmopolitan circles towards 'individuality' ('no mind of his own') and 'enthusiasm' ('never in any doubt'). But he assumes that the word 'provincial' is beyond reclamation from its pejorative implications; and so he concentrates his attention on the paradoxical purification of the word 'parochial' from derogatory nuances. The 'parochial' writer for Kavanagh (and Hardy and Faulkner obviously qualify) works with the intimately known rural society and landscape and is successful if these come alive and work in the realized artistic creation: the writer's 'parish' provides authenticity, and a self-dependent myth upon which the writer can build. He must, however, guard against the 'bravado which takes pleasure in the notion that the potato patch is the ultimate' with 'the right kind of sensitive courage and the right kind of sensitive humility'. We must ask a little later, in the light of Kavanagh's own achievement, what he meant by this.

Yeats, writing about his own early novel, shows that he had learned from Irish regional fiction the aesthetic principle of 'parochial' writing. He saw that it should focus on those who love their native places without perhaps, loving Ireland, exploiting the way that they make their native town into their whole world. While *John Sherman* does not as a novel add distinction to this formula, *Tarry Flynn*, Kavanagh's most sustained major achievement certainly does. But Yeats also acknowledged the strange double-bind of which the Irish writer's preoccupation with provincialism is symptomatic when he said of such novels that their characters 'do not travel and are shut off from England by the whole breadth of Ireland'. He could not help being aware of the further dimension with which the Arnoldian 'frame' could trouble 'parochial' writing.

B

'Shancoduff' (1934) shows how early these considerations were affecting Kavanagh. It is a celebration of his own locale as a complete and self-contained world; but by virtue of this fact it has to recognize the alternative view:

> My black hills have never seen the sun rising,
> Eternally they look north toward Armagh.
> Lot's wife would not be salt if she had been
> Incurious as my black hills that are happy
> When dawn whitens Glassdrummond chapel.

Words like 'black' and 'north', the depressive sound of the mundane place-names, Shancoduff, Glassdrummond, the inveterately rural and provincial ring of 'Armagh' almost allow us to take up the vernacular pejorative implication of 'Eternally'. The stanza hinges on that word, which finally retains its traditional (religious and artistic) force in association with the perpetually arrested vision of whiteness artistically heightened by a 'north light', the chapel backed up by the ancient religious capital of Ireland. Somewhere behind the poem, the knowledge that Armagh was once the 'metropolis', the bishop's seat, is balanced against the fascination with the wicked city which had ruined Lot's wife. And the concern with provincialism conditions the impeded development, the openendedness of the poem. Against the mainly euphoric literary clichés of the speaker in the second stanza ('They are my Alps and I have climbed the Matterhorn') is set the dour realism of the (mobile) cattle-drovers:

> 'Who owns them hungry hills
> That the water-hen and snipe must have forsaken?'

The ambiguity of 'poor' in the penultimate line does not (and is not intended to) resolve the issue entirely:

> 'A poet? Then by heavens he must be poor'
> I hear and is my heart not badly shaken?

With his migration to Dublin five years later this central conflict was to become more urgent and painful for Kavanagh. He always resisted the simple assumption that the 'centre' was a better place to be. But it is only rarely that the 'parochial' writer in Kavanagh's sense, having achieved through his own mobility a new perspective, a point-of-vantage from which to view his own parish, can afford to exclude some formal or dramatic equivalent from his art. Examples would be the figure of the 'returned native' who often acts as the ironic focus of disillusionment and regret in Hardy's novels; or Faulkner's carefully staged re-enactment of his provincial drama at an ostensible cultural centre with the 'sophisticate' Shreve as ringmaster. *Tarry Flynn* works successfully without such devices because of its triumphantly concrete style, its assured address to the reader (who is persuaded by its very openendedness to agree that Tarry is 'not a country man, but merely a man living. And life was the same everywhere'). But despite the 'parochial' virtues of *The Great Hunger*, freshness, clarity, authenticity and compassion, it lacks a formal centre of control and judgement: and falls back too readily upon overbearing sententiousness or the deliberate use of bathetic rhythms to define its attitude to central figure (Maguire) and central theme (rural provincial deprivation).

The important thing about the formal and dramatic points-of-vantage in Hardy and Faulkner referred to above is that they function ironically. In mid-nineteenth-century writing (for example, *Middlemarch, Shirley, Villette*) comparable devices at least partially implied the validity of a more expansive mode of life beyond the provincial milieu: but in Hardy and Faulkner they tend to suggest the moral bankruptcy of bourgeois-genteel 'central' culture, and formally reinforce the reverberations of the 'parochial' drama. How could Kavanagh, in lyric poetry with no obviously experimental tendencies, achieve a similar ironic perspective?

One strategy, after moving to Dublin in 1939, was to write about the Second World War from a national viewpoint rather as Hardy and Edward Thomas wrote about the First. The speaker in 'Peace' wonders whether he should be 'here' in neutral Ireland rather than in war-torn Europe ('Ireland is most provincial when most peaceful'?); 'here' becomes precise, however, only in a characteristic local landscape ('leaf-lapped furrow', 'old plough', 'weedy ridge', 'saddle-harrow') which breaks through the immediate pretext of the poem (England/Ireland) to reveal the tensions arising from Kavanagh's departure from his childhood landscape for Dublin:

> Out of that childhood country what fools climb
> To fight with tyrants Love and Life and Time?

The attempt to equate Monaghan with Ireland (in the phase of his verse which he later condemned for its exploitation of a pseudo-Irish poetic identity) is not successful. In fact, he is thrown back on a vocabulary of rhetorical abstractions (as in that final line of 'Peace') by the out-dated poetic strategy he has chosen.

Another over-literary frame of reference in the poetry of this period is the ninetyish idea of Parnassus. 'Temptation in Harvest', explores the personal implications for the poet of the life objectively realized in *The Great Hunger*. The poem depicts a 'returned native' reliving the desire to be an uncomplicated countryman 'on an ash-tree's limb / Sawing a stick for a post', to love the local landscape and care for his ricks without intellectual ambition; he tries to ignore the inevitable fate of such men, left 'on their backs in muddiness'. But the opposite alternative, the journey, is imaged (rather emptily) in the inviting glance of a passing girl (the muse). The speaker remembers asking himself

> Could I go
> Over the fields to the City of the Kings
> Where art, music, letters are the real things?

In the memory, labourers, animals, landscape and an old country woman (the poet's mother?) urge him to stay at home ('You cannot eat what grows upon Parnassus / And she is going there sure as sin.'); but he turns

> Away from the ricks, the sheds, the cabbage garden,
> The stones of the street, the thrush song in the tree
> The potato pits, the flaggers in the swamp;
> From the country heart that hardly learned to harden

to 'follow her who winked at me'. The poem's strength resides in its 'parochial' vividness. But it is sabotaged by the clichéd attempt to fuse Kavanagh's real-life migratory experience with a symbolic Parnassian journey.

The poet was soon experiencing and expressing the traumatic conflicts arising from his failure to adjust to the Dublin literary situation: but the best poems of the period find subtle new uses for his familiar Monaghan materials. 'Innocence', for instance, is an attempt to counter the pejorative view of the poet's provincial background, the urbane conviction that he is limited by his origins:

> They laughed at one I loved –
> The triangular hill that hung
> Under the Big Forth. They said
> That I was bounded by the whitethorn hedges
> Of the little farm and did not know the world.
> But I knew that love's doorway to life
> Is the same doorway everywhere.

As the poem proceeds an initial repudiation of his roots ('Ashamed of what I loved') is succeeded by a mystical or magical state ('back in her briary arms') in which

> I know nothing of women,
> Nothing of cities,
> I cannot die
> Unless I walk outside these whitethorn hedges.

The poem is an advance upon 'Temptation in Harvest' in the way that the feminine figure (both muse and mother) is now imperceptibly present in the local imagery giving concrete particularity to the central assertion that 'love's doorway to life / Is the same doorway everywhere'. The symbolism functions delicately to persuade us that the local scene is a 'universal stage' as it does in *Tarry Flynn*. But Kavanagh is still excluding rather than ironically encompassing the patronizingly urbane stand-point which was perturbing him, looking backwards rather than towards the resolution of his present conflicts. One sees this evasion in 'Auditors In', which turns away from 'the sour soil of a town where all roots canker', claiming to have arrived at 'The placeless Heaven that's under all our noses'. Kavanagh could not write well about a 'placeless Heaven'. His strength was his capacity for a deep and intense engagement with place, and he was still coming to terms with a new location.

He achieved this in two stages: the first was necessary for his emotional and intellectual development but produced bad poetry; in the second, however, he seems to me to have achieved at times the kind of ironic perspective which gives formal completeness to 'parochial' writing. The low point of his poetic career (and a temporary betrayal of what it represents) came with the writing of drab satiric poems about the provincial mediocrity of Dublin which invoke the superior cosmopolitan alternatives (London and Paris) recognized by 'Stephen Dedalus', Yeats and the O'Casey of *Inishfallen, Fare Thee Well* ('The Paddiad'). In these poems there is no doubt that Kavanagh becomes a provincial in the sense of his own later definition. He has ceased to trust what his eyes see and directs his aspirations towards a superior 'metropolis'. In so doing he gives temporary assent to the nineteenth-century genteel 'frame' and all its superior assumptions. Ironically, he takes this position in order to attack a literary establishment which is urging the celebration of Irish culture as 'the last preserve / Of Eden' where genius walks 'with feet rooted in the native soil' ('The Defeated') as well as arranging cosmopolitan opportunities for its politically influential members ('Irish Stew'). He seems later to have regarded this phase of his poetry as one of spiritual death from which the next phase emerged as a kind of spiritual rebirth.

This painfully devastated period ended with his libel suit against *The Leader*: an occasion which can be seen as a ritual punishment of the hubristic outsider who was refusing (Kavanagh said this) to play the inferior role allotted to him. In some ways it was like the drubbing Hardy received after the publication of *Jude the Obscure*, though in Kavanagh's case the wounds were self-invited. The crucial recognition wrung from him during the traumatic trial proceedings was his commitment to Dublin as locale: 'I love the place. Why should I come and stay in it if I didn't?' It seems to be with this acceptance of his love for the place he had journeyed to (in full recognition that it was as 'provincial' as the place he had left) that the final fruits of his genius emerged. (Though we are in a position, as he was not, to recognize the characteristically Irish overlap of two social situations which made this resolution possible.)

A number of late lyrics which many people (including the poet) have considered to be the height of Kavanagh's poetic achievement hinge upon the fully dramatized and minutely realized motif of a completed journey. When he found himself experiencing in 1955 'the same emotion' on the Grand Canal Bank as back in Monaghan his poetry reached some kind of parallel resolution: 'Canal Bank Walk' and its companion poems celebrate his new ability to 'grow with nature again as before I grew'. Earlier he had said (still drawing on his vapid ninetyish idea of poetry) 'In the presence of the Parnassian authority we are provincials nowhere'. But now the minute particulars of Dublin as locale (canal seats and bridges and water, city streets and trees and hospitals) allowed the affectionate superimposition of one provincial milieu upon another, the discovery in concrete terms that we are provincials everywhere.

The late poetry is still very uneven. Its anti-genteel centre is Kavanagh's self-presentation as one of the Dublin dispossessed: sometimes with the makings of a folk-hero ('If Ever You Go to Dublin Town'); more often as a down-and-out migrant 'enduring' the spare deprivation of streets, hospitals, bridges, benches, garages. The 'I' of this poetry is as recognizably a scapegoat figure as is Hardy's Jude in his latter days in Christminster. ('Poetry made me a sort of outcast . . .', wrote Kavanagh, introducing his *Collected Poems*, 'I do not believe in sacrifice yet it seems that I was sacrificed'.) But he is consciously a scapegoat — recognizing in 'Come Dance with Kitty Stobling' how Dublin society had recalled him to his familiar rural social role:

> I had a very pleasant journey, thank you sincerely
> For giving me my madness back, or nearly.

He is the scapegoat as comic poet: he brings with him from his rural past spells and exorcisms for the urban present; and the subtle gaieties of his late rhythms play with transformative power over his deep sense of his double role as provincial victim. As he walks 'this arboreal street on the edge of a town':

> The breeze too, even the temperature
> And pattern of movement is precisely the same
> As broke my heart for youth passing. Now I am sure
> Of something. Something will be mine wherever I am.
> I want to throw myself on the public street without caring
> For anything but the prayering that the earth offers.
> It is October over all my life and the light is staring
> As it caught me once in a plantation by the fox coverts.
> A man is ploughing ground for winter wheat
> And my nineteen years weigh heavily on my feet.
>
> ('October')

The sharp ambiguities, indicative of unresolved tensions, of poems like 'Shancoduff' have relaxed into a new rich solving movement consistent with 'the prayering that the earth offers': this movement, however,

plays against the unease of the half-rhymes; and unearned securities
are excluded by the placing of 'I am sure' at the end of the line, the
hint of misgiving in the repeated 'something'; and also the ominous
associations of 'staring', 'caught', 'ground for winter wheat', 'weigh
heavily'. As in the best writing of this kind (compare some of Emily
Dickinson's poems as well as Hardy's) the isolation and curtailment of
life's possibilities induced by the provincial milieu (past and present)
is subtly universalized by the seasonal landscape (so concrete in the
past, so consciously abstract in the present). The ritual permanance
discovered in this double perspective *is* the poem. And the successful
formula which reveals a rural provincial spareness, a traditional ritual
stance, in a shabby urban landscape works with other juxtapositions,
other recognizable journeys:

> Only thus can I attune
> To despair an illness like winter alone in Leeds.
>
> ('Winter in Leeds')

> The winkers that had no choke-band
> The collar and the reins . . .
> In Ealing Broadway, London Town
> I name their several names . . .
>
> ('Kerr's Ass')

Seamus Deane points out that Kavanagh has had more influence
than Yeats over recent Irish poetry. I am suggesting that Kavanagh may
be having the same kind of effect on the development of Irish writing
('because he was there') as Hardy has had on the development of
English writing: the arrest and reversal of a whole nineteenth-century
way of thinking about literary location. (Since my emphasis has been on
the power of social roles and ideas as well as on the influence of poetry,
it is only fair to point out that Hardy's influence in England was rein-
forced by social changes which have established less genteel assumptions
about literary location; and which are less advanced in Ireland.) The
poetic careers of John Montague and Seamus Heaney offer two
interesting test-cases for this hypothesis.

Montague began writing earlier than Heaney, assimilating as Heaney
did, London modes like that of *New Lines*, but looking towards Dublin
as his nation's literary capital. The two dominant models for an Irish
poetic career in the late fifties were still the naïve nationalistic
peasant-poet and the cosmopolitan (who should now look to Rome, Paris
or the U.S.A. rather than London). In the latter category, a poet like
Thomas MacGreevy had been (according to his dust-jacket) identifying
himself 'with the European intelligences in Irish poetry — Montgomery,
Coffey and Devlin'; a poet like Desmond O'Grady was just then moving
from Paris to Rome and the patronage of Ezra Pound. It is not

surprising that Montague should have adopted the explicit notion of a
tradition of fruitful cosmopolitanism which he later traces in his essay
'The Impact of International Modern Poetry on Irish Writing' from
Yeats and Joyce through Denis Devlin to himself. The poems in his
first book are not unlike some of Kavanagh's in their delicate and
authentic use of the rural childhood landscape and society. But the
search for a point-of-vantage seizes on cosmopolitan possibilities, Rome
visited, Auschwitz remembered or an abstracted aesthetic tradition:

> One stood until the bucket brimmed
> Inhaling the musty smell of unpicked berries,
> That heavy greenness fostered by water.
>
> Recovering the scene, I had hoped to stylize it,
> Like the portrait of an Egyptian water-carrier . . .
>
> ('The Water Carrier')

In a brief satiric poem 'Regionalism or Portrait of the Artist as a Model
Farmer' he impersonates an Irish rural poet who shields the 'tuber' he
has planted from

> Foreign beetles and exotic weeds,
> Complicated continental breeds

in the incoherent belief that the purity of his gift will comfort him in
his 'fierce anonymity'. The sheer vigour of the impersonation suggests
that Montague has some instinctive sympathy for the position he is
satirizing. But his over-all aesthetic commitment at this point in his
career is clear enough.

His second book, *A Chosen Light* (1967) assumes in the title
sequence that an appropriate point-of-vantage has been achieved in a
cosmopolitan setting; that a symbolic journey has been accomplished,
'from Tyrone to the rue Daguerre'. Such a journey is assimilated into
the make-up of the volume: the Paris locale is used to encapsulate
(always sensitively) the remembered Irish past. But this principle of
development is not sustained. A fragile retractive sequence in the next
book *Tides* (called, significantly, 'The Pale Light') moves away from the
cosmopolitan perspective achieved in *A Chosen Light*: it begins by
contemplating 'the shelf of Europe', 'the dome of the casino' ('North
Sea'), 'the Stadz-muzeum at Bruges' ('Coming Events') but goes on to
register (in terms of human relationship and poetic development) the
need for a diminuendo, for

> the slow
> climb
> down.

After this, the cosmopolitan point-of-vantage as such disappears from

Montague's poetry. And his next book, *The Rough Field* (1972) returns to rural Tyrone for its subject matter, reprinting several earlier poems in the search for some kind of new locally-rooted perspective.

How are we to explain this reversal? Kavanagh's *Come Dance with Kitty Stobling* was published in 1960, his *Collected Poems* in 1964. And in 1966 Heaney was widely praised for his first book, *Death of a Naturalist* about which he said: 'I have no need to write a poem to Patrick Kavanagh; I wrote *Death of a Naturalist*'. But the possibility of being a 'parochial' poet in Kavanagh's sense was clearly there in Montague's early poetry too. A selection of his poems appeared in an anthology *Six Irish Poets* in 1962; and the editor, Robin Skelton, praised in his introduction, the way Irish poetry could still base itself firmly on 'natural resources . . . the sense of belonging' and thereby gain a 'real vitality'. It was about this time, Montague says, that he began to plan *The Rough Field*.

Despite the affectionate re-creation of the locale, there is, throughout Montague's book, a careful, ruefully hesitant poetic voice to be heard conceding, movingly, an alienation, a lack of ultimate direction, summed up in the refrain-line: 'for all my circling, a failure to return'. One is reminded of the central preoccupation of Kavanagh's later poetry, 'return in departure'. But Montague is unable to achieve that kind of vitally ironic point-of-vantage, formally vindicated, which distinguishes Kavanagh's best last poems. And the selfconscious attempt to construct an over-all viewpoint for the book, using historical quotations, woodcuts, and verse-reportage to universalize the poet's local materials by reference to the 'Ulster Crisis' is no substitute.

That it is intended to be a substitute, and to remind us in an underhand way of the poet's cosmopolitanism is clear from the back cover: ' . . . the New Road I describe runs through Normandy as well as Tyrone. And experience of agitations in Paris and Berkeley taught me that the violence of disputing factions is more than a local phenomenon.' One is reminded of Kavanagh's primary stipulation for the 'parochial' writer: that he should never show 'any doubt about the social and artistic validity of his parish'. The importance of this stipulation, his definition implies, is that any concession to genteel cosmopolitanism in the context of such writing would devitalize the poetry. This would be my complaint about *The Rough Field*. Whether from the nature of his gifts or because of an accident of timing, Montague has not shown himself so far to be capable of following and profiting from Kavanagh's achievement. Heaney, on the other hand, has never shown any doubt about the social and artistic validity of his parish.

In Heaney's earlier poems the imaginative implications of the local society and terrain, viewed often with a childhood intensity, are presented with subtlety and vigour, and with no hint of selfconscious humility. It is probably this essential confidence in the utility of the re-created internally consistent region of his poems that he was admitting to having inherited from Kavanagh. But this is possibly not the whole of his debt. In his second and third books he too begins to embody in key poems a crucial relationship between poetic development and the motif of the journey away from roots. In 'Bogland', 'The Wool Trade', 'Westering' and 'The Tollund Man' he shows himself to have learned how to work with specific ironic vantage-points which may seem to illuminate, but are in fact illuminated by the 'parochial' materials.

We are probably now in a position to see what Kavanagh meant by his injunction that the parochial writer should guard against the bravado that takes the potato patch for the ultimate with 'the right kind of sensitive courage and the right kind of sensitive humility'. He did not mean that the writer should avoid technical influence from literary mainstreams; Auden is as important to the making of Kavanagh's own later rhythms as Roethke and Hughes have been to the growth of Heaney's poetic idiom. What he was advocating (for a particular *kind* of writer) was the delicate adjustment of social and poetic strategies to the changing pressures of the poet's own most authentic experience. The aim was to remain free of the sapping and enervating currents of establishmentarian uniformity (which in Ireland still tended to keep alive the nineteenth-century tradition of genteel cosmopolitanism and its subordinate convention of naïve peasant pastoralism). Kavanagh was an innovator in Ireland as much by what he stood for as by what he wrote: the wastefulness, the false directions, the personal over-assertiveness which sometimes characterize his poetic career, also provide pointers to directions in which his successors need not move because he did. Heaney's writing to some extent emerges from the same ambiguous concern with provincialism that we find in Kavanagh and Montague. But because of Kavanagh he could begin from a position of strength. In his work the personal and intellectual underpinnings are entirely hidden, leaving us to respond to the way the local materials emerge into the constantly developing, fluid yet certain poetic point of view.

Austin Clarke and
Padraic Fallon
by Donald Davie

TWO JUSTLY admired poems of our time are by the same hand and have virtually the same title. They are Edwin Muir's 'Horses' of 1925, and 'The Horses' of 1956. The poems are significantly different: Muir was a late starter, and 'Horses' is in many ways a touchingly incompetent poem, helplessly dependent at one point on Yeats ('Perhaps some childish hour has come again') and at another on Keats ('Ah, now it fades! it fades! and I must pine'); whereas 'The Horses' is thoroughly achieved, a sustained and frightening vision provoked by the possibility of an atomic holocaust and the impossibility of imagining its aftermath:

> . . . That old bad world that swallowed its children quick
> At one great gulp. We would not have it again.
> Sometimes we think of the nations lying asleep,
> Curled blindly in impenetrable sorrow,
> And then the thought confounds us with its strangeness.
> The tractors lie about our fields; at evening
> They look like dank sea-monsters couched and waiting.
> We leave them where they are and let them rust:
> 'They'll moulder away and be like other loam.'
> We make our oxen drag our rusty ploughs,
> Long laid aside. We have gone back
> Far past our fathers' land.
>   And then, that evening
> Late in the summer the strange horses came.
> We heard a distant tapping on the road,
> A deepening drumming; it stopped, went on again
> And at the corner changed to hollow thunder.
> We saw the heads
> Like a wild wave charging and were afraid.
> We had sold our horses in our fathers' time
> To buy new tractors. Now they were strange to us
> As fabulous steeds set on an ancient shield
> Or illustrations in a book of knights.
> We did not dare go near them. Yet they waited,
> Stubborn and shy, as if they had been sent
> By an old command to find our whereabouts
> And that long-lost archaic companionship . . .

Different as this is from the technical gaucheries that Muir had per-
petrated thirty years before, at another level altogether one is struck
by how alike they are, this late poem by Muir and that earlier one. For
plainly in the lines above Muir is not imagining (what is indeed unimaginable), the actual consequences of an atomic war. He is not
looking into the future, any more than in the poem of 1925 he was
looking into the past of his Orkney Island childhood when he said of
the horses there:

> Their eyes as brilliant and as wide as night
> Gleamed with a cruel apocalyptic light.
> Their manes the leaping ire of the wind
> Lifted with rage invisible and blind.

Past, present and future are categories that do not apply when we
consider what takes place in either of these poems; as in nearly every
poem that Muir wrote, the action takes place in a visionary or fabulous
time that clocks and calendars do not measure.

In other words Muir is a mythopoeic poet. And I recall him so as to
present the bleakest possible contrast with Austin Clarke, who is
further from mythopoeia than any poet one might think of. For Clarke
too has his poem about horses, 'Forget Me Not' (1961), and Muir's
line about 'that long-lost archaic companionship' is glossed in Clarke's
poem:

> Good company, up and down
> The ages, gone: the trick of knife left, horse cut
> To serve man. All the gentling, custom of mind
> And instinct, close affection, done with. The unemployed
> Must go. Dead or ghosted by froths, we ship them
> Abroad. Foal, filly, farm pony, bred for slaughter:
> What are they now but hundredweights of meat?

But Clarke's poem is as insistently *in* historical time as Muir's is out
of it. For it is provoked by the revelation in the years just before the
poem was written that the Irish were indeed raising their horses so as
to slaughter them or have them slaughtered, and export them either
on the hoof or as carcasses to feed the poor of the Continent.[1] And it
is as usual for Clarke's poems to be thus occasional and highly topical
as it is for Muir's poems to be nothing of the kind.

The contrast is even more striking and instructive if we look for the
lines in 'Forget Me Not' which correspond to Muir's

> As fabulous steeds set on an ancient field
> Or illustrations in a book of knights.

In order to make the same point about the horse in the Age of Chivalry
Clarke treats us to a capsulated history of Western Europe:

                    Yet all the world
Was hackneyed once—those horses o' the sun,
Apollo's car, centaurs in Thessaly.
Too many staves have splintered the toy
That captured Troy. The Hippocrene is stale.
Dark ages; Latin rotted, came up from night-soil,
New rush of words; thought mounted them. Trappings
Of palfrey, sword-kiss of chivalry, high song
Of grammar. Men pick the ribs of Rosinante
In restaurants now. Horse-shoe weighs in with saddle
Of meat.
                    Horseman, the pass-word, courage shared
With lace, steel, buff.
                    Wars regimented
Haunches together. Cities move by in motor
Cars, charging the will. I hear in the lateness of Empires,
A neighing, man's cry in engines. No peace, yet,
Poor draggers of artillery.

The comparison could be extended; for instance Muir's 'Horses'
corresponds to a passage in his *Autobiography* (1954), and in the same
way passage after passage in 'Forget Me Not' can be matched in
Clarke's autobiography, *Twice Round the Black Church* (1962). But it
is better to pause here and to face the awkward fact that, given kinds
of poetry as different as Muir's and Clarke's, no one's taste is, or
can be expected to be, so catholic and unprejudiced as to respond to
both kinds with equal ardour. We may *respect* both kinds; but we
cannot be expected to love them both equally. And it is worth considering what might be said of Clarke's poem by some one who
responds very immediately and fervently to Muir's.

   In the first place such a reader might very justly point out, as
regards what we have looked at so far, that in one case a single line
by Muir is matched by seven lines from Clarke, in the other case two
lines of Muir correspond to sixteen in Clarke. Muir then is the more
economical writer; he says as much in altogether smaller compass,
and this is what we expect of poetry as compared with prose. So we
might conclude that Clarke is a more 'prosy' writer than Muir, and
this damaging imputation will be strengthened if our imagined reader
goes on to say, as he well might, that Muir's writing on this showing
is more musical than Clarke's, that 'The Horses' has a melody which
he can hear, whereas 'Forget Me Not' hasn't. (And to this objection,
the only practical answer is to urge the reader to listen to Clarke
reading on gramophone record.[2]) Then, our reader might point out
that he need bring to Muir's poem no more than imagination, sympathy and seriousness, whereas to Clarke's poem he has to bring a
modicum of learning — he has to know and remember for instance that
Rosinante was the mount of Don Quixote. Finally, a related point —

noting in the second passage particularly the high frequency of puns ('hackneyed' and 'staves' and 'stale' are all puns; so are 'weighs in' and even 'saddle'; and so is 'Hippocrene' if we remember that 'hippos' in Greek means 'horse'), our reader may confess that he doubts whether Clarke is serious, whether his overt theme is more than a pretext for him to play word-games and juggle with allusions. It takes courage to raise this last objection nowadays, when we have all been bullied into tolerating the allusiveness of a poem like Eliot's *Waste Land*, and have been dazzled and bemused by William Empson's demonstration of the puns and near-puns in Shakespeare's sonnets. But it ought to be agreed that, though punning and allusiveness can appear in poetry of the utmost seriousness, there is other poetry in which such features do indeed indicate a fundamental frivolity in the poet. And so there is a case to answer: Clarke's punning must be shown to be however modestly of the Shakespearean sort, not of the sort of 'The Groves of Blarney'.

Counter-attack is the best form of defence, and so an admirer of Clarke may say that Muir's poem, much as he admires its grave music, suffers from the lack of just that verbal energy and continual play of quick intelligence which throws up puns and allusions in 'Forget Me Not'. (He may also remark — though it's beside the point of the present argument — that there is a presumably unintended and unfortunate allusion in Muir's poem: to Wordsworth's 'Resolution and Independence', in the lines where the abandoned tractors are compared, surely implausibly, with 'dank sea-monsters'.) Once one has acquired a taste for the way language is used in 'Too many staves have splintered the toy / That captured Troy', the language of Edwin Muir is bound to seem, however worthy and responsible, undeniably *tame*. And as for economy of expression, Clarke's word 'staves' means first the staves of the barrel-body of the wooden horse by which Troy was taken; but also as a variant of 'staff', all the sticks that have thwacked horses' hides through the centuries when the horse was man's servant; and finally 'stave' in its technical sense in music delivers the sense, 'Too many songs since Homer's have devoted themselves to the matter of the Trojan war; the theme has been done to death (splintered)'. If this isn't to say much in a little space, it's hard to know what is!

There is in any case a sense in which a mythopoeic poem will always be shorter than a poem which, so far from rising into visionary timelessness, trusts the categories of past, present and future, and ranges to and fro among them. For in order that a myth may be made which will shape and encompass the multitudinous variety of historical experience, that experience must be stripped of what is local and contingent; it is the rendering of the contingencies — of place as well as time — which in a non-mythopoeic poem takes up the space that the mythopoeic poem can do without. And Austin Clarke is an extreme case of the poet who trusts the local and contingent through thick and thin, who refuses to rise above the congested heterogeneity of the world as we experience it through our senses, enmeshed in particular circumstances, of *this* time in *this* place. What makes him an extreme case is that he lived his days in a place, the Irish Republic, which has been and is in many ways anomalous, where social and political life has taken on forms hardly to be found in other English-speaking societies of the twentieth century. W. B. Yeats, surviving into this socio-political situation, exerted himself — like the mythopoeic poet he was — to show that underneath the peculiarities of Irish life there could be found the lineaments of myths which encompassed and made sense of the life of the Irishman as of the rest of mankind. That is not Clarke's way; on the contrary he immerses himself in the life of modern Ireland in all the eccentric particularity of that life. And the upshot is that issues which bulk larger in Ireland than in other English-speaking countries — for instance, the breeding of horses for slaughter, or again the non-availability of contraceptive devices inside the Republic — bulk disconcertingly large in Clarke's poems also. This means that for the non-Irish reader, on top of the difficulties that come of Clarke's being unashamedly a *poeta doctus*, a proudly learned poet, there arises another set of difficulties altogether — the need to know in considerable detail the history of modern Ireland, especially the history of public opinion inside the Republic, as well as the history of Ireland through previous centuries. This makes Clarke sound like a very provincial, even a parochial poet. And in one sense he is so, quite consciously and defiantly. It means in any case that the non-Irish reader, and for that matter many Irish readers also, have to work much harder to get what Clarke has to offer them, than to get at Edwin Muir. And so Clarke will always be caviare to the general, as Muir isn't.

To put it another way, there are good hard-headed reasons for the modern Irish poet to take the mythopoeic path which Clarke set his face against. Moreover that had been by and large (not altogether) the path taken by W. B. Yeats; and the worldwide fame which Yeats achieved, it might seem, must have impelled the Irish poets after him to tread in his mythopoeic footsteps. In fact, however, very few of the first-rate talents have struck out in this direction, though one who did — Padraic Fallon — will engage our attention later in this essay. The reason is not hard to find. When a poet so great as Yeats is born to a country as small as Ireland, this is a wonderful windfall for everyone in that country *except the poets*. For them it is a disaster. For, if the young Edwin Muir could not prevent his own voice from being at times drowned out by the organ-voice sounding from across the Irish Sea, how much more difficult it must have been for a poet like the young Clarke, moving about the very city where the master-poet was housed, where the ringing and imperious voice sounded in his ears, as it were, every hour of the day. Even today, for Irish poets as for poets as far away as the Antipodes, Yeats must figure as the great ventriloquist; if they relax their concentration for a second, or become any more familiar than they must with the highly distinctive Yeatsian idiom and cadence, they find themselves transformed into puppets sitting on the great ventriloquist's knee, using not their own voice but his. This at any rate I take to be the right context in which to consider Clarke's mostly feline and mischievous comments on Yeats. Dublin gossip will have it that, at the time when Yeats could decide on which younger brow to place the laurel of his approval, he conspicuously favoured F. R. Higgins above Clarke; and that Clarke has never forgiven him. This may well be the case. For that matter there were plenty of other reasons for mutual antipathy between Clarke, urban, petty bourgeois, and Roman Catholic; and Yeats, shabby-genteel, Protestant, admirer of rural peasantry and landowners. But a degree of antipathy to Yeats would have been inevitable for any ambitious and serious Irish poet of Austin Clarke's generation; only by making himself deaf to Yeats's voice could any such poet save himself poetically and forge a style true to the integrity of his own different temperament and concerns.

This necessity for the young Clarke to keep his distance from Yeats must be borne in mind when we see him in the 1920s choosing to exploit just those centuries of Irish history which Yeats had least cultivated — the centuries of Celtic Romanesque, after the heroic age and before the Elizabethan plantations. The great symbol and metropolis of that Ireland is the Rock of Cashel, the hill in Tipperary still crowded with the ruins of Romanesque churches; and if Yeats at times invokes the Rock, Clarke has a better right to do so. He earned that right by many poems in the two collections, *Pilgrimage* (1929) and *Night and Morning* (1938). In *Pilgrimage* occurs 'The Scholar', which is a free paraphrase of an anonymous Gaelic poem, 'An Mac Leighinn':

> Summer delights the scholar
> With knowledge and reason.
> Who is happy in hedgerow
> Or meadow as he is?
>
> Paying no dues to the parish,
> He argues in logic
> And has no care of cattle
> But a satchel and stick.

The showery airs grow softer,
He profits from his ploughland
For the share of the schoolmen
Is a pen in hand.

When mid-day hides the reaping,
He sleeps by a river
Or comes to the stone plain
Where the saints live.

But in winter by the big fires,
The ignorant hear his fiddle,
And he battles on the chessboard,
As the land lords bid him.

I cite this in the first place as a clear and winning example of the poems that Clarke could draw from what he has called 'our forgotten mediaeval Ireland when we almost had a religion of our own'. But it serves also to isolate the extraordinary technical innovation, or body of innovations, by which Clarke has made available to other poets writing in English a whole kit or cabinet of erstwhile undiscovered musical resources. For the assonantal pattern of 'The Scholar' approximates very closely to a structural principle informing the Gaelic original. In the first quatrain, the second syllable of 'knowledge' chimes with the first syllable of 'hedgerow', which word chimes with both syllables of 'meadow'; in the second quatrain, there is a chiming link between the first syllables of 'parish', 'cattle', and 'satchel'; in the third quatrain, 'softer' chimes with 'profits' as well as 'schoolmen' with 'pen'; in the fourth, 'reaping' with 'sleeps', and 'plain' with 'saints'; while in the last stanza the word 'ignorant' is at the centre of a web of chimes and echoes which link its first syllable with 'winter' and 'bid', its second with 'lords', and its last with 'battles' and 'land'. And on top of this Clarke end-rhymes, consistently though never straightforwardly. Of these matters he has written:

> Assonance, more elaborate in Gaelic than in Spanish poetry, takes the clapper from the bell of rhyme. In simple patterns, the tonic word at the end of the line is supported by a vowel-rhyme in the middle of the next line . . .
> The natural lack of double rhymes in English leads to an avoidance of words of more than one syllable at the end of the lyric line, except in blank alternation with rhyme. A movement constant in Continental languages is absent. But by cross-rhymes or vowel-rhyming, separately, one or more of the syllables of longer words, on or off accent, the difficulty may be turned: lovely and neglected words are advanced to the tonic place and divide their echoes.

It is not fanciful, hearing the interlacement of sounds in the poem, to think it an equivalent for the ear of what strikes the eye when we look at the interlaced curves and angles on the geometrically curved shaft of a Celtic cross or at illuminated letters in the Book of Kells. But,

faced with the solid symmetries of 'The Scholar', we cannot fall into
the error denounced by Hugh MacDiarmid, speaking of the Gaelic
music of the *pibroch*: 'the idea that the Celt has no architectonic power,
that his art is confined to niggling involutions and intricacies'.[3] Yet
'niggling', I fear, is what some English readers may be saying under
their breath; for the characteristically English liking for the insouciant
and slapdash amateur, in the arts as in other fields, is affronted
by the scrupulous professionalism of Clarke, alike in the poem and in
his note just quoted. But this is typical, if not of Ireland (for the Irish
produce their own brand of sometimes engaging amateurish harum-
scarums), at least of the Gaelic Ireland which produced the bardic
schools. And Clarke is unashamedly *poeta doctus* no less in the fashion-
ing of his poems as artefacts than in the learnedness of his allusions
and references. 'Irish poets, learn your trade.' Thus Yeats; and Clarke
has obeyed the injunction, having schooled himself indeed in a harder
school than Yeats dreamed of.

It would be quite wrong to see Clarke's need to distance himself
from Yeats as the sole or even the main reason why he was drawn to
the Celtic Romanesque. In the words of Augustine Martin, 'The most
obvious reason is that implied in his tendency towards separatism: a
deeply religious man, he found himself repelled by the Victorian and
Jansenistic version of Catholicism in which he was reared.' Clarke's
need for an alternative Roman Catholicism, and his search for it in
medieval Ireland, were implicit in the wistfulness with which he
spoke of 'our forgotten mediaeval Ireland *when we almost had a religion
of our own*' (my italics). And yet one may suspect that Clarke
would have been mutinous and irreverent inside any church at all. For
the poet who is opposed to mythopoeia is obviously going to have a
difficult relationship with the Christian myth along with all the rest.
And to say so is not to impugn the sincerity of any profession he may
make of belief in the Christian verities. However, the Jansenistic
temper of the Roman Church in modern Ireland is what few people
will dispute; nor is anticlericalism much less common in the Republic
than in other Roman Catholic countries. And anticlericalism, angry,
needling and insistent, informs many poems that Clarke has written
since the Second World War.

It is not for nothing that Hugh MacDiarmid's name has cropped
up. For MacDiarmid's quarrel with the culture of post-Reformation
Scotland, and his appeal beyond John Knox to the Scotland of James
IV and Dunbar, is in important respects very like Clarke's appeal from
the Jansenistic Romansim of modern Ireland to the medieval Catholicism of Cashel and Clonmacnoise. To the Scottish poet as to the Irish
one, what has been cramped and thwarted by an arrogant and hysterical
Church (Protestant in the one case, Roman in the other) is above

all the capacity for joyous sexuality. And so they are both insistently erotic poets, defiantly obscene when they judge that is called for.

Clarke's anger at the attitudes of the Irish Church, particularly at the inhumanity (as he sees it) of the Church's attitude to sex, grew ever harsher and more explicit, not always to the benefit of his art. Two poems which ask to be compared, from this point of view, are 'Martha Blake', which appeared in *Night and Morning* (1938), and 'Martha Blake at Fifty-one', written in the early sixties. Both poems are very harrowing, and the later one is relentless in the particularity with which Clarke conveys the indignities to which Martha Blake is condemned by her sick body, sufferings which her piety and the ministrations of her Church do nothing to assuage. The earlier poem, much shorter and harder to understand, is a great deal more subtle, as Denis Donoghue intimated very helpfully when he spoke of ' "Martha Blake" . . . where the pain is given in the cadence':[4]

> Before the day is everywhere
> And the timid warmth of sleep
> Is delicate on limb, she dares
> The silence of the street
> Until the double bells are thrown back
> For Mass and echoes bound
> In the chapel yard, O then her soul
> Makes bold in the arms of sound.

Here the 'pain' — to the reader's inner ear — comes in the fifth line, where the extra syllable at the end, 'back', disturbs cruelly the expectation of easy pleasure built up through the liquid three/four time of the lines that precede it, and unsettles the otherwise very rich pleasure of the lines that follow, bringing the positively plummy bell-note of the perfect rhyme, 'sound'/'bound'. When we notice that 'back' chimes with 'Mass', and that there is vowel-rhyme between 'thrown', 'echoes', and 'soul', we perceive that 'cross-rhymes or vowel-rhyming . . . on or off accent', precisely to the degree that they can please the ear, can also pain it, whenever expected pleasures are harshly denied. And thus the assonantal interlacings that Clarke invented for English verse turn out to be not just structural devices, nor a source of delightful grace-notes, but *expressive* also.

The remaining seven stanzas take Martha Blake through all the stages of the Eucharist, drawing out how in her experience of the sacrament sensuous delight is necessarily confounded with spiritual exaltation. In the sixth stanza, one of the most difficult, this confounding or compounding of allegedly distinct realms of experience exacts a step even beyond cross-rhyme and produces a 'rhyme' that is an anagram ('silent'/'listen'):

> But now she feels within her breast
> Such calm that she is silent,
> For soul can never be immodest
> Where body may not listen.

In the poem as a whole there is nothing to offend the most devout Christian, and indeed it could have been written only by a poet who had experienced the Eucharist very fervently. He feels along with Martha Blake the whole way; and the only sign that he is also detached from her, feeling for her and about her as well as with her (feeling for instance that she does not understand how spiritual experience *must* be mediated through the senses), is in the calculated harshness with which from time to time the cadence is blocked from providing the reader with the pleasure it has led him to expect. The effect is extraordinarily poignant; and such reticence sustained with such subtlety is something which it is hard to parallel.

A poem that goes along with the two Martha Blake poems is 'Ancient Lights', which deals with another sacrament, Confession, somewhat as 'Martha Blake' had dealt with the Eucharist. 'Ancient Lights', which gave its name to a slim and flimsy booklet of 1955, has a special place in my experience of Clarke's work, for it was this poem, encountered in this unlikely format, which introduced me to his poetry. I well remember, what indeed I recorded in print, the startled incredulity with which I learned that poetry of such avant-garde brilliance and power was the work of a man who had been a figure on the Irish literary scene for forty years, whose earlier writings moreover — prose-romances and verse-plays as well as poems — had displayed similar or equal virtues over many years. Augustine Martin, in a valuable essay, suggests that my experience was not unrepresentative; that the collection called *Ancient Lights* 'marks the period when readers of poetry in Ireland were beginning to turn again in guilty recognition to the forgotten but relentless genius of Austin Clarke'. Such readers were right to feel guilty, and the shabby story of how the Irish treated their poet must be told again, in Augustine Martin's words. The story does not begin with Yeats, nor can the burden of guilt be shifted on to his shoulders; but it is fair to guess that the cold shoulder which the Irish public turned to Clarke became intolerable for him when, in 1936, Yeats pointedly excluded him from *The Oxford Book of Modern Verse*. Mr Martin reflects:

> Writers react differently to neglect; Irish writers in general do not tolerate it. Wilde, Shaw, Yeats, Stephens, O'Casey and Behan were not self-effacing men; it is unthinkable that they would have allowed the world to ignore them, even if the world had been that way inclined. But Austin Clarke reacted differently: if his countrymen did not want his poems he would not tout them; in fact he would make them a little harder to come by; he would bring them out privately in severely limited editions . . . If the public could not be both-

ered he would be at pains not to bother them. So, throughout his middle period, from the appearance of *Night and Morning* (1938) to *The Horse-Eaters* (1960) he published all his original poetic work under the imprint of his own Bridge Press, Templeogue, Dublin. It is strange to think that some of the finest lyrics and satires, not only of modern Ireland but of modern times, made their appearance in this obscure and unpretentious manner in a city where Patrick Kavanagh dominated the poetic skyline on the strength of two very slender, if very distinguished, volumes of verse.[5]

Amends have been made since, but they were sadly belated. Moreover, though of course there were honourable exceptions, Irish readers in general began to esteem Clarke only after non-Irish readers had begun to notice and applaud him.

Ancient Lights ('This edition is limited to two hundred copies') is subtitled, 'Poems and Satires, First Series'. This is not helpful, and indeed it must be said that Clarke is not just proudly reticent but positively perverse in the obstructions which he erects between himself and his readers. This is true not only in how he describes and categorizes his poems (in the present case, for instance, are we to conclude that a satire is not a poem?), but also in some aspects of his writing. His obscurity is sometimes irresponsible and inexcusable, and although I would not unsay any of the admiration that I expressed for 'Ancient Lights' in 1956, I have to take account of the fact that, over the years since, neither I nor any one I have consulted has been able to say what it is that happens in the crucial fourth and fifth stanzas. Some sort of natural epiphany, undoubtedly; but just what sort, and just how? For this reason 'Ancient Lights' seems to be ultimately unsuccessful, and inferior to 'Martha Blake', despite the difficulties in that poem also. The coarser, more emphatic and extended writing of 'Martha Blake at Fifty-one' must be thought more effective than either 'Martha Blake' or 'Ancient Lights' if, as we must suppose, Clarke's purpose by 1960 was to reach and unequivocally *hurt* as many Irish readers as possible.

Augustine Martin says, of 'Ancient Lights':

> This powerful poem with its theme of spiritual release projects Austin Clarke into a new phase of creativity, and this phase is reflected in the poems which accompany it in the volume. These poems, mostly satires on modern Ireland, reveal that the poet has abandoned his objective correlative, and withdrawn from the medieval landscape. Now he confronts his experience in the first person, and grapples fiercely with the living scene around him.[6]

By describing these later poems as 'mostly satires', Martin is taking up Clarke's own hint, as we have seen. Yet in many cases 'satire' is a misnomer, or at least, if it applies at all, it applies too loosely to be useful. Rather often, a more appropriate description might be 'epigram' or 'lampoon'; and the names of Landor on the one hand, of Swift on the other, should remind us that there can be great writing in both these genres. Marmoreal finish and emblematic aptness may well recall Landor in for instance the grave and witty epigram, 'St. Christopher' (from *Too Great a Vine*, 1957):

> Child that his strength upbore,
> Knotted as tree-trunks i' the spate,
> Became a giant, whose weight
> Unearthed the river from shore
> Till saint's bones were a-crack.
> Fabulist, can an ill state
> Like ours, carry so great
> A Church upon its back?

And it is the direct savagery of the lampoon that we hear in a poem about sixty orphans burned alive in a dormitory without fire-escape, and about a statement issued by the local bishop:

> Martyr and heretic
> Have been the shrieking wick!
> But smoke of faith on fire
> Can hide us from enquiry
> And trust in Providence
> Rid us of vain expense.
> So why should pity uncage
> A burning orphanage,
> Bar flight to little souls
> That set no church bell tolling?
> Cast-iron step and rail
> Could but prolong the wailing:
> Has not a Bishop declared
> That flame-wrapped babes are spared
> Our life-time of temptation?
> Leap, mind, in consolation
> For heart can only lodge
> Itself, plucked out by logic.
> Those children, charred in Cavan,
> Passed straight through Hell to Heaven.

This is invective. Its quickly construed sarcasm is the only concession it makes to the indirections by which a Dryden or a Pope constructs elaborate satirical structures so as to baffle and implicate his reader. It is surely open to question whether a true satire can ever be as short as most of the poems by Clarke that we are now considering. I am not sure that we can ask the satirist for a consistent viewpoint, though Augustine Martin thinks that we can and that Pope and Dryden would pass the test; it seems clear that we cannot ask this of the lampooner. As lyrics by the same hand on facing pages may contradict each other, so I would guess may lampoons or epigrams. And surely Martin himself must be uneasy when, uncovering a particularly flagrant contradiction between two poems of Clarke's, he decides, 'One is therefore inclined to ask Mr. Clarke how *he* would solve the employment problem . . .' (This is not to say that all Clarke's lampoons are equally justifiable; 'Medical Missionary of Mary' is one that strikes me as *cheap*.)

When Martin asks of Clarke that he be qualified to act as Minister of Labour, he sounds rather like another critic who decides of 'Forget Me Not': 'I have seen too many people dying of starvation in Shimbashi slums to become greatly exercised over man's inhumanity to horses. If an export horse trade can boost a nation's economy and help eliminate poverty, I find nothing short-sighted or stupid in it, Lemuel Gulliver and Austin Clarke notwithstanding.'[7] I dare say most of us feel that this bluff humanitarian good sense is somehow beside the point, but it's not at first easy to see or to say why. The truth is, I suppose, that 'Forget Me Not' does not declare it to be wrong to raise horses for slaughter, to slaughter them, or to eat their meat; what it *does* say, I think, is that a decision to set this process in motion cannot be taken on merely quantitative computations ('the greatest good of the greatest number') but should take into account imponderable because qualitative considerations like 'All the gentling, custom of mind / And instinct, close affection, done with'; and the poem surely says or implies with justified indignation that this decision, like all such decisions in modern societies, *was* taken after merely quantitative computations of short-term profit and loss — precisely such computations as those of the critic quoted above. One of the qualitative costs that must be counted in the disappearance of the horse as man's workmate — not one of the most grievous costs perhaps, but one of the most surprising — is counted sardonically at the end of Clarke's poem:

> Tipsters respect our grandsires,
> Thorough-breds, jumpers o' the best.
> Our grass still makes a noble show, and the roar
> Of money cheers us at the winning post.
> So pack tradition in the meat-sack, Boys,
> Write off the epitaph of Yeats.
>   I'll turn
> To jogtrot, pony bell, say my first lesson:
>
> > *Up the hill,*
> > *Hurry me not;*
> > *Down the hill,*
> > *Worry me not;*
> > *On the level,*
> > *Spare me not,*
> > *In the stable,*
> > *Forget me not.*
>
> *Forget me not.*

The same artless lines, except for the repeated 'Forget me not', had opened the poem, which had then gone on:

> Trochaic dimeter, amphimacer
> And choriamb, with hyper catalexis,
> Grammatical inversion, springing of double
> Rhyme

— which is a prosodist's learnedly exact description of just those italicized verses. And these are (so the poem tells us a few lines later) the 'work-a-day, holiday jingle' which the poet as a child learned to say when riding in a neat pony-trap or horse-drawn cab with his Uncle John, who figures largely in *Twice Round the Black Church*. After the prosodist's analysis, we have:

> So we learned to scan all, analyse
> Lyric and ode, elegy, anonymous patter,
> For what is song itself but substitution?

And what this means to say is that some of the patterns of rhythm which sound, or used to sound, in the head of verse-making man were the several patterns of varied but regular recurrence beaten out by a horse's hooves as the horse trotted or walked, cantered or galloped. In fact Clarke is inverting and yet endorsing the point made by T. S. Eliot in a much-quoted guess that man's sense of rhythm and measure may have been permanently altered by the internal combustion engine. The characteristic pun on 'substitution' makes the point for those who look: it is a technical term of prosody, but 'what is song itself but substitution?' means also that in poetry we substitute a pattern in the reality of language for patterns that we discern and want to express in reality outside of language. Among those linguistic patternings are those, peculiarly important to verse, which reveal themselves to the ear, and can be analysed by counting syllables, counting the beat, counting metrical feet. Yeats's epitaph — 'Horseman, pass by!' — we must indeed 'write off'; and with it we write off all the centuries in which no rhythms were so insistently present to man, from earliest childhood, as the rhythms beaten out by horses' hooves — rhythms so insistent that one may indeed wonder whether they were not imprinted on man's nervous system.

But this consideration, though it brilliantly and intriguingly frames Clarke's poem (and makes it a post-symbolist poem, in as much as we now see it describing itself), is far from accounting for the indignation and outrage which are at its heart, which inform also his 'Knacker Rhymes' in a booklet of 1960 ('Poems and Satires, Third Series') where the title, *The Horse-Eaters*, forces the theme on our attention. Hasn't Clarke got the whole thing 'out of proportion'? No! For what Clarke sees and protests against is *sacrilege*. And thus it is just here that we find the grounds for saying, with Augustine Martin, that Clarke is 'a deeply religious man'. 'Forget Me Not' reminds us that in the ancient world the horse was a sacred animal; for Clarke what is sacred is not the horse, but the relationship between horse and man. The sanctity of that tie is the non-quantifiable cost which is left out of account if with W. J. Roscelli we refuse 'to become greatly exercised over man's inhumanity to horses', because of 'too many people dying of starvation in Shimbashi slums'.

And this brings us full circle to where we started, with *mythopoeia*. Clarke's poetry seems to make no new myths, and to celebrate no old ones; more often it exerts itself sardonically to puncture and explode myths, in the sense of dangerous fictions with which the Irishman deludes himself about his national identity and his supposedly peculiar virtues. And yet the poems about the horse-trade show that at the heart of Clarke's world, as in the strikingly different mythopoeic world of Muir, there *is* myth since there is a belief in the sacred. To find this belief professed in a tone of voice that is still sardonic is especially arresting; it gives us pause, as Muir's voice cannot. On the other hand the sardonic tone misleads all but the most careful reader; for the tone makes us look anywhere but where, since sacrilege is denounced, sacredness is affirmed. And so there is that much excuse for a misreading like Roscelli's. One can go further indeed, and suggest that Clarke at times deceives himself as he deceives many readers. In 'Medical Missionary of Mary' a nun injures herself by falling from her bicycle, her habit caught up in a pedal; she is taken on a stretcher to Lourdes, despite her devotions there she is not cured, and

> worse than ever, came back
> By London, lying on her back,
> Saw there, thank Heaven, a specialist
> And now is on the recovery list.

If we declare this, despite the delightfully raucous interjection of 'thank Heaven', none the less *cheap*, we mean in the first place to protest that the woman inside the nun's habit is suffering and frightened just as Martha Blake was; but one may object also that to deny a miracle-working sanctity at Lourdes is one thing, to deny that such sanctity exists or may exist elsewhere is something else again. The poem certainly invites us to make this second denial, and to think that the notion of such imponderable and unprovable sanctities is a dangerous fiction which only stops us looking for help, for salvation, to the one quarter where it can be found — in the scientific humanism of the London medical specialist. If so, this poem is at odds with 'Forget Me Not', and invites W. J. Roscelli's impatient misreading of that poem. We may hesitantly conclude that the poet's task is ultimately and essentially, if not mythopoeic, at any rate religious; and that it is dangerous for any poet to think otherwise.

*

Padraic Fallon (b. 1905), though a younger poet than Clarke, may be considered along with him for a number of reasons. One is that, although he has been a respected figure on the Irish literary scene through several decades, the literary world of Ireland has not recognized its obligations towards him any more generously than it did its obligations to Austin Clarke. Fallon's poems have to be hunted up for the most part in the files of magazines; and his *Collected Poems*,* long promised from the Dolmen Press, has still not appeared as I write this. However, as I hinted on an earlier page, to set Fallon beside Clarke is to be struck by the contrast between them more than by anything they have in common.

Fallon too has written 'horsey' poems. But in pieces like 'Gowran Park, Autumn Meeting' or 'Curragh November Meeting', we look in vain for the arresting perception common to Clarke and to Muir — that in their lifetime they have seen what looks like a quantum jump in man's development, for good or ill; the ending of man's dependence on the horse as a work-mate or servant, and the disappearance of the horse from the human scene except in contexts of sport or pleasure. Fallon's poems, like Philip Larkin's poem 'At Grass', have to do with race-horses, not work-horses; and this by itself is enough to remove from them the historical resonance of Muir's 'Horses' or Clarke's 'Forget Me Not'. The poet who chose for his epitaph, 'Horseman, pass by!' must have been equally blind to how in his lifetime man's relationship to the horse had changed radically and momentously. And this should make us think again about putting Yeats and Muir together as 'mythopoeic poets'. In particular, it should give us a new respect for Edwin Muir; his myth, it now seems, could take note of and encompass a radical historical change. Indeed, 'The Horses' judges modern times unequivocally: it says that man is rushing to his doom by relying on inert machinery, technological ingenuity, to do for him what can safely be done only by comradely care for other creatures than himself. (It says moreover, very touchingly and sombrely, with no sentimentality at all, that if mankind is ever to have a 'second chance', it can only be on these creaturely terms, and will depend on domesticated creatures like the horse agreeing, as it were, to 'try again'.) Yeats is by all counts an infinitely greater poet than Muir. Yet on this point a comparison between them does not work in Yeats's favour; it is not at all clear that any of Yeats's myths can stoop to notice and make sense of any one distinguishable and observable historical change as surely as Muir's does. This to be sure flies in the face of accepted opinion about Yeats. For the author of 'The Second Coming' is often presented as *par excellence* the tragic historian of western man's twentieth-century times. Yet is it not the case that

* Published in October, 1974. Ed.

Yeats the philosopher of history works on a time-scale too grandiose ever to be tripped up by particular instances of the changes that history brings about? Does not Yeats's concern for the Dionysian 'great year' release him from the pain of the years that we tick off on the calendar? And does not his cyclical theory of history, like every such theory, say in the end *Plus ça change, plus c'est la même chose*, in a tone that is ultimately consoling and anaesthetic? One imagines Clarke answering a venomous 'Yes' to all these questions.

At any rate the same Yeatsian tone, and the same unformulated assumptions, crop up in Padraic Fallon in poems like those cited, or in much better ones like 'Peasantry' and 'Weir Bridge', which seem to say or to imply that there is nothing new under the sun. In a better poem still, such as 'The Dwelling', everything depends on whether what the poem gives us is offered as what *is*, or as what *should be*:

> At night the house grows
> Around the blackshawled woman. Harsh
> And sparse the bony room
> But with the lamp
> All the pieces give their lights:
> She shines among her satellites.
>
> Man-chairs of oak, scrubbed; a rack
> Of cups and blue plates;
> The tabled jug:
> The oilcloth spreading from the wick;
> The spindled stair without a rug
> But scrubbed, scrubbed to the quick.
>
> The tiny window's shut its eye;
> Let the strand roar
> And the white horses tumble on the shore,
> Here catgreen
> The salt driftwood purrs inside the fire
> And the sea ends that pours around the world.
>
> Somewhere an old working clock,
> Weights and chains, ticks on and tells
> The woman's hours;
> The wether's wool in the knitted sock,
> The world weather in
> Her knotted face, her knotted talk;
>
> How men come home
> From the ocean drip, still rocking, ill at ease
> Till she gathers them;
> Here she sets them down in peace
> Inside the lamp, the house, the shawl.
> Here is the centre of them all.
>
> And all the pieces hang

> In one. The man is on the chair
> Who winds the clock
> Who'll climb the stairhead after her,
> Adjust the wick
> Till the great night idles, barely ticking over.

'*Barely* ticking', but still ticking . . . And does the sea that pours around the world really 'end' in this seemingly primordial scenario, or only seem to? (That's to say, *is* it primordial, or does it only appear to be?) Has Women's Liberation no hope of unsettling this Tolstoyan vision of 'the woman of the house' as stable centre and unwavering vehicle of man's culture? The poem is too cunning to answer these questions; it is careful to keep its options open. Yet there is not much room for doubt that those who are charmed by the poem are responding to it as a vision of what unalterably *is* (and will be seen to be so, after temporary aberrations), rather than as a vision of what ought to be, but is no longer, and perhaps never will be again. And this means that the poem stays securely within the Yeatsian universe, not moving outside into the more problematic areas where in their different ways Clarke's poems live, and Muir's.

However, Fallon is not always quite so cagey, nor are his poems always thus furnished with the cottage properties of J. M. Synge. At the end of a long, splendid and ambitious poem, 'Boyne Valley', he writes:

> Jaguars roll from the meet, trailing
> Horseheads and dogfoxes. History perhaps
> Is slowly reaching some conclusion.
> And here is the usual tentative dusk
> As day runs out of silver
> And one flintnebbed swan owns all the Boyne;
> No afterglow or
> Gold bowl to sail home the antlered one,
> Surrogate, heraldic sufferer,
> Cerumnos, Arthur, Bran.

Here, though Fallon still keeps his options open, he only just does so. The 'perhaps' with which History is said to be 'slowly reaching some conclusion' is a possibility rather firmly excluded by the 'usual tentative dusk', and the final impression is that, despite the different appurtenances (Jaguar cars hauling horse-boxes) the hunt is still the unchanging and necessary ritual that it always was.

In any case, it will be seen that Fallon stands in a curious relation to Yeats. And his direct and unabashed dialogue with that overbearing predecessor is strikingly at odds with Austin Clarke's evasive obliquities, his talking around the inescapable monument. Fallon, that is to say, has not kept his distance from Yeats, as Clarke and other prudent poets found it necessary to do. And Fallon pays the price; his

'Wexford to Commodore Barry' is a poem in which the heroic cadences of the great ventriloquist overwhelm Fallon and push him into unintended parody. But as I read Fallon, he knows the risks he runs and is prepared to live dangerously. It is thus that he seems to define himself in the poem he calls 'Odysseus' — that legendary voyager who figures in so many poems by Fallon that we may without absurdity think the Odyssean paradigm not much less important for him than for Joyce:

> Last year's decencies
> Are the rags and reach-me-downs he'll wear forever,
> Knowing one day he'll sober up inside them
> Safe in wind and wife and limb,
> Respected, of unimpeachable behaviour.
>
> Meanwhile he goes forward
> Magniloquently to himself; and, the fit on him,
> Pushes his painful hobble to a dance,
> Exposing in obscene wounds and dilapidation
> The naked metre of the man.

If Yeatsian idioms and cadences are 'last year's decencies', Fallon will wear them, at whatever cost in occasional absurdity. And if it comes to a push between the graduate of the Bardic schools and the harum-scarum, Fallon is with the harum-scarums.

Fallon's more or less direct dialogue with the shade of Yeats is in the following poems: 'Fin de Siècle' (where there is a tinge — no more — of the jealous rancour we sometimes find in Clarke); 'Yeats at Athenry Perhaps' (which is charming but slight, and accordingly too long); 'Stop on the Road to Ballylee'; 'On the Tower Stairs' (which is principally about Lady Gregory, and is a dazzling performance, entertaining and audacious); and 'Yeats's Tower at Ballylee' — a list to which I would add 'Johnstown Castle', a poem where Yeats's presence is less overt but not much less insistent.

Written in 1951, 'Yeats's Tower at Ballylee' is very explicit indeed, certainly too much so for its own good as an independent poem. The Yeatsian turns and resonances are snatched up as opportunity offers, by no means 'placed' nor made new. Yet the piece is central to Fallon's work because it reveals, better than any other, and precisely by being so vulnerable, the earnestness with which Fallon meditates on the significance of Yeats's career. The poem has for epigraph Yeats's lines:

> Is every modern nation like the Tower
> Half-dead at the top?

And Fallon comes to grips with this, two-thirds of the way through his poem:

I climb to the wasting storey at the top.
His symbol's there where water and watery air
Soak through the plaster. The higher we clamber up
Into ourselves the greater seems the danger;
For the wider the vision then
On a desolate and more desolate world
Where the inspirations of men
Are taken by man and hurled
From shape into evil shape;
With the good and the grace gone out of them
Where indeed is there hope for men?
So every civilization tires at the top.

Around me now from this great height
Is a vision I did not seek. I have avoided it
And now I am forty-five
And wars blow up again, the east is lit,
Town burn, villages are bombed,
With people everywhere in flight,
Their households on a handcart, or entombed
In homes that fell about them in the night,
And dragging children homeless in the air;
A mass migration of the humble
Before some war-mad general.
O the higher we climb up the wider our despair.

The poem ends:

Everywhere is the world. And not less here
Because the stream, dividing, moats the place.
To live a fairy tale he bought this tower
And married a woman with a pleasant face;
And built in bookshelves, cupboards, hung
His pictures up and walked around
His beehive and his acre, wrung
Some civilization from the ground:
And yet instead of rhyming country ease
As in the eighteenth century we find
Him raving like a man gone blind
At the bloody vision that usurped his eyes.

Below me in the road two countrymen
Are talking of cattle and the price of wool,
Glad of the gossip and something held in common.
That scene would have been peaceful
An hour ago, but now I stumble down
In horror, knowing that there is no way
Of protest left to poet or to clown
That will enlarge his future by one day.
I could beat a policeman, bawl in a square, do gaol
For something silly. And what avails it? I
Step into the drizzle of the sky
Despairingly, to talk of the price of wool.

The assertion that 'every civilization tires at the top', with the preceding lines that seek to validate it ('The higher we clamber up / Into ourselves the greater seems the danger; / For the wider the vision then') is so important, both in itself and as a gloss on Yeats's verses, that any middle-aged reader should pause to ask if his own experience bears it out. And by earnest doggedness earlier in the poem Fallon has earned the right to this sort of attention. It's a pity that his language is not crisp nor memorable enough to enforce it, yet his diction, if it's more patchy than Edwin Muir's homespun, is by that token more flexible. Certainly the dull thud that the poem ends on enacts the despair it is talking about. And in any case what we are presented with beyond possibility of quibble is what is poignant at certain comparable moments in Yeats himself: a man who believes in ritual or heraldic patterns subsisting unchanged below the phenomena of history, admitting that the belief does not sustain him or itself in the face of evidence that in history real changes do occur, and for the worse — for instance between the eighteenth century and the twentieth.

Moreover the dogged discursiveness of Fallon's style in this poem is not at all characteristic of him, but rather (we may suppose) something that the pain and gravity of one particular experience impelled him to. What comes to him more naturally is a style altogether more colourful. It may be exemplified from a poem where he is altogether clear of Yeatsian territory, and approaching indeed — in subject but also in style — the territory of Clarke. It is a poem on the Immaculate Conception, entitled 'Magna Mater':

> A dove plus an
> Assenting virgin is
> An odd equation; the bird of Venus,
> Shotsilk woodhaunter and
> A country shawl
> In congress to produce
> The least erotic of the gods . . .

'Shotsilk woodhaunter' for 'dove' is all Fallon; a note struck no more by Clarke than by Yeats. Characteristically, the poem (which is thoroughly devout, and strongly and interestingly conceived) falls away from this first stanza through four more which are makeshift. And indeed 'makeshift' is exact for Padraic Fallon; he is a brilliant opportunist, and content to be so. Nor is this necessarily so disparaging as it sounds. For certainly in Fallon's case his *trouvailles* are as astonishing as his misjudgements, his unfortunate puns for instance, are outrageous; and in almost every poem he veers from blunder to felicity, the one as breath-taking as the other. What happens when Fallon tries to be flawless and relatively sober, can be seen in another poem on the Virgin, 'Mater Dei':

In March the seed
Fell, when the month leaned over, looking
Down into the valley.
And none but the woman knew it where she sat
In the tree of her veins and tended him
The red and ripening Adam of the year.

Her autumn was late and human.
Trees were nude, the lights were on at the pole
All night when he came,
Her own man;
In the cry of a child she sat, not knowing
That this was a stranger.

Milk ran wild
Across the heavens. Imperiously He
Sipped at the delicate beakers she proffered him.
How was she to know
How huge a body she was, how she corrected
The very tilt of the earth on its new course?

By Fallon's standards this is almost classical. And yet oddly enough
its marmoreal finish is nearer being vulgar than is the audacity of
'Magna Mater'. It seems that Fallon is true to himself only when he
is immoderate; and in very different ways this is true of Yeats also,
and of Austin Clarke.

NOTES

1. See Clarke's note to his Knacker Rhymes in *Later Poems* (1961).
2. Cf. *Beyond the Pale. Austin Clarke Reads His Own Poetry*, Claddagh
Records, Dublin, 1964.
3. Hugh MacDiarmid, 'Charles Doughty and the Need for Heroic Poetry',
1936.
4. Denis Donoghue, *The Ordinary Universe*, London, 1968, p. 30. In the
analysis which follows I am indebted to members of a graduate seminar at
Stanford, particularly Michael Stillman and Gareth Reeves.
5. Augustine Martin, 'The Rediscovery of Austin Clarke', in *Studies. An
Irish Quarterly Review*, LIV, 216 (winter 1965).
6. Martin, op. cit., p. 424.
7. W. J. Roscelli, in *The Celtic Cross*, Purdue University Studies, 1964, p. 69.

N.B. *Irish University Review*, IV, 1 (1974) is an 'Austin Clarke Special
Issue'. Among contributions by Maurice Harmon, Brendan Kenelly, Thomas
Kinsella and others, it contains a Bibliography compiled by Gerard Lyne.
Susan Halpern's *The Life and Works of Austin Clarke* (Dolmen, 1974) con-
tains biographical information as well as criticism, with chapters on Clarke's plays
and prose, and a bibliography. Ed.

On Other Grounds:
The Poetry of Brian Coffey
by Stan Smith

BRIAN COFFEY is an Irishman who has constructed, from the very casualness of his exile, a poetry which transcends the familiar categories of residence and expatriation. Coffey's stance is not the Joycean *non serviam* which, with its *frisson* of adolescent apostasy, implicitly subscribes to the allegiance against which it revolts. For Coffey, where one finds oneself is the result of an accumulation of circumstances, accidents and omissions, not a willed and single act of defiance or flight. And it is with one's circumstantial self that reckoning, for the poet, must always be made, as he concludes in 'Missouri Sequence', his most ambitious and successful work to date:

> No servant, the muse
> abides in truth,
> permits the use of protest
> as a second best
> to make clean fields,
> exults only in the actual
> expression of a love,
> love all problem,
> wisdom lacking.

For,

> The true muse fleshed
> nor was, nor shall be,
> is a torment of oneself,
> cannot be done without.

In Coffey's thought, with its undertones of Taoism and Christian neo-platonism, exile is not so much a social condition as an ontological given, the necessary ground of existence. An aside in 'Syllables for Accents' which speaks of 'the patient pale exiles, waiters, / Shells voided and beached by the sea' seems almost a joke at Joyce's expense, exploiting the tension latent in the concepts both of service and of waiting, a tension which is also that between the registers of philosophic discourse and workaday experience. But it also, ironically, hints at an

existential dilemma, turning Sartre's familiar analogue for self-definition
— a waiter is a man acting the part of a waiter — against itself. Coffey's
phrase catches the contingency of being, the forfeit of autonomy that is
paid in assuming a reductive and defining role. The waiter is, in his
very choice of an occupation, other-defined, attendant on a social
reality from which he stands back, deferentially. At the same time he is
flotsam, casually cast up into this identity by a world that delivers him
to his own emptiness.

For all particularity is to some extent a rupture with the seamless
web of undifferentiated being, a fall from grace. In 'Third Person' the
recognition of the otherness of others carries with it the shock of one's
own strangeness, as a part which seeks to grasp the whole from which it
is split off by the very fact of consciousness:

> She is one part of all
> as I am as I hold all
> as no stone does
> mine in her way
> hers in mine
> By glens of exile
> if she turned
> love was needed

To each, the world's body belongs less to self than to the other who
seems part of that body in a way one's own self never does: the stepping
back to take hold results in a necessary estrangement. Here, characteristically, the verbal play stresses the linguistic distance, suggesting that
consciousness is caught up in a grid of language necessarily divorced
from the concrete world it maps, and never reducible to it. Meaning is a
system of exchanges, independent of the objects signified. The Romantic
cult of the image, which sought, through metaphor, to close the gap
between tenor and vehicle, denied that disjunction which, for Coffey, is
the necessary ground of freedom and volition:

> She is no stone no lilac
> no bird more beautiful than stars
> takes what she takes by right of grace
> to make hearts equal
> unequal were strange

'Third Person' deploys the parts of speech as its central metaphor: it is
only in the eyes of a third that self and other become reconciled, as
figures in a single field, unequivocally located in a common space which,
for each of them, seems to belong inequitably to the other. Language
is the celebration of this dispersal, as language too is the force-field
where the centrifugal parts are held in unstable equilibrium:

> She finds pain
> he she you we they
> this one that one

> other the same
> how why when where
> before once often after now
> never end
>
> Who speaks to whom
> of whom
> these three.

The world, as 'Headrock', the postlude to this collection,* indicates, is everything which is the case, an '*ipso facto* paper' where one is instructed to 'Answer all questions taking all your time', but lacks the necessary information, insight or honesty to answer what are often, in any case, loaded or unanswerable metaquestions ('*one* What have you forgotten . . . *four* Are you pushed for time yet . . . *six* When you were beating your wife did she smile and if so why'). The very shape of the poem on the page, with its words run together and arbitrarily end-stopped to present the image of a solid rectangular headstone with, at its base, the capitalized words 'NO ESCAPE', seems to propose a contrast between the undifferentiated mass of experience and the orderly patterns to which intellection reduces it.

The opacity, the impenetrable, obstructive otherness of such a world, can come upon the self with a sense of numbing shock: it is, again and again, a revelation that induces the recoil of silence, withdrawal, nihilism:

> so many have come this way
> the flash the sight the dark
> fading on and heart
> bruised by unthought-of walls
> on way of purpose
> Alienated Us
> Like nothing there at all
> all opting for fair times stunned
> to silence by close wall.

And indeed the quotidian state explored in the sequence from which this comes, 'How Far from Daybreak', is an unpromising and unalleviated deprivation, the barrenness of an exile in the wilderness. The verbal dislocation of the poem mimes the inconsequentiality of consciousness in a centreless void, lost in space:

> There is he Space all ways
> up deep-in down around.

In a world where there seems no immediate correspondence between the sterile endless overlaying of process and the fatuous excess of the human gesture, the contrast of mind and its objects conceals a deeper similarity, which in turn provokes a further, distinguishing excess

* *Selected Poems,* New Writers' Press, Dublin, 1972.

hardly different from the Beckettian cry of anguish; honest because involuntary, pointless, extreme, abruptly cut short:

> No promise in the coloured light
> green the like sand and white
>
> But feed your nettles to the desert
> compassionately scatter clay
> The sand moves moving the sand
> Stripped and naked
> what will you do some day
> when you die
> Howl man Woman scream
> Be dead

Within this endless inanition, randomness, under pressure of a human necessity, coalesces into form: an eye desperate for promise and for confirmations discerns, or invents, limits and relations, centres and margins:

> Moonlike Bright on sheet silk
> with stretch of white sand
> unterminated
> until surround of hill
> touched bright by brightness
> Moonlight indeed
> Dead centre out of mind.

The ambivalence which correlates exactitude and nullity — 'Dead centre' — introduces a harrowing tension, taken up at once:

> But in mind
> the dead centre
> like like yawning
>
> yawning away
> in shadows
> straight and still
>
> Nothing that flickers
> for sidelong glances
> Nothing Period
>
> O moon of dead desire
> for ever motionless.

From the peak of selfhood, both inner and outer landscapes slip abruptly away into nothingness. Consciousness is a pit of shadows, a void that flickers with dull, reptilian langour, living only in its deflections, extinguished in the very act of turning to contemplate itself. The repeated, subversive 'like' proposes a being that lives only in its capacity to establish relations, in a world which is itself radically centreless. These yawning interiors in and out of mind are the 'glens of exile'

within which each self lives, needing the intercession of another to assure
him, by analogy, of his own existence:

> Who is sitting
> by what fire
> and knows
> another watching him
> We guess at others
> and of ourselves
> pretend to guess
> to blind our pain.

   The ratio of survival in Coffey's poetry sets the ordinariness of loss
and need against the rare, reverential patience which may deserve but
can never arrogate grace. This is not resignation, but an attendant and
attentive openness, a humility before events which is neither stubborn
stoical indifference nor the impatient, desperate greed of hedonism,
but a calm readiness which salvages assurance from the dispossessing
flux:

> Yet is the open heart free
> to brush all hesitancy from court.

To remain 'patient always / in scenes of casual strife' ('Dreams What
Returns') cannot guarantee these momentary redeeming intuitions:
there is no causal relationship between patience and grace ('How it pains
me to say / the possible not probable'); but survival keeps open the
improbable possibility. Grace is gratuitous, 'Happening from nowhere /
unhappening right away', and it is, he says in 'Missouri Sequence',
'such a grace / as comes only to awaken / but does not stay to
strengthen'; yet its very unpredictability makes it perpetually possible,
undetermined by necessity or logic, a 'green chance':

> Take the residue
> chance effects
> to offset what must be
> Let what is sudden unforseen
> unforseen and wonder bide . . .
>
> Green it was green of chill water
> green to turn patience
> from a habit to peace . . .
>
> It was meeting every green
> for no reason at all
>
> A happening that raised one up
>
> Consider dear against all backdrops
> this is a world where what's not planned
> the unnecessary can be.
>
>   ('How Far . . .')

At this moment of epiphany, direct address becomes possible, as space recedes to its proper, its humane distance.

There is no facile movement from desire to gratification in Coffey's verse, but rather an uneasy, shifting rhythm of partial gaining and loss, of opportunities and omissions, in some adjustment of freedom and necessity, casual and causal, 'some equation between God's will and mine, / rejecting prudence . . .' But the mutuality of selves is a sustaining fiction of all his work. The poems abound in the intertexturing of pronouns and possessive adjectives which creates a self-sufficient world of human exchanges, one self 'mindful', and 'mind full' of another:

> Never forever
> though in mine yours
> and in yours mine
> random should stray
>> ('Mindful of You')

The opening lines of 'Bridie' establish a self-enclosing circularity of relationship which transcends the sordid situation:

> His old bat and her boy
> sip in the soiled saloon;

while 'The Nicest Phantasies are Shared' uses the device to distinguish between a superficial and an authentic reciprocity:

> Taking her garments
> while she takes his
> does not make theirs
> a single robe

> Their holding hands leaves each
> aware of self and other
> Their touching skins
> breast to mouth mouth to breast
> their planting kisses in hair
> sunders uniting if he in her
> unmatched is by a her in him.

Neither self nor other is solely the autonomous, tangible body, the empirically demonstrable object, but a whole mode of being and relating, communicated and realized through the body and its gestures. This is an incarnational ontology quite distinct from Descartes' threadbare sartorial imagery (taken up later in a pun on 'suit') — an integral exchange of significances which can be expressed only in terms of *information*, the self informed in its own fullness in the act of informing, giving to another. Individuation is a function of relatedness, generated in a system of exchanges in which subject and object are both integers of the integrating verb.

The language of giving and taking, of finding and losing, is not incidental in Coffey's poetry, but intimately bound up with his insistence
on responsiveness. Love is no ravishment of a reluctant ego, but the
completion of a movement from enclosure to openness, an unfolding
and a giving which is radical and yet endlessly regenerative; so that, in
'The Nicest Phantasies . . .', the unexpectedly blunt 'mating' is justified
by its illuminating reference back to 'unmatched', setting up a counterpoint between carnality and the strangely archaic, spiritualizing accents
of *amour courtois*:

> What then, is love
> for lovers mating
> with naught spoiled
> though all uprooted
> but completing natural skill
> forever giving him to her
> giving forever her to him
> for them joying
> in every difference
> love decrees.

The conception of love as the exercise of an innate skill, rather than
a transfer of spiritual capital, is precise, proposing a giving which
strengthens rather than depletes. The alternative, and more common
mode of relating seems to be encapsulated in 'One Way', the one-way
transactions of mercantilist economics, which subsists in a slow dis-
sipation of energy:

> Giving what he has not given
> he sees what he has not seen
>
> Taking what he has not taken
> he hears what he has not heard . . .
>
> constraint constrained
> to work himself out.

Such constrictions are the fruits of a culture of hoarding and reten-
tiveness, fixated on the principles of duty and reward, penalty and
compensation, whose primal metaphors for selfhood are derived from
the cash-nexus and power-politics. 'Latin Lover' seems to be a parody
of such an ethos, the grotesque, unnatural contortions of a latinate
syntax aping the rhetoric and postures of a love which weighs invest-
ment against return, estimates the relative values of properties, and
consistently fuses a fay imagery of enchantment and enthralling with
that of imperial domination befitting a Roman. The poem seems to
grow out of the collision between an impulse to generosity and a bitter
carping that counts the small change of resentment, fluctuating between
a sense of the intrinsic worth of the other and a suspicion of over-
valuation: 'fair exchange', 'good bargain', 'currency in love':

> When once pleasing I was to thee
> didst thou wonder at it ask why it was I turned . . .
> Princess thee to worship small O of poor domain. . .
>
> What showed as impairment in thee
> manners mincing the tare of bitchiness and lies
> features thine all others bettered
> skin breath hair nose and mouth these I accepted loving thee.

Against such deformations of speech and attitude Coffey's own style offers itself, fluid, moving, insubstantial, yet gathering substance and resonance, like that incorrigible, deft lucidity, without rigidity or rancour, praised in his master, Su Tungpo, suitor to a Muse

> [whose] lovers . . . work a light
> Peering tyrants will not see . . .
>
> Who did show
> Himself yours and free.
>
> Unperturbed by tigerish spite
> He honoured an honesty
>
> In winter muse-like, reckless, right—
> Crane ash-grey when snow
> Shrouds willow
> Southwards blown swiftly—
>
> His style, its brook-song cloud-flight
> Your gift unmistakably.

The alienated world of reductive visions, of 'peering tyrants', 'self-elected' ideologies cramped by their vast ambitions, receives its contemptuous dismissal in 'The Monument', whose Nietzschean *Uebermensch* is reduced by the opening lines ('Up! up! And away!') to the status of a comic-book Superman. The language of these technological over-reachers abounds in imagery of closure and constriction, calculation and manipulation, despite the ostensible aspiration to 'egress / from limits which had halted progress'. For what they mean by progress is a further circumscription of human and natural worlds by the dominative rationality of the machine:

> The vision we had constructed
> of a renewed earth had contracted
> to make-shift patching with obtuse men
> who withheld the blind faith we demanded
> as the price of an epoch when
> conflict would have ended. . .
>
> Perfect our reliance
> on shaping matter as we willed. . .
> Yet in our plan their full consent
> Would have sealed closure of the great argument.

> The neatest solution
> suggested men accept their dissolution.

The Utopia planned by such technological existentialists is a 'termitary' of totally regulated, determined beings, quite different from the platonic Eden of a nature undisturbed by man —

> executive trees, determinate season,
> form-moved beasts, ecological reason.

The inexplicable but 'exact betrayal' of this experts' millennium by the 'multitudinous unskilled' who do not appreciate its astringent beauty breeds schemes of retributive genocide, the poisoning and pollution of the planet from which the 'proud skymen' take flight to the next star. Yet they themselves become victims of the technology they have invented, mutated by 'arbitrary machines' to fit the instruments with which they sought to dominate the alien terrain. Their pride, finally, shrinks to that of having foreseen, and 'exactly answered' in advance, the queries of the visiting stranger who, on some alien planet, now reads the monument on which is inscribed all that remains of their titanic hubris.

What the parable contrasts to this degenerate titanism is the relaxing into being of the 'lovers', left behind, 'mazed in no lie', 'tend[ing] heart's flame in patient toil':

> rest no death but present being,
> in perfected incorruptible seeing.

The opposition of Promethean and Orphic modes, the aspiring 'metric' of technology and the celebratory 'measures' of music and poetry, is not so much a contrast of *Verstand* and *Vernunft*, as of dominative and responsive forms of perception and relation. Thus, while the skymen need to contain even the unpredictable within a 'scheme of uncertified possibilities', it is sheer, intuitive *nous* that warns the 'regressive' multitude against their fanaticisms ('How they guessed, we do not understand'). Guesswork is a crucial component of Coffey's epistemology, an affirmation of capricious freedom in face of the certitudes of reductive reason. The Faustian striving after an ever-elusive consummation ('longing heart / going always longing on / beside another's heart of longing') is seen, in 'How Far from Daybreak', as graceless ingratitude, the ambition of the 'drinker of ocean' 'who what was offered did not see / . . . wanting what day does not give'; an ambition quite capable, at some crux of choice, to betray the actual loved other, as Faust betrayed Gretchen, in the name of an imaginary absolute. Orpheus, on the other hand, seeks perpetually the reclamation of his lost bride, the muse encountered momentarily in 'Muse, June, Related', and his quest is not for transcendence but for recovery and

reconciliation, though it may end in the poet's metaphoric dis-
membering:

> If he turned his head
> in his course
> he saw her through branches
> a slip of light
> until the leaves took her
>
> He went imagining
> her tears at morning
> spent on the green.
> In song he poised her,
> lauded victory
> over his muse.
>
> What he fancied ended
> she smiled at as begun,
> knowing him no freeman. . .
>
> He did not know, not yet,
> him hers, his elements
> scattered on shore and shore. . .

The unexpected reversal turns mastery into service, but a service which
is perfect freedom. Individual muses are 'casual stimulants', but the
grace they embody 'cannot be done without'. Guessing at such a
possibility initiates, in 'How Far . . . ', the return from the underworld
of abandonment, to the prospect of renewal:

> In oneself seeing who sees oneself
> a flash smell of sprinkled leaves
> growth again in a possible world
> black Orpheus made glad
>
> absence made amiable by default;

and, once conceded, reality is transfigured by the prospect:

> To have been made over
> to light and song
> birds a garden rose
> her peace calm
> gracious immeasure
>
> To have guessed it possible
> merely to have guessed
> His whole sky alight
> perfect clarity
> joy flaming
>
> ('Mindful of You')

Grace is immeasurable. Yet there is measure, as there is rhyme and
reason, in Coffey's poetry. The ambiguity explored in 'Syllables for

Accents' is that of a tangible social world, 'riotous winter in Paris'; but it is also an ambiguity latent in the title: syllables for which accents must be found, syllables found to fit some existing metric; prosody become a metaphor for the relationship between the moments of an individual life and the momentum they assume. Men are made over into poetry, certainly: 'Of Teng Pang what were known had Po not read his verses?'

But this in turn is only the extreme case of a universal process, not confined to art alone:

> Many young people visited me,
> Sontag, then poet, now newsman,
> Miailhe, comrade, now gendarme,
> And Rudy translating lust love
> For a greedy bourgeois girl
> Circled the city explaining:
> 'I levelled her, so.
> I levelled her, so.'

The translation is an attempted self-justification, a fiction woven from the self for the benefit of the self and of others, a pretended guessing at act and motive; so that laying a girl, in Rudy's conveniently broken English, is metaphorically transmuted into a levelling, a pro-letarianization of the bourgeois. This self-production along the line of a fable is one variant of a universal fictive impulse, suggested also in that repeated distinguishing of past and present selves. The poem moves from particulars to generalization:

> By their firm choices they split at forked paths
> And such firm choices raised walls between
> Who now survive gardening their new strange hearts.

This apparently arbitrary allusion to Borges' story 'The Garden of the Forked Paths' in fact embodies a device recurrent in Coffey's verse. Borges' 'Fiction' too concerns the varying inflections and deflections which the trajectory of a single life can undergo. A parable constructed on the principle of a 'detective' or 'spy' story, it moves between shifting identities with fixed names and fixed identities with changing names, and its denouement depends upon guessing correctly a name hinted at by a complex allusiveness. But its most central relevance, perhaps, lies in its juxtaposition of two contrasting attitudes towards time — one, the initial maxim of the narrator, an assassin at once fleeing and seeking assassination, the assertion of rigid, linear progress: 'The author of an atrocious undertaking ought to imagine that he has already accomplished it, ought to impose upon himself a future as irrevocable as the past.' The other is revealed to him in the garden where, on entering, he is greeted by 'a high pitched almost syllabic music [which] approached and receded in the shifting of the wind'. He is admitted to the secret of an interminable labyrinth which is both this garden and a book quite unlike all other books: 'In all fictional works, each time a man is confronted with several alternatives, he chooses one and eliminates all the others;' whereas in this work he chooses all options simultaneously, creating diverse futures and pasts which themselves fork and proliferate, so that, for example, 'all possible outcomes occur' when a stranger calls at the door. All variants, however, are inflections of one basic plot, in which the parts and actions are continuously redistributed in an infinite regress. Against, then, the 'exact distributors of limits' of a one-track universe, Coffey balances a world of infinite possibilities, constantly redefined and rearranged by the evolving fictions of its many converging and diverging characters; a world in which, as for Borges' narrator, one can be the enemy only of the moments of other men, not of their lifetimes or their countries:

> If I talked with a lover of wisdom
> Of men, their changes, mutinous then
> Would he so gladly listen?

The sentence itself enacts the mutiny of which it speaks; yet the poem goes on to postulate an essence ('the same She'), revealed nowhere but in the particular awakenings to which a name and a due season must be given, thus establishing a radical tension between openness to all possibilities and the inevitability of choice. The discrepancy between the wished self and its ripening, the 'strange new heart' one becomes, a tension between the merely putative and the merely achieved, is embodied in the poem's counterpointing of casual utterance, an apparently random accumulation of memories, with the artifice of the construction. The poem itself is the labyrinth which opens backwards and forwards, a fiction at once circumscriptive and centrifugal. But so, too, is the real Paris within which these various lives circled, and the wider and wider gyres in which they moved, in the endless reforging of their momentary selves. (Cf. Borges: 'Centuries and centuries and only in the present do things happen; countless men in the air, on the face of the earth and sea, and all that really is happening is happening to me'):

> Now as then seed falls
> Then as now unfruited trees,
> As it was it is.
>
> I weep for what I remember
> Of faithfulness, credulity,
> Acquaintance, its calculus,
> And her I did seek
> Like a climber without maps
> Finds and loses highest peaks,
> And them all unlike the ripening of those wished selves
> For good reason and all,
> For good reason and all.

Faithfulness runs into credulity because it involves a readiness, 'against the grain' of individual will and of circumstance, to persist in one's conviction of the other's singleness,

> Each time each one awakens the same She whose beauty
> Of his conceiving is granted him. . .

The stubborn ordinariness of Coffey's poetry, despite or because of its cryptic intonations, its inflections of cliché into oracular utterance, all insist on this interplay of the casual and the fictive. Conventions of speech are subverted in their very use, normal syntactic patterns are dislocated, displaced, cut short; the poetry abounds in anacolutha; and what this indicates is a willingness to change direction, a refusal of linear progression, of the ruthless irrelevance of logic. Once a sentence's development is assured, and it moves inexorably to its predetermined goal, a moment of freedom has been surrendered, plenitude has been made over to necessity. Consistently, Coffey disposes of these expectations with a throwaway flourish. In 'Davy Byrne's of a Saturday Night', the closeness and tightness of the rhyme scheme, unusual in Coffey's verse, is counterpointed against the randomness, the incoherence of the perceptions, at times lurching into the surreal:

> But to continue meditating on life:
> There are a number of ways of irritating people.
> Observe the big black woman with a knife
> Chasing Poe's raven up that steeple.
>
> You may wonder why the grass is green.
> Nothing is green but thinking makes it so.
> You may ask why flies fly into cream.
> Have they any better place to go?

The irony of 'meditating' is plain, for the succession of thoughts is meditative only in that wider, unphilosophical sense of the word in everyday use, a synonym for daydreaming. The directions life takes may be dictated by nothing more pointed than a urinal revelation:

> Then you will observe often a man at wine
> In a four-square tavern for no better reason
> Than that he saw the Silk of the Kine
> In a convenience accusing him of high treason.

'Convenience' here takes on a new, moral significance, and there is a mutual recharging of everyday and philosophical language in its interplay with 'reason'. One suspects an undercurrent of subliminal connections beneath this gossipy inconsequentiality, and indeed, a context of sorts seems to be supplied by the Davy Byrne's sequence in *Ulysses* (pp. 160-9, 1937 edition) — itself cohering around the concept of love — which contains many images and words gratuitously rearranged in the poem. (That there is a correspondence seems to be confirmed by the appearance of 'High sheriff, Coffey the butcher' in Joyce's sequence, an allusion which fits in with the self-accusations above.)

What in fact happens in the poem is that the stage props, cribbed from *Ulysses*, are returned to their location in the ordinary, stripped of the mythic dimension in which Joyce had implicated them with such cunning mock realism ('And I remember / I wanted to be a sailor,' the poem notes, reducing the Ulyssean myth to the terms of 'career and all' from which he has been cast up to love). Persistently, Coffey parodies the mythologizing of the self endemic, not only to literature, but to the idea of a career itself, with its subordination of possibility to a partial destiny (a tension revealed too, in 'reflect[ing] / On the different things that may happen to a man', in the contrast between 'wife' and 'another also-ran'). The conclusion of the poem is at once an evasive slipping out of — or into? — commitment, and a delineation of Coffey's own style, in poetry as in experience, of keeping the options open,

> 'Paddy!'
> 'Love's at the door, Sir, promising turmoil.
> 'I'll be going now, if you don't mind, quiet-like, casual.'

The subversion of expectations is a central feature of 'Missouri Sequence', whose four sections, in their reversals, circlings back, and displacements, have a much more casual interdependence than the linear sequential logic their title implies. Section III, 'Muse, June, Related', suggests the primary principle of organization in the poem: 'related' — kinship, not identity. The double plane of narration on which this section operates, powerfully fusing a landscape and a woman's body into a single image of a muse, by unifying them in a linguistic field which describes both simultaneously, indicates another aspect of this structure. For statements about poetry become, by extension, statements about love, about relationship to others and to landscape: 'relationship', in its many forms, is the informing theme of the poem. The sequence is a gathering together, briefly, of a tangle of threads which have converged and intertwined in this particular life. The dedications of the sections, suggesting in turn epistle, address, elegy and love letter, sustain a centrifugal impetus that pushes against the containing momentum, out towards a polycentric universe in which

> Many loves exist
> concur concretely
> in this pendant world.
> Only in twisted man
> does love scatter and disperse.

The poem is about the attempt to hold together these tangential loves within the provisional unity of a life, to make of the self a garden of forked paths in which all are reconciled. It is itself the creation and resolution of many tensions.

'Missouri Sequence' repudiates the musical rigour of the *Four Quartets*, avoiding any simple chronological or imposed schema. Though the first section, for example, moves from midwinter nightfall to perfected midnight, it immediately spills over, on the note of closure, into a proliferating displacement in time and space:

> Tomorrow early we shall make lunches
> for the children to take to school,
> forgetting while working out the week
> our wrestling with the sad flesh
> and the only Ireland we love
> where in Achill still
> the poor praise Christ aloud
> when the priest elevates
> the Saviour of the World.

Events are the shape we give to time, and the working out of the week is akin to the rituals which transmute the mundane into the sacred. The transposition from horizontal into vertical planes, here, as a deliberate human intervention, recurs in a variety of forms throughout the poem; but the cyclical myths we allow to shape our experience are gradually demonstrated to be an inadequate, reductive attempt to impose symmetry on the open-ended exfoliating rhythms of a reality neither linear nor cyclical. It is introduced, at the beginning of the poem, as a child's strategy, a play of directedness which gets nowhere, which can assume meaning only within the invented space of a game or a house:

> Our children have eaten supper,
> play Follow-my-Leader,
> make songs from room to room
> around and around;
> once each minute
> past my desk they go.

Set against this, in the adult world, is a multiplication of relative perspectives where the self can drown — inside/outside, proximity/distance, from/towards — all of them functions of a particular point of view with no absolute hold on space, sensitive to the negativity and absences with which the present is pervaded, capable both of more and more minute discriminations of the particular (tree/branch/leaf), and of wider and wider margins of error (Canada, Ireland, the far bank of the river, all equally inaccessible):

> Inside the house is warm.
> Winter outside blows from Canada
> freezing rain to ice our trees
> branch by branch, leaf by leaf.

> The mare shelters in the barn.
> On the impassable road no movement.
> Nothing stirs in the sky against the black.
> If memory were an icefield
> quiet as all outside!
> Tonight the poetry is in the children's game:
> I am distracted by comparisons,
> Ireland across the grey ocean,
> here, across the wide river.

The echo, in the last line, makes sense of what otherwise seems like an unnecessary, distracting footnote: 'In Missouri most people pronounce Missouri to rhyme with Shenandoah.' To invoke that other river valley, far to the east, is to recall the man 'bound, bound away, 'cross the wide Missouri', for whom Missouri is an outpost of exile. To go west is restlessness, not return to the cradle. Every settlement was first a frontier and then a point of transit, before it lapsed into its proper autonomy.

> We live far from where
> my mother grows very old.
> Five miles away, in Byrnesville,
> the cemetery is filled with Irish graves. . .
>
> People drifted in here from the river,
> Irish, Germans, Bohemians,
> more than one hundred years ago,
> come to make homes.

> Many Irish souls have gone back to God from Byrnesville.

What the poem celebrates is a natural and inevitable vagrancy, rather than exile, which presupposes some determining locus in space and time. Drifting together, drifting apart, men live; all settlements, of the spirit or of the body, provisional, a making over of the self in the making of a home. That demographic convergence, the movement of actual human history, which produced this particular place, with its ludicrously hybrid name, is more than a mere metaphor for the genesis of personal identity. The self is not a rigidly fixed ego, but a precarious congruence of forces, discovering its bounds only in the encounter with resistance and incapacity. It is a settlement because it is what one settles for, where one is, but it is also what one settles in, settles into, with the incipient fissures, cracks that may widen, the imminent collapse. The security of walls is an illusion; minute pressures and strains accumulate, foundations stir:

> When in this settlement of walls
> forcefields of hurt and bruising
> not boundaries on show
> the sudden start towards hares

and open fields halts
lest wall enough to stem action
kill joy foretasted or
or quick wall interpose an opposite.
                              ('How Far from Daybreak')

Against the expansive movement to open fields it is easy to opt for
the contrary movement of regression, the conserving of an established
self which, initially protective, in the end seals the self in its own
labyrinthine desolation. The thickening of the senses into vitrifaction
('Glass bounds / shelter him') culminates in petrifaction. A windowless
monad, beyond language and communication, the self recoils into
foetal indifference:

There was a sort of place
call it a bowl
encompassed a maze
of growing walls
Let's say there was no way out
all ways led within

There walls grew strong
around a central waste
grew petrified
'til small distant soul
encurled in wordless haven
and withdrawal.
                              ('How Far . . .')

Such a solution is indeed canvassed, and rejected, in the poem's
second section. The more frequent variant of this is that recoil of
nostalgia, the flight from contingent being to the assurance of surrender:

the fictive form of heaven on earth,
the child's return to motherly arms, . . .
flight from where one is.

But, though he reaches in sentiment to the hills behind Dublin, the
soul's parochiality has been eroded by a deeper conviction of the
relativity, the contingency of origins, and of the disabling paralysis of
affiliation:

There is a love of Ireland
withering for Irish men.

Does it matter where one dies,
supposing one knows how?

The stress on knowing is significant; for identity is a cognitive
myth, a matter of what one happens to come to know, where and when
one comes to it. Thus his own children have learnt another set of
images, and, with them, a different cultural and personal identity. For

them the extraordinary has become mundane. The learning of objects
is a learning of love and loyalty, peculiar to its own place:

> They know nothing of Ireland,
> they grow American,
> They have chased snakes through the couch grass
> in summer, caught butterflies and beetles
> we did not know existed... ·
> observed the pupa of the shrill cicada
> surface on dry clay,
> disrobe for the short ruinous day. . . ·
> paid homage to dead men
> with fire-crackers in July,
> eaten the turkey in November.
> Here now they make friendships,
> learn to love God.

From this essential residue that transcends locality, that which survives
when the sustaining pupa of custom is shed, the self can create its own
proper grounds. Constructed in one place and time, its here and now
can never be circumscribed by the externally given; a necessary tension
impels it beyond the improvised allegiances, into a final schism. This
last pain is that of shedding, not only what one has grown out of, but
what one has grown into, the adopted locus. But there is a complementary movement, back to enclosure, as the free self is incorporated into
the collaborative fiction of parenthood 'for one / charged with care of
others'.

This systolic/diastolic movement is characteristic of Coffey's poetry,
which operates recurrently through a complex overlapping of rhythms
of opening and closing, unfolding and infolding, rising and dispersal.
'Muse, June, Related' opens with one such instant, the first words.
themselves catching a moment of closure which is also a liberation; and
the image of children gathered, in poised fullness to burst beyond the
husk where they have grown, is easily extended into a metaphor, or
embodiment, of the momentum of human history, coalescing, uncoiling:

> School is out.
> The house is full of children.
> How fast they grow, how far
> they cast their glances janus-wise
> back to last June's butterflies,
> forward to the yet uncaptured Mourning Cloak.
>
> All the passions meet at the dinner table,
> all men's history ever was or will be
> uncoils its features while we serve the food.

'March, Missouri' begins with a similarly expansive gesture, in
response to the unseasonable mildness of the March weather:

> one opened windows, one allowed
> doors to swing, one lived at last
> between times, charmed carefree,
> dreaming daffodils.

The euphoric openness, with its expansive calm, its declaratory casualness, is cut short by the return of normative winter weather, its chiaroscuro candour:

> black wind wedged the candid snow
> weather and earth between
> driving day-long victory home
> to massive drifts.

The balancing of 'home' against 'drifts' reactivates that antithesis which had pervaded the previous section, resonating through the reluctant accommodations with which the return of routine is greeted:

> Unreadied, we faced winter again
> with half-hearted shifts.

'Missouri, Midsummer, Closure' is aware of the slipping moment, of the firm ground unsteady beneath the feet. There is a strange tension between the immemorial fixity of the place, locked in its own rhythms of renewal, and the transitory significance with which it is endowed by its tenants. The leisurely itemization of the trees with which it opens implies both the diversity of the place and the attempt to hold on to a property that is merely rented, which is already sloping away into a different kind of distance. The trees are 'rooted', yet their composure is itself extempore, an illusory quiet at the intersection of chance and necessity, the 'casual fall of seed', the 'astonishing rise of sap', that causes them to flourish in the casually determined spot. Not accidentally, the passage recalls Yeats's 'great-rooted blossomer',

> the perfect leaves
> compose with boughs and branches
> the vivid temples poets contemplate,

for the next phase moves (in its reflections of the insufficiencies both of spontaneous natural growth and the 'struggle towards the exact muse' associated with Yeats at the close of section I, and 'that perfect self sages praise', which 'grows mastering the unthought-of change' in section II) to the central preoccupations of 'Among Schoolchildren' and the 'Dialogue of Self and Soul'. It evokes, in fact, Yeats in his most accomplished attitudinizing, that 'monument to Celtic self-importance', the Preface to *Responsibilities:*

> Forty-eight years after my birth, tonight
> when faint heart counsels
> my concerning me

> with family cares and crises
> and decline, tonight
> I write verses at my desk.

The careful ordinariness here, the falling rhythms of doubt and decline, so different from Yeats's rhetorical crescendos which convert apologia into braggadocio, flaunting the unpoetic particularity of age in the daring exposure of rhyme ('Although I have come close on forty-nine'), mutes any sense of triumph with a guilty acknowledgement of irresponsibility, and yet in the end redeems more, by refusing to substitute an empty histrionic gesture for the fretful circling within the confines of an acknowledged conflict.

The allusive richness of 'Missouri Sequence', evoking in the subsequent lines, by echoes of rhyme, image and theme, the concluding stanzas of the 'Dialogue of Self and Soul', modulates into a meditative abstraction reminiscent of *Four Quartets*, whose river imagery, as an emblemism of beginnings and ends, is here followed to its source, the Missouri of Eliot's birthplace:

> Our eyes do not see
> the act's issue in the act.
> Beginnings we see,
> and continuings,
> and endings in due course.
> Will, we know, if good will
> wills beyond what thought holds,
> so present joy
> assuages earlier or later woe,
> so, if one fail,
> others onelike fail.
> But beginnings entrance us,
> breed our hopes,
> dispel our fears.

It becomes clear that 'Missouri Sequence' is, in part, a poetry made out of a quarrel with the rhetoric of others, a polemic on the process of self-justification, on the modernist idea of art as a redemption, an excusing, of the fecklessness and failure of life, which disputes the self-abnegation of Eliot's Senecan Christianity as much as Yeats's invention of a strutting persona. The whole disjunction of art and life, 'Beauty' and 'Truth', is an aesthete's myth, for the 'willing suspension of disbelief' is as much a prerequisite (the pun on 'entrance' suggests) for participation in the 'supreme fiction' of 'reality' as of 'art'. Art is merely life grown to its most consummate fullness, not a dimension different from the 'real', but its epitome. 'Poetry becomes humankind' — it is the shape that will feature him, a moment of communion where many loves concur, set against 'the habit of withholding love' which 'unfits us for poetry':

And so, seek wisdom wholly always
refuse as you must
the shape that will not feature you
nothing withheld give,
give love.

Out of such patience
I am seated here

hoping the weightless flight
of a poem born aright.

The 'exact relation' between freedom and necessity, spontaneity and order, is one in which the perfection of utterance *is* the necessary fulfilment of that which is uttered, in which there is neither redundancy nor deficiency. Neither the internal emigration of the poet who 'dreamed himself / watched him go', nor Eliot's flight from self to the womblike reassurance of tradition reaches this resolution, which is a moment of reconciliation and infolding, rooted in a mutual attentiveness, an acceptance even of loss and gracelessness:

It bears the truth of all,
freely attends on who
keeps constant watch
lives whenever everywhere,
awakens when our love
says yes to all, accepts
even the viper vibrant in the vine.

Such attendant readiness is that wisdom with which Su Tungpo greeted adversity, who 'when it came time / . . . fared forth gentle with reason'. Wisdom is a knowing how to deal with the adventitious, a preservation of options at the moment which invites to closure and despair:

To greet unwisdomed change of season
is to fail the unexpected
test, ruin completed.

If 'Fortune beyond their foresight / masters most with shifting wind', wisdom is no simple contrary growth to mastery over circumstance, but a skill called forth only occasionally, residing partly in the very ability to decide when it is required:

So are the wise not perfect
here and now . . .
their difference shows
when questioning event
requires exact response,
when it is wisdom to avoid
the routine answer,

> when love alive alone proffers
> love's unpredictable reply.

Significantly, the metaphor here is of speech, of some catechism of love in which there is a perfect adequation of question and answer. Such exactitude is not the consonance of two pre-existent parts, but a new, whole creation, a moment of closure and release. The world's body is the host to our self-creative, self-discovering enterprise, a fiction made true in that movement of question and response, twining and un-twining, dispersal and convergence, which is the fundamental rhythm of biological and social life. To begin the journey is to ensure the out-come, for men are their own source, their destiny implicit already in their determination, bound together, bound to find their own bounds, and 'bound away, 'cross the wide Missouri':

> Never was despair imperative,
> never are we grown so old
> we cannot start our journey,
> bound to find
> an eternal note of gladness
> in loves true for men,
> the source whence they flow,
> the ocean whither they go.

This source is not dependent on eventuality, but 'abides in truth', in 'a love true for men' on other grounds:

> And all begins again,
> each time other, each time same,
> cycles of rising and resting
> which do not fit our bounds.
> We face a testing
> based on other grounds than nature's;
> not on weather's may we shape our features,
> any weather is good weather
> for the loving soul,
> spring show, summer its perfect noon,
> autumnal moon, winter snow.

W. R. Rodgers & John Hewitt
by Terence Brown

W. R. RODGERS'S POETRY recreates for its readers an apprehension of conflicts, clashes, tensions and resolutions, that was for the poet the primary datum of his experience. To read his poems is to enter a poetic universe where

> The world moves, not with meant and maintained pace
> Toward some hill-horizon or held mood,
> But in great jags and jerks, probed and prodded
> From point to point of anger, exploded
> By each new and opposed touch.
>
> ('Awake')

For Rodgers the natural world is experienced as an arena of continual activity, of vigorous process in which the fleeting particulars of the world take part in a swirling, confusing but exhilarating dance of life. Initially this activity appears for the poet to be mere random disorder, a very plenitude but without pattern or structure:

> Of the Mournes I remember most the mist,
> The grey granite goosefleshed, the minute
> And blazing parachutes of fuchsia, and us
> Listening to the tiny clustered clinks
> Of little chisels tinkling tirelessly
> On stone, like a drip of birds' beaks picking
> Rapidly at scattered grain.
>
> ('Ireland')

The world appears primarily as an endless proliferation of 'All things counter, original, spare, strange'; objects and events observed 'wriggling', 'niggling', 'frothing', 'magotting' dominate the surfaces and textures of his poems so that the opening of 'Europa and the Bull' seems an entirely characteristic passage expressing the poet's fundamental awareness:

> Naked they came, a niggling core of girls
> Magotting gaily in the curling wool
> Of morning mist, and careless as the lark
> That gargled overhead. They were the root

> Of all that writhing air, the frothing rock
> Of that grey sea in whose vacuity
> Footless they stood, nor knew if it or they
> Were moving now.

The primary sense here is of idiosyncratic, almost grotesque movement and of a Nature alive with its own energies. It is in these energies that Rodgers detects a principle that takes his sense of the natural world beyond mere nominalism, that allows him to discern pattern in its profusion. For the energies at work in Rodgers's Nature are he believes generated by the friction of conflict, clash and opposition, by what he called in an essay 'that fructifying struggle . . . that life which is born from the rub of opposites, from coming and going . . .'[1] Many of his poems are present when the energy so generated has sparked into a vigorous life. Many of them open in the midst of activity. 'Stormy Day' begins:

> O look how the loops and balloons of bloom
> Bobbing on long strings from the finger-ends
> And knuckles of the lurching cherry-tree
> Heap and hug, elbow and part, this wild day,
> Like a careless carillon cavorting . . .

while 'Awake', 'Spring-dance', 'The Train', 'Spring' open with similar *élan*. Other poems begin in the midst of a chase, in mid-conflict between hare and hound, god and goddess, force and force:

> Across the heavy sands running they came,
> She like his shadow shot on before him . . .
>
> ('Pan and Syrinx')

> Over rock and wrinkled ground
> Ran the lingering nose of hound,
> The little and elastic hare
> Stretched herself nor stayed to stare.
>
> ('Beagles')

Conversely others of Rodgers's poems are present at the moment just before the energies of Nature erupt into life and movement. 'The Fountains' is an obvious example:

> Suddenly all the fountains in the park
> Opened smoothly their umbrellas of water . . .

The poet seems fascinated by the instant before the release of energy, the collapse of structure into violently disintegrating fragments, the moment before transmutation and transformation. 'Ireland' concludes:

> all these names lie
> Silently in my grass-grown memory,
> Each one bright and steady as a frog's eye;
> But touch it and it leaps, leaps like a bead
> Of mercury that breaks and scatters

> Suddenly in a thousand shining strings
> And running spools and ever-dwindling rings
> Round the mind's bowl, till at last all drop,
> Lumped and leaden again, to one full stop.

The 'steady' moment gives way to a collapse into transmuting activity ('mercury' to 'leaden'). Interestingly it is pressure on the eye that fragments it in this release. Often the natural energies that the poet focuses on at the moment of their generation, are those that result not simply from conflict and clash but from containment and constriction. Pressure induces an explosive escape:

> The rooks boil and bubble above the woods . . .
>
>   ('End of a World')

> War shot its spark, and our shut chimneys
> Shed and vehemently vomited
> Their woolly volumes.
>
>   ('Action Station')

Nature therefore for Rodgers is an endless profusion of phenomena, grotesque, individual, colourful — most of all colourful for his work displays a finer visual sense than most Irish poets can command. His work is full of shades and contrasts minutely observed. 'Why', he asks

> . . . must people think of colour in terms of great panoramic sweeps and brilliantly drawn-out seasons. It is the small momentary contrasts: a deceptively sunny morning in March with snow on the ground, and the golden-brown bees emerging from the cherry tree and clustering sleepily on the snow-drops: or an Ulster garden in June suddenly sugared with hailstones that strike a million puffs of smoke from the heavily pollined yew trees: a yellow fire burning on green grass, the golden flutings of water on the Liffey, or the pink and green light of an Armagh apple orchard in blossom.[2]

His poetry captures, sometimes quite brilliantly, colours and physical impressions such as these, evokes the palpable physicality of the world. So Michael Longley can assert that 'one of Rodgers's central achievements is to have revealed, as under a magnifying glass, the wonder of life's surfaces . . . with his almost frenzied scrutiny' his 'obsessive close up'.[3] But Nature for Rodgers is also the clash and conflict of forces and the energies they release; it is the process that they set in motion, the explosions and releases that containment or tension inevitably produce.

In Rodgers's mind words seem to share the properties he discerns in Nature. They appear to him to have a life of their own, independent of the poet. He feels himself almost overpowered by a rush of verbal possibilities; they crowd, push and thrust themselves into his mind. As he suggested in a broadcast talk, 'There's power of words that is imprisoned, and like underground water-springs they are bursting to be let out.'[4] His poem 'Words' celebrates the moment of words' arrival:

> Always the arriving winds of words
> Pour like Atlantic gales over these ears . . .

So, many of Rodgers's poems allow words simply to crowd into the reader's consciousness. Others are structured as hectic paced, one or two sentence stanzas, suggesting a poet struggling to keep up in a chase after a verbal universe fleeing before his mind. The first stanza of 'Express' is a fine example:

> As the through-train of words with white hot whistle
> Shrills past the heart's mean halts, the mind's full stops,
> With all the signals down; past the small town
> Contentment, with the citizens all leaning
> And loitering parenthetically
> In waiting-rooms, or interrogative on platforms;
> Its screaming mouth crammed tight with urgent meaning,
> — I, by it borne on, look out and wonder
> To what happy or calamitous terminus
> I am bound, what anonymity or what renown.

The poet is breathless with his own poem's pace. Characteristically in his poetry the verb is often the highlighted syntactical unit of a stanza, since the poet feels 'the flitting verb is important, more than the sitting noun or the clinging adjective; by means of the verb words link and copulate and concepts are born . . .'[5] For the energies of words derive from the same source as those he celebrates in the natural world, from clash and struggle. He believes of words that they '. . . have their times and tides and double meanings and motions; their oppositions, their yea and nay, their rub and rob, they are never static, never one in meaning . . . Nothing pleases me so much in writing as to be able to sit on both sides of the sense, and if there were six sides I would sit on them all.'[6] Rodgers wishes his individual words to shade into conflicting meanings as shot silk changes colour with the change of light. For Rodgers 'Knowledge is the enemy of knowing and to name is to numb',[7] so he is delighted when in his poetry he can allow words a multiplicity of meanings, of relationships and conflicts, for '. . . words like to leap, to laugh, to be at two places at once, to have double meanings and double-crossings, to flash from likeness to likeness of image, and branch to branch of sound, and bid farewell to each welcome'.[8] Rodgers suggests this kind of verbal life in his poems by a variety of strategies: by heavy alliteration binding words together (this sometimes gives his verse a gothic, overly ornate texture which can repel);[9] by puns, echoes, jarring dissonances and sometimes by investing his diction (especially in his poems on religious themes) with what seems to me a rather mannered, *faux naïf* quality, as if to suggest that the language exists at a level prior to or beneath rational meaning, knowledge or social experience.

But Rodgers, for a significant period in his life, was also a parson; and as such he was all too aware of a different function for Language: analysis, homily and abstract theological statement. The son of a staunchly Protestant puritan family in Belfast, his youthful consciousness had been stamped with the stark outlines of Calvin's highly abstract vision of a choosing and rejecting deity. The shadow of that God is cast on his early poetry, where, despite a natural inclination towards pagan acceptance of life and its contradictions, he seemed driven to probe experience, to interpret and to judge. His first book *Awake and Other Poems* is therefore marred by a too frequent tendency to gesture towards the rhetoric of allegory and sermon. Moral abstractions are always close. It was, I think, the poet's strained attachment to the highly structured yet compelling demands of Calvinist religion, rather than any awareness of prevailing literary fashions in thirties England, that led so many of his early poems in the direction of parable and social comment. Words, for Rodgers, the Presbyterian Minister in Co. Armagh had, often twice a week, to be used in the service of an unpleasantly clear meaning. It was hardly likely that when he came to write his poems he could escape his other role entirely.[10] Yet sometimes in fact the energies of his best early poems derive from the tension created by their languages' dual nature. For although in many of his early poems words as moral abstraction and words as extra-rational activity appear to inhabit two separate, unconnected areas of experience, in some others the poet seems to wrestle to control with meaning a verbal flux that breaks away from his constraint into an exciting release of verbal life which is the linguistic equivalent of those moments of natural escape that some of his poems attend to. These are, for me, among his finest poetic effects. At the conclusion of 'Directions to a Rebel' a list of intensely abstract injunctions gives way to a verbal and emotional release from the poem's steady build up of premisses and statements.

> So,
> Gay in the midst of growling things, you'll go
> Tip-toe, songs in your ears, sights in your eyes,
> That blind and deafen you to compromise.

The psychological equivalent of Rodgers's sense of Nature and Language is his awareness of tension and conflict in human relations and in his own relation with God. Many of his poems focus on a moment of human conflict. 'The Lovers', one of his best poems, is a terrifying recreation of the moment when human energies, anger and passionate recrimination, erupt:

> After the tiff there was stiff silence, till
> One word, flung in centre like single stone,
> Starred and cracked the ice of her resentment

> To its edge. From that stung core opened and
> Poured up one outward and widening wave
> Of eager and extravagant anger.

'Paired Lives' treats an emotional war of attrition, 'Stormy Night' is a powerful poem of psychological clash and release, a disturbed love poem, while 'Scapegoat' is a poem in which the Ulster Calvinist God, a conglomerate of Special Branch, local party hack and Orange lodge, confronts the poet in a violent nightmare:

> God broke into my house last night
> With his flying squad, narks, batmen, bully-boys,
> Procters, bailiffs, aiders and abettors —
> Call them what you will — hard mouthed, bowler-hatted.

Psychologically, constraint and clash create energy and activity in Rodgers's view of life, as they do in Nature and Language. This is reflected in the fact that many of his poems dramatize not only human conflict but suggest breaking through puritan inhibition and self-protective prudence to sexual and emotional risks and satisfactions. 'The Net' is a finely effective statement of the inter-relationship of constraint and release in a developed sexual experience:

> Ah, shifty as the fin
> Of any fish this flesh
> That, shaken to the shin,
> Now shoals into your mesh,
> Bursting to be held in;
> Purse proud and pebble-hard,
> Its pence like shingle showered.
>
> Open the haul, and shake
> The fill of shillings free . . .

So one of the successful aspects of 'Europa and the Bull' — which must over all be judged a flawed, self-indulgent poem (I am thinking especially of some of its more baroque puns) — is its exploration of the psychology of sexual desire, with its blend of fear and aspiration, holding back and giving, that creative tension that induces ecstatic release:

> He longed to stop this longing, to burst
> The thong, to be beholden to no one,
> To wander at will, to squelch and to squander
> Without regard . . .

'The Fall' is poised before the moment of emotional risk as the poet longs

> To float out on the rootless raft of air
> With flowing hold . . .

In the psychic and spiritual dimension, as in the sexual, conflict and fear — 'dread / On whose jellied edges each joy is dandled' — have brought the poet to the moment in which tension is creative; release must follow.

Rodgers saw Ireland too as an arena of clash and conflict, but was, and this is surely significant, unable to bring his poems on Ireland to the moment when the tensions could become creative in any way. Writing of the country he suggested: 'By nature hers are a dramatic people, loving clash and contrast . . . '[11] and 'The Irish mind has always had a liking for drama and a fond eye for the oppositions of things, and it is this which lends such friction and fire to its politics. By comparison, other countries seem grey and tame and toothless after the clash and colour of the Irish scene.'[12] As an Ulsterman the clash he most deeply understood of course was that between Orange and Green in his native province. He believed that each faction is the other's opposite, which accounts for the clash, but that they could complement one another:

> These characters, Protestant and Catholic are complementary. One takes a long view of life, the other a short view. One is thoughtful and individual, the other emotional and communal. One tends to a democratic and progressive view of life, the other to a hieratic and established way . . . They are, by nature, complements of head and heart.[13]

He also believed

> Where two racial patterns meet each gives definition to the other. The impact may be painful, but at length a new man is born, a new pattern is made. It happened when the contact of Gael and Saxon brought that peculiar product, the Anglo-Irishman, on the scene. But, as I see it, the field is set in Ireland for a vaster happening . . . It will be a meeting of equals.[14]

Given such a sense of Ireland and her possibilities, a sense so analogous to his main preoccupations and obsessions, one might have expected that Rodgers's poetry would have treated both the clash of Irish life and politics and the possible birth of the 'new man', the release of the tension. Strangely his poems on Irish subjects are few and mostly topographical. If we except such a poem as 'Directions to a Rebel' (which is more a defence of psychological extremism than a political poem) only 'Home Thoughts from Abroad' and 'Epilogue' advert to the 'matter of Ireland' in any direct way. The former is an entertaining, but superficial salute to Ian Paisley; 'Epilogue' is the partially complete poem on Ireland that Rodgers at his death had been working on, from time to time, over a period of years. It was to form the epilogue to a book he and Louis MacNeice were editing together, *The Character of Ireland*. The poem, I think, despite his apparent dilatoriness in addressing himself to its final composition, meant a good deal to Rodgers. 'Working on it' he wrote to a friend, 'both excites and depresses me, and I realize that to write about it is like opening an old wound which is Ireland.'[15] The poem, his notes reveal, was to have attempted a comprehensive response to Ireland by focusing, as Louis MacNeice had done in Section XVI of *Autumn Journal*, on political and social concerns in terms of personal and familial history. Apart from a few witty lines the fragment is not impressive. Rodgers wrote of working on the poem:

> I sit here with a little hill before me, of notes, comments, reminiscences, confessions, phrases, lines of verse, thoughts unthought of, all gathered over mountainous years of trouble and love, and I wonder which way the water — the poetry — which shows the shape of the land, is going to run down it. Will it run, and will the stones obligingly melt? . . . But I wish I could get the first wilful run of it, and then find the easy will-less expansion of it.[16]

The clue to the poem's abandonment and an explanation for the scarcity of poems on directly Irish themes in his *Collected Poems* is, I think, in this passage. Rodgers hopes the poem will come to him as did those poems which celebrate natural and psychological clashes, processes and releases. But whereas Nature as he saw it moved inevitably from birth to death to birth, and the personal and sexual life could for him move through its own processes towards psychic release, the cultural neuroses and psychoses in the collective mind of Ireland (the sum of her inhabitants' warring myths and identity problems) could admit of no such simple therapeutic resolution, seemed impelled by no necessarily benign natural or historical process. Perhaps Rodgers, at a level deeper than his rational analytic mind, knew this and abandoned his attempts at comprehensive statements about his country in poetry, preferring to write those poems which excitingly suggest the flux and process, the endless toing and froing of the natural world and of the self.

One cannot, I fear, help regretting this, for when in prose Rodgers explored the psychological differences between Catholic and Protestant in Ulster, he brought to bear on the subject a subtlety of insight and imaginative sympathy with both groups that has rarely been equalled. His analysis of the Ulster Protestant psyche (published in Dublin in *The Bell* in 1942) is particularly perceptive:

> The Protestant Ulsterman has halts and suppressions of feeling in his speech, is slow to communicate, reserved, self-conscious, inarticulate, and therefore makes his connections with other people through logic rather than emotion . . . For the Northern Protestant's feelings are deep because they are not extensive and have not been dissipated in words. He would *like* to have eloquence. But he suspects and hates eloquence that has no bone of logic in it. It seems to him glib, spineless and insincere.[17]

There is much general truth in this, though Rodgers's own personality might well be thought of as the exception that proves the rule, or maybe could serve as warning that such cultural generalities must be treated with scepticism. Yet as if to render scepticism unfounded the work of Rodgers's friend John Hewitt displays most of the characteristics

Rodgers identifies as essentially Northern Protestant.

John Hewitt's poems, which have appeared steadily in periodicals, newspapers, pamphlets and books (*No Rebel Word* 1948 and *Collected Poems* 1968[18]) since the 1930s have throughout maintained a clear, sober, uninflated diction, a control of prosody and rhythm and an integrity of feeling, that are at the opposite pole to the inflated rhetoric or dishonest linguistic afflatus the Ulsterman is supposed to mistrust. His poems are almost always held in a quiet dignified reserve from his readers. They maintain their privacy by a syntax of careful logic which is never allowed to become the intellectual equivalent of emotional or verbal imbalance. The conditional is the syntactical embodiment of his stance in life as for Rodgers it was the verb or participle. Poem after poems manages its connectives with 'but', 'if', 'perhaps', 'maybe' and establishes its tone through diffident parenthetic interruptions of rhythmic regularity. This address to the peasantry in rural Ulster is a characteristic stanza:

> You are coarse to my senses, to my washed skin;
> I shall maybe learn to wear dung on my heel,,
> but the slow assurance, the unconscious discipline
> informing your vocabulary of skill,
> is beyond my mastery, who have followed a trade
> three generations now, at counter and desk;
> hand me a rake, and I at once, betrayed,
> will shed more sweat than is needed for the task.

('O Country People')

Most of Hewitt's poems begin in low key, in moments of conscientious observation (less intense than Rodgers, he still sees exactly) or unexcited retrospection. There is no sense that they ever emerge from sudden internal strife or violent changes in outlook as events dramatically overtake him. Even the pamphlet of poems Hewitt published in 1971 as a 'release for my sense of frustration in verse'[19] as his native province once again physically tore itself apart, stylistically continued to suggest a poet speaking after long reflection with 'feelings that are deep because they are not extensive and have not been dissipated in words'. 'Minister', the most successful poem in a not entirely successful collection, reflects on the career of Brian Faulkner:

> Not one of your tall captains bred to rule,
> that right confirmed by school and Army list,
> he went to school, but not the proper school.
> His family tree will offer little grist
> to any plodding genealogist;
> his father's money grew from making shirts.
> But with ambition clenched in his tight fist,
> and careful to discount the glancing hurts,
> he climbed to office, studiously intent,
> and reached the door he planned to enter, twice

> to have it slammed by the establishment.
> A plight that well might sympathy command
> had we not watched that staff of prejudice
> he'd used with skill, turn serpent in his hand.[20]

But all this care, quiet zeal for verbal accuracy and emotional control would only be of minimal interest if it were not put to the service of some significant theme. In Hewitt's work that theme has always been his own problem of identity, his personal quest for true belonging. 'The Protestant', wrote W. R. Rodgers 'has an *inner* opposition, his conflict is, first and last, a private one: it forces self-awareness on him.'[21] In Hewitt's poetry we overhear such a private drama of enforced self-awareness. Hewitt primarily feels himself a man who is most at home in a natural environment. He acknowledges that, 'I live my best in the landscape, being at ease there . . .' ('The Ram's Horn'), and that it is in Glens of Antrim

> I have won
> by grace or by intention, to delight
> that seems to match the colours mystics write
> only in places far from kerb or street.
>
> ('Conacre')

The town or city for all its poetic possibilities cannot fully engage his imagination. Its details

> make up the world my heel and nostril know,
> but not the world my pulses take for true . . .
> and leave the quiet depths unmeasured still . . .
>
> ('Conacre')

Yet he openly recognizes his distinctiveness from the Glens people he celebrates. He is the stranger in their midst:

> I recognise the limits I can stretch;
> even a lifetime among you should leave me strange,
> for I could not change enough, and you will not change;
> there'd still be levels neither'd ever reach.
>
> ('O Country People')

He therefore writes of their lives, their rituals and customs and of the countryside they inhabit in terms of ironic pastoral, recognizing his own alienation. This alienation is complicated for Hewitt (and this rescues it from the level of cultural commonplace) by his sense of the tradition that some of his writing most naturally extends. For much of Hewitt's verse is reminiscent of that by English practitioners of landscape and nature poetry. He himself realizes 'I draw upon an English literary tradition which includes Marvell, Crabbe, Wordsworth, Clare . . .'[22] So, many of Hewitt's poems are in the English manner — accurate, steady, cumulative natural observation, blending the rustic prosaicism of Crabbe with the tenderness of Clare. Now, of course, this should not matter. The Anglo-Irish poetic tradition has always drawn more on

English and Continental models than on the native Irish. And did not John Montague in quest of a 'rhythm to write a public poem'[23] about the 1969 battle of the Bogside, find himself satisfied only by 'the oldest metric in English, the only public one, the Anglo-Saxon line'.[24] But it was easier for Montague, secure even if troubled in his nationality, to seek abroad for 'experiments and exchanges' which will 'serve to illuminate the self, a discovery of the oldest laws of the psyche'.[25] For Hewitt, a Northern Protestant with an English name, writing of the Glen's people in a manner which relates him to an English tradition must complicate his social alienation from them as urban man, by national and racial insecurities. Those insecurities are persistently present in Hewitt's verse and form a further element in the private drama his work enacts. He knows the history of his province. His verse play *The Bloody Brae*, written in 1936, openly admits the hideous violence of the seventeenth-century Plantation of Ulster, while 'The Colony' chronicles a history of dispossession, servitude and colonial insecurity:

> We took the kindlier soils. It had been theirs,
> this patient, temperate, slow, indifferent,
> crop-yielding, crop-denying, in-neglect-
> quickly-returning-to-the-nettle-and-bracken,
> sodden and friendly land. We took it from them.

'Sunset over Glenaan' remembers:

> when the clansmen broke
> and limped defeated to the woody glens ...[26]

so that now when the poet finds

> a peace and speech I do not find
> familiarly among my kin and kind[27]

in conversation and social intercourse with the descendants of a disinherited people, he ponders uneasily:

> Maybe, at some dark level, grown aware
> of our old load of guilt, I shrink afraid,
> and seek the false truce of a renegade ...

The truce that Hewitt in fact proposed in the 1940s in poems, essays and manifestos, was the concept of regionalism. In 'Conacre', written in 1943, he recognized

> This is my home and country. Later on
> perhaps I'll find this nation is my own ...

In an essay published in 1972, Hewitt reminisced about the feelings that produced those lines and the poem in which they appeared:

> During this period my thought stimulated by the ideas of Le Play and

Patrick Geddes, mediated through the successive books of Lewis Mumford, found itself directed towards and settled upon the concept of Regionalism. This proposed that since the world about us is so vast and complex, strangled by bureaucratic centralisation . . . we must seek for some grouping smaller than the Nation, larger than the family, with which we could effectively identify, with which we could come to terms of sympathetic comprehension, within which our faculties and human potentialities could find due nurture and proper fulfilment. In a word, the Region, an area of a size and a significance that we could hold in our hearts.

It seemed obvious to me that the Province of Ulster was indeed such a Region; so I set about deepening my knowledge of its physical components, its history, its arts, its literature, its folklore, its mythology scrupulously examined and assessed, its weaknesses confronted, its values recognised. It seemed also to hold the hope and promise that in this concept might be found a meeting-place for the two separated communities which dwelt within its limits, where the older and less old peoples might discover a basis for amity and co-operative promise.[28]

Hewitt hoped that his own poetry in texture and diction might, by blending the speech characteristics of the province's inhabitants, lay the ground-work for a unique regionalist poetry that would contribute to a developing regionalist consciousness:

> Our speech is a narrow speech, the rags and remnants
> of Tudor rogues and stiff Scots Covenanters
> curt soldierly despatches and puritan sermons,
> with a jab or two of glaar from tangled sheugh,
> the cross-roads solo and the penny ballad.
> . . . .
> We can make something of it, something hard
> and clean and honest as the basalt cliffs . . . [29]

Hewitt thought in the forties that such a resolution of an ancient quarrel could be effected. Yet his own poems, in fact, reveal how difficult a task he had set both himself and his province, for they do not achieve that cultural and imaginative synthesis that his essays and poems assert he hoped for. He remains from first to last a man of liberal, humane sympathies, whose primary instinct is to live in harmony with Nature and with his neighbours, earnestly debating with himself how on earth this can be managed in the province of Ulster to which he gives his loyalty. Consequently, much that is central to Irish experience, to the psychic condition of the country and probably to all essentially peasant societies, seems absent from his work, or comprehensible to him only as a spectator commenting upon it, despite a lifelong concern to be fully involved. For example, his feelings for the dead suggest that they are basically benign; they are 'my dead' who

> lie in the steepled hillock of Kilmore
> in a fat country rich with bloom and fruit . . .

('The Glens')

They are 'the buried men / in Ulster clay' who, together with the changes effected by work and by climate,

> rock and glen
> and mist and cloud and quality of air . . .
>
> ('Once Alien Here')

have substantiated his rights to acceptance within the Irish community. They are never the 'dark fathers' who have deeply acknowledged rights of their own:

> I have no ghosts.
> My dead are safely dead . . .
>
> ('Ghosts')

His sense of relationship to the fields men work, to the earth they depend on, is also one of fundamental, almost Wordsworthian calm, except when he remembers the guilt of dispossession or is moved to a William Morris-like social concern. Indeed many of his finest, most skilful poems ('Sonnets in October', 'Late Spring', 'First Snow in the Glens', for example) are the serene meditations of a rationalist/materialist who believes that —

> talk of weather is also talk of life,
> and life is man and place and these have names.
>
> ('Landscape')

Passage after passage has the poet in the landscape at ease, content to celebrate natural and physical well-being in a poetry that, often with extraordinary tact, moves from prosaic statement to a controlled lyricism or evocative verbal music. He knows himself to be

> a happy man who seldom sees
> the emptiness behind the images
> that wake my heart to wonder, I derive
> sufficient joy from being here alive
> in this mad island crammed with bloody ghosts
> and moaning memories of forgotten coasts
> our fathers steered from, where we cannot go
> the names so lost in time's grey undertow.
>
> ('Conacre')

To the old pre-Christian gods of the countryside, Hewitt gives affectionate respect. His heart in 'May Altar' rejects Catholic ritual and practice for the pagan rites of spring:

> but my heart hankers for the pagan thorn
> that none dare break a spray from and bring in.[30]

He trusts the mythic salmon of Celtic legend and lets its ancient rule hold sway over his imagination without the apprehension or sense of the numinous most men feel before their gods:

> The nuts drop in the pool: the Salmon there
> is wisest of all creatures, old and wise
> who equally can hope and fear outstare
> with the cold focus of unblinking eyes:
> this, from the ancient legendry I share
> simply by breathing in the drifting air
> near the swift waters of a mountain glen,
> and with it, knowledge also, of the kind
> that jingles in the pockets of the mind
> but has the smallest currency with men.[31]

The pagan unchristened earth does not terrify him, and when it momentarily threatens to do so, he dismisses such dark imaginings:

> So our troubled thought
> is from enchantments of the old tree magic,
> but I am not a sick and haunted man . . .
>
> ('The Colony')

But Ulster's and Ireland's sense of the dead, of the land and of the gods, is not the calm thing it is in the quiet-toned discourse of Hewitt's poetry. It is closer to the clashes and eruptions, the deaths and resurrections that Rodgers's sense of life represented, but which he never expressed satisfactorily in terms of a directly Irish subject matter. So when Hewitt writes of Ulster's 'mythology scrupulously examined and assessed, its weaknesses confronted' one wonders: Does he know on his pulses what that might entail? Seamus Heaney in 1972 introduced an anthology of recent Irish poetry: 'Soundings can mean two things: the activity of taking readings of the sea's depths and the area within which this activity is possible. It implies a notion of geographical limits and an exploration of depth within those limits.'[32] In the same year Hewitt wrote of his poem 'Once Alien Here': 'But that was in some way a physical identification with the earth, with the climate; it was little more than locating my place on the map, mine by a respectably long tenure.'[33]

Hewitt's poetry has not taken readings of the depths from which, as Heaney asserts, 'too comes the monster, and how with this rage shall beauty hold a plea'.[34] For out of the past, from myth, folk memory, racial and national grievance, from sources in communal human imaginings, can come stranger manifestations than Hewitt's poetry can comprehend or include. That poet's imagination, disturbed to its private depths only by fears of a final homelessness, remains a limited one that, moved by landscape and locale, concerns itself with boundaries, the definition of cultural areas, the drawing and redrawing of maps.

Seamus Heaney's third volume, Wintering Out, employs his province

as he tells us Hewitt, by example, enabled Northern Irish writers to do
(and this is an aspect of Hewitt's achievement that deserves recognition):
'as a hinterland of reference, should they require a tradition more
intimate than the broad perspectives of the English literary achievement . . . '[35] He explores the significance of place name, celebrates
rural magic or laments its passing, ponders linguistic tensions in a
colonial situation. Heaney's book also contains the strange, terrifying,
imaginatively daring poem 'The Tollund Man'. One doubts whether
such a poem represents exactly what Hewitt meant when he suggested
that Northern Irish writers scrupulously examine Ulster's mythology.
It is a poem certainly 'regionalist' in its deepest frightening implications,
that has broken through to universal areas of psychic and cultural truth
in a way Hewitt's verse fails to, as it achieves its more limited but
necessary ends of definition and debate.

Rodgers, although it never got into his poetry in any direct way,
knew something of these dark truths too when he concluded his essay
in *The Bell* on Catholic and Protestant:

> For is it not true that all of the civilization, all its sparkling towers and
> spiritual pinnacles, all its spreading branches of knowledge and fine leaf
> of achievement, are rooted in the earth? And all the promise and multiplicity
> of attachments which you denote by 'love of country' is adumbrated by the
> peasant's love of land.[36]

With his sense of eruptive forces in life, Rodgers must have known that
love can do strange things, can overwhelm a man in passion, can bury a
sacrificial victim. Hewitt appears not to. Perhaps Rodgers remains a
minor poet since he could not finally face and control what he knew
and produce the poem on the 'matter of Ireland' that he might have
done. Perhaps Hewitt remains minor since in the end despite the
integrity of his vision, imaginatively, he does not know enough. Yet
each has left us memorable poems. Rodgers's flux and dance of words,
his fine eye for colour and movement can be marvellously invigorating;
Hewitt's sober joy in man's natural life, his sense of stability and con-
tinuities in a country that often appears to be governed only by
principles of clash, force and by dark imaginings can console and
fortify. Neither should go unread.

NOTES

1. W. R. Rodgers, 'Time to Kill', *New Statesman*, 21 March 1953, p. 336.
2. W. R. Rodgers, *Ireland in Colour*, London, 1957, p. 10.
3. Michael Longley, in *Causeway* published in Dublin by the Arts Council of
Northern Ireland in association with Gill and MacMillan, 1971, p. 99.
4. Republished as 'Balloons and Maggots', *Rann*, 14, p. 11.

5. W. R. Rodgers, 'The Dance of Words', *New Statesman*, 1 August 1953, p. 126.

6. 'Time to Kill'.

7. 'The Dance of Words'.

8. ibid.

9. The most cogently argued attack on Rodgers's verbal practice was mounted, admittedly for strategic reasons, by Kingsley Amis in 1953. See 'Ulster Bull: The Case of W. R. Rodgers', *Essays in Criticism*, III, 4 (October 1953), pp. 470—5.

10. See Darcy O'Brien, *W. R. Rodgers*, Bucknell Univ. Press, Lewisberg, 1970, where Rodgers's dream books are examined as they reflect the guilt and sense of confused identity his role of parson/poet induced: 'One situation recurs frequently. He stands before his congregation, unable to speak for one reason or another. Either he has lost his voice or, more often, has forgotten to prepare his sermon' O'Brien, pp. 42—3.

11. *Ireland in Colour*, p. 9.

12. ibid., p. 26.

13. W. R. Rodgers, 'Black North', *New Statesman*, 20 November 1943, pp. 331—2.

14. ibid., p. 333.

15. Quoted by Dan Davin, Introductory Memoir, *The Collected Poems of W. R. Rodgers*, London, 1971, p. xviii. All quotations from Rodgers's poetry are from this volume.

16. ibid., pp. xvii—xix.

17. 'An Ulster Protestant', *The Bell*, IV, 5 (August 1942), p. 309. This article, which was unsigned, has been identified as from Rodgers's pen. I am grateful to Michael Longley for this information. The article is a fuller statement of the ideas Rodgers was to publish the following year in the *New Statesman*, under his signature, as 'Black North'.

18. Published in 1968 in London by MacGibbon and Kee. All quotations from Hewitt's poetry are from this volume unless stated otherwise.

19. Foreword to *An Ulster Reckoning*, privately printed by the author, 1971, p. 1.

20. ibid., p. 13.

21. 'An Ulster Protestant', p. 310.

22. John Hewitt, 'No Rootless Colonist', *Aquarius*, 5 (1972), p. 91.

23. John Montague, 'The Impact of International Modern Poetry on Irish Writing', in *Irish Poets in English*, edited by Sean Lucy, The Mercier Press, Cork and Dublin, 1973, p. 157.

24. ibid.

25. ibid.

26. John Hewitt, *The Day of the Corncrake*, published by the Glens of Antrim Historical Society, 1969, p. 10.

27. ibid., p. 11.

28. 'No Rootless Colonist', p. 93.

29. John Hewitt, 'Overture for Ulster Regionalism', *Poetry Ireland*, 1 (April 1948), p. 14.

30. *The Day of the Corncrake*, p. 14.

31. John Hewitt, *Those Swans Remember*, privately printed in Belfast by the author, 1956, p. 3.

32. Editor's Note to *Soundings*, The Blackstaff Press, Belfast, 1972.

33. 'No Rootless Colonist', p. 93. In the rest of this article Hewitt attempted to argue beyond this point, predicating that a colony slowly becomes native, in a distinctive way. However, he cannot, or chooses not, to enlarge on how this

distinctively native population then relates to the older population, although he hints that he has not lost faith completely in Regionalism.

34. Editor's note to *Soundings*.

35. Seamus Heaney, 'The Poetry of John Hewitt', *Threshold*, 22 (Summer 1969), p. 73.

36. 'An Ulster Protestant', p. 314.

The Neolithic Night
A Note on the Irishness of
Louis MacNeice
by Michael Longley

I

LOUIS MACNEICE found his voice early. This doesn't mean that he
didn't develop. He moved forward through a series of minute adjust-
ments — a progress which would seem to parallel the course of the
central tradition of poetry in English. His work, like that of Yeats and
Auden, was new without being novel. He never succumbed to the
stylistic *volte face*. There was in fact little over the years to jolt
critics and reviewers out of their preconceived notions. A poetic
personality which was so soon assured and recognizable allowed
critics and anthologists to find *their* voices very early when they came
to deal with him.

Misconceptions and misjudgements dogged MacNeice throughout his
career. A cursory glance through the bibliography at the back of
William T. McKinnon's recent study, *Apollo's Blended Dream*, indicates
that praise has often been grudging, that MacNeice's critics have usually
blown hot and cold. Here are some essay titles: 'Louis MacNeice:
Poetry and Commonsense', 'Evasive Honesty: the Poetry of Louis
MacNeice', 'Louis MacNeice and the Line of Least Resistance'. He has
consistently been billed as a sort of poetic Everyman, a talented
spokesman for the man in the street, a purveyor of decent liberal
middle-class values — plenty of common sense but not much vision. We
are encouraged to believe that he lacked depth and penetration, that if
he does ask a pertinent question, he doesn't linger long enough to
collect an answer, that he is really not much more than a highly professional entertainer. He has been attacked for his attraction to the
showy aspects of language, linguistic gimmicks, 'the whole delightful
world of cliché and refrain'.

In his pioneering study of W. B. Yeats MacNeice comments, 'Poetry
gains body from beliefs, and the more suited the belief is to the poet,
the healthier his poetry', and in *Modern Poetry* he writes, 'The good
poet has a definite attitude to life: most good poets, I fancy, have

more than that — they have beliefs (though their beliefs need not i
explicit in their work).' MacNeice's own philosophy is usually implicit
It is many-faceted, adaptable and changeable. It seldom surfaces in any
handily detachable form, and is continually tugged and swirled by
doubts and reservations. 'Leaving Barra' has this stanza:

> For fretful even in leisure
> I fidget for different values,
> Restless as a gull and haunted
> By a hankering after Atlantis.

In his search for Atlantis MacNeice was never able to align himself
wholeheartedly with any aesthetic, political or religious creed, to borrow
somebody else's map and compass. He was always less likely than most
to succumb to 'the pitiless abstractions', to be beaten down by 'the
shuddering insidious shock of the theory vendors'. He wanted to
approach his concerns with all of himself and with all of life: 'we only
can discover / Life in the life we make'. He aimed at 'A life beyond the
self but self-completing'. The search had to be organic, open to all the
possibilities. No systems could be imposed. His friend and countryman,
W. R. Rodgers, has commented on MacNeice's empirical attitudes:

> Critics sometimes say that MacNeice perhaps lacks an over-all view, a deep
> intention, an inherent and linking philosophy. Quite untrue. If MacNeice's
> poetry — or his life — at first sight appears fragmentary or lacking in
> cohesion, it is not because he failed to edit or order it; it is simply because
> he positively refrained from editing or ordering his sensations in advance. He
> preferred to leave himself open to experience, to the infinitely possible and
> the suddenly surprising, to the *given*. This, I would suggest, is the very basis
> of poetry.

II

MacNeice, then, is a difficult figure to pin down and label. To the Irish
he is an exile, to the English something of a stranger. He was an
Ulsterman, and Ulster is a limbo between two (three?) cultures. Although he is still closely associated with Auden, Spender and Day Lewis,
he was never really a card-carrying thirties poet. His contribution, the
Celtic 'Mac', detaches with proper ease from the front end of Roy
Campbell's famous composite monster, MacSpaunday. Lastly, he does
not with any neatness slot into the pantheon of Anglo-Irish literature.
(A recent depressing symptom of this last fact is John Montague's
inclusion of only two poems by MacNeice in *The Faber Book of Irish
Verse* — half the allocation he allows himself or Thomas Kinsella.)

But it is in Ireland that any attempt to define MacNeice's achievement must begin. In Canto XXIII of *Autumn Journal* he writes:

> I admit that for myself I cannot straighten
> My broken rambling track
> Which reaches so irregularly back

> To burning cities and rifled rose-bushes
> And cairns and lonely farms.

In 'Eclogue from Iceland' Auden, who is called Craven, and MacNeice, who has christened himself Ryan, are cross-examined by Grettir. Grettir asks MacNeice (Ryan):

> And you with the burglar's underlip,
> In your land do things stand well?

Ryan replies:

> In my land nothing stands at all,
> But some fly high and some lie low.

Later in the poem he says:

> I come from an island, Ireland, a nation
> Built upon violence and morose vendettas.
> My diehard countrymen, like dray-horses,
> Drag their ruin behind them.
> Shooting straight in the cause of crooked thinking
> Their greed is surfaced with pretence of public spirit.
> From all which I am an exile.

Vigorous love/hate tensions shaped his relationship with Ireland. On the one hand he could celebrate for his lover in 'Train to Dublin'

> the smell of Norman stone, the squelch
> Of bog beneath your boots, the red bog-grass,
> The vivid chequer of the Antrim hills, the trough of dark
> Golden water for the carthorses, the brass
> Belt of serene sun upon the lough.

On the other hand he describes in 'Valediction' the Belfast where he was born:

> Built on reclaimed mud, hammers playing in the shipyard,
> Time punched with holes like a steel sheet, time
> Hardening the faces, veneering with a grey and speckled rime
> The faces under the shawls and caps:
> This was my mother-city, these my paps.
> Country of callous lava cooled to stone,
> Of minute sodden haycocks, of ship sirens' moan
> Of falling intonations — I would call you to book,
> I would say to you, Look;
> I would say, This is what you have given me —
> Indifference and sentimentality,
> A metallic giggle, a fumbling hand,
> A heart that leaps to a fife band.

In 'Woods' MacNeice notes the difference between English and Irish landscapes and explicitly indicates his own Irishness. English woods, he says,

> are not like the wilds of Mayo, they are assured
> Of their place by men; reprieved from the neolithic night
> By gamekeepers or by Herrick's girls at play.

Ireland in various ways introduced MacNeice to 'the neolithic night'.

The fine autobiographical fragment, *The Strings are False*, tells us a lot about his childhood in Ulster, his early responses to that complex scene, its unforgettable blend of the frightening and the picturesque. The extremes of Irish life touched him early — the bloody banging of the Lambeg drums, the squalor in which the Carrickfergus Catholics lived. In relation to these extremes MacNeice himself was in a special situation. His parents had come to Ulster from the west of Ireland. His father was a Church of Ireland clergyman and a Nationalist. (He wrote a famous series of letters to the press in support of Home Rule.) Even the apparently cushioned state of being 'the rector's son, born to the Anglican order' was a further midway position, both religiously and socially. 'The lower classes were dour and hostile. . .and the gentry not much better.' In MacNeice's eyes Ulster seems for some time to have held a monopoly of Ireland's 'neolithic night':

> And the North, where I was a boy,
>   Is still the North, veneered with the grime of Glasgow,
> Thousands of men whom nobody will employ
>   Standing at the corners, coughing.
> And the street-children play on the wet
>   Pavement — hopscotch or marbles;
> And each rich family boasts a sagging tennis-net
>   On a spongy lawn beside a dripping shrubbery.
> The smoking chimneys hint
>   At prosperity round the corner
> But they make their Ulster linen from foreign lint
>   And the money that comes in goes out to make more money.
> A city built upon mud;
>   A culture built upon profit;
> Free speech nipped in the bud,
>   The minority always guilty.

Ulster was for MacNeice a place hard with basalt and iron, cacophonous with 'fog-horn, mill-horn, corncrake and church bell', 'the hooting of lost sirens and the clang of trams', 'the voodoo of the Orange bands'. The place was dark and oppressive with religion — 'devout and profane and hard'. The West of Ireland 'became the first of my dream-worlds'. Years later he could portion out the darkness more evenly between North and South. 'As with Belfast it took me years to penetrate its outer ugliness and dourness, so with Dublin it took me years to see through its soft charm to its prickly core.' MacNeice worked gradually towards a balanced conception of Ireland, seeing North and South as complementary, one in a way deeper than politics. In his study of Yeats he implies just how difficult it is to capture Ireland whole. 'Most Irish people cannot see Ireland clearly because they are busy grinding axes. Many English people cannot see her clearly because she gives them a tear in the eye.' Because of his Irish and English and Ulster viewpoints MacNeice was able to respond with flexibility and objectivity to the complexities of Ireland, her 'jumble of opposites', her 'intricacies of gloom and glint'. In 'Dublin'

> the days are soft,
> Soft enough to forget
> The lesson better learnt,
> The bullet on the wet
> Street, the crooked deal,
> The steel behind the laugh,
> The Four Courts burnt.

He sees Ireland as simultaneously glorious and debased, life-enhancing and death-dealing. Ireland gave MacNeice a considerable range of theme, exercised and focused a comprehensive consciousness which he would apply to experience in general. When MacNeice wrote about Ireland, he wrote about life.

This painful but poetically fruitful relationship with his native land is summed up in the retrospective poem, 'Carrick Revisited', a crucial statement:

> the green banks are as rich and the lough as hazily lazy
> And the child's astonishment not yet cured.

Here is the second stanza:

> Who was — and am — dumbfounded to find myself
> In a topographical frame — here, not there —
> The channels of my dreams determined largely
> By random chemistry of soil and air;
> Memories I had shelved peer at me from the shelf.

Despite his English education at Marlborough and Oxford, despite his choosing to work in England, and despite (or because of) all his justly harsh judgements on Ireland, MacNeice was never able to divorce himself from his 'topographical frame':

> Torn before birth from where my fathers dwelt,
> Schooled from the age of ten to a foreign voice,
> Yet neither western Ireland nor southern England
> Cancels this interlude. . .

'Carrick Revisited' ends:

> Whatever then my inherited or acquired
> Affinities, such remains my childhood's frame
> Like a belated rock in the red Antrim clay
> That cannot at this era change its pitch or name. . .

'Time and place,' he says earlier in the poem, make up 'our bridgeheads into reality'.

Narrow religion and life-denying puritanism mark the point at which Ulster's darker attributes shade into the more personal aspects of MacNeice's childhood. When he was still very young he was looked after by a woman whom he represents in *The Strings are False* as a blend of the least desirable Northern Irish qualities. 'Her face was sour and diehard puritanical. . .she knew all there was to be known about bringing up children: keep them conscious of sin, learn them their sums, keep the windows shut tight.' 'Religion encroached upon us steadily.' He was afraid of his father's 'conspiracy with God':

> My father made the walls resound,
> He wore his collar the wrong way round.

He was terrorized by a precocious sense of sin and feelings of guilt, by dreams and shadows which, as the autobiographical writing indicates, were connected with early encounters with death and mental illness:

> When I was five the black dreams came;
> Nothing after was quite the same.

'On Good Fridays I made a great effort to be Christian, would read the Crucifixion through in all the four Gospels on end, and then walk up and down the garden, keeping my face austere, trying not to be pleased by the daffodils.' Fantasies, games of make-believe and above all a sensuous relishing of the external world were the antidotes he evolved to vanquish religion, darkness, loneliness and fears of death. These childhood antidotes anticipated in miniature the strategies of the adult poet. MacNeice's poetry began and continued as a reaction against darkness and a search for light.

III

Under the pressure of his childhood experience MacNeice seems to have assembled early the nucleus of his imagination. There is the dark side: 'the web of night', 'creaks and cawings', 'the murderer on the nursery ceiling', 'the watchers on the wall'. The grim backcloth and properties of nightmarish darkness include stone, bells with their 'skulls' mouths', clocks, 'the dull, / The taut and ticking fear / That hides in all clocks', the 'tyrant time' who is 'shown with a stone face':

> The nightmare noise of the scythe upon the hone,
> Time sharpening his blade among high rocks alone.

And, of course, dominant in the darkness is death, 'the drift of death / In the sombre wind'. Beyond all these recurring images stretches 'a larger emptiness, the spaces of the universe'.

Darkness in MacNeice's poetry is overpowering, but is is answered by an intense brightness. On the side of light we have sensuous response, imagination, women, water, birds — 'the drunkenness of things being various'. Light itself flashes through his work: lamps, candles, firelight, embers, sparks, 'the dazzle on the sea', 'glitters of dew' and, of course, the sun in all its moods and seasons, but especially spring, summer and morning, the sun on field, mountain and building, 'the sunlight on the garden', which connects with another key image — flowers. These recur frequently as life-symbols. In 'Death of an Actress', for instance, Florrie

Forde '. . .threw a trellis of Dorothy Perkins roses / Around an audience come from slum and suburb / And weary of the tea-leaves in the sink.' She creates for them 'cowslip time'. Favourite colours are sun-colours — yellow, gold: favourite flowers yellow and golden — daffodils, primroses, dandelions, sunflowers. The light of MacNeice's imagination plays over natural and manmade phenomena, encompasses landscapes, seascapes, townscapes, weathers and seasons, animals, all kinds of people, business and pleasure, eating and drinking, talking and sex. I can think of few poets who convey so fully what being alive can mean. When he cherished variousness in his own life, MacNeice was cherishing the structure of his imagination.

The gaudy paraphernalia of MacNeice's poetry, the riot of imagery, the dizzy word-play add up finally to a reply to death, 'the fear of becoming stone'. In *Modern Poetry* he writes, 'Nearly all poets have selected surface details with reference to inner or spiritual criteria.' Too many critics have been unable or unwilling to see in his work more than 'the twanging dazzle, or the dazzling noise'. Many English commentators are clearly not attuned to his qualities and procedures. And some of his countrymen are not much better. Judgements would be more precise if the Northern Irish context were taken more into account. As I have suggested, the seeds of darkness were sown during MacNeice's Ulster childhood.

Ireland must be one of the very few remaining areas in the English-speaking world which are still likely to produce poets who write out of a response to religion. The vividness of MacNeice's work was projected partly as an assault on religious narrowness and cultural restriction. In so many ways he seems a touchstone of what an Ulster (that is to say Irish) poet might be. It is too easy to dismiss him as a free-wheeling epicurean, a flashy juggler, a poet too worldly to be really wise. He himself answers this charge adequately: 'The word *worldly* is always used pejoratively — which proves what hypocrites we are.' MacNeice's games are funeral games. The bright patterns he conjures from the external world and the pleasures of being alive are not fairy light and bauble but searchlight and icon.

Time was Away: The World of Louis MacNeice, *edited by Terence Brown and Alec Reid (Dolmen, 1974) has pertinent contributions by Derek Mahon, John Montague and Terence Brown. Ed.*

The Poetry of
Patrick Kavanagh:
From Monaghan to the Grand Canal
by Seamus Heaney

'I HAVE never been much considered by the English critics' — in the
first sentence of Kavanagh's 'Author's Note' to the *Collected Poems* it is
hard to separate the bitterness from the boldness of 'not caring'. It was
written towards the end of his career when he was sure, as I am, that he
had contributed originally and significantly to the Irish literary tradition,
not only in his poetry and his novel, *Tarry Flynn,* but also in his
attempts to redefine the idea of that tradition.

Matters of audience and tradition are important in discussing
Kavanagh. How do we 'place' him? It will not do to haul the academic
net and mention peasant poets like John Clare or Stephen Duck. The
poetry of these men is a bonus in an already abundant poetic tradition;
their achievements can be displayed and cherished like corn dollies,
adornments, lovely signals of the total harvest. Their consciousness
could hold on to the rungs of established norms, there was a standard
accent against which their dialect could be evaluated. And if the English
parallels are unrewarding, it is almost equally difficult to posit an Irish
lineage. Kavanagh's proper idiom is free from the intonations typical of
the Revival poets. His imagination has not been tutored to 'sweeten
Ireland's wrong', his ear has not been programmed to retrieve in English
the lost music of verse in Irish. The 'matter of Ireland', mythic, historical or literary, forms no significant part of his material. There are a
few Yeatsian noises — 'why should I lament the wind' — in *Plowman*
(1936), but in general the uncertain voice of that first book and the
authoritative voice of *The Great Hunger* (1942) cannot be derived from
the conventional notes of previous modern Irish poetry. What we have
is something new, authentic and liberating. There is what I would call an
artesian quality about his best work because for the first time since
Brian Merriman's poetry in Irish at the end of the eighteenth century
and William Carleton's novels in the nineteenth, a hard buried life that
subsisted beyond the feel of middle-class novelists and romantic
nationalist poets, a life denuded of 'folk' and picturesque elements,

found its expression. And in expressing that life in *The Great Hunger* and in *Tarry Flynn* (1948) Kavanagh forged not so much a conscience as a consciousness for the great majority of his countrymen, crossing the pieties of a rural Catholic sensibility with the *non serviam* of his original personality, raising the inhibited energies of a subculture to the power of a cultural resource.

Much of his authority and oddity derives from the fact that he wrested his idiom bare-handed out of a literary nowhere. At its most expressive, his voice has the air of bursting a long battened-down silence. It comes on with news in the first line — 'Clay is the word and clay is the flesh', 'I have lived in important places' — and it keeps on urgently and ebulliently to the last. It never settles itself into self-regard; it doesn't preen itself in felicities; it has a spoken rather than a written note — which means that when unsuccessful it sounds more like blather than bad verse — and it runs with a lovely jaunty confidence against its metrical norm. In his *Self Portrait* (1964) Kavanagh imagined himself jumping ditches with a load of white flour on his back, and this could be an image for the kind of risky buoyancy his best work achieves, a completely different kind of discipline from Austin Clarke's 'loading himself with golden chains and trying to escape'. Kavanagh is closer to the tightrope walker than the escape artist. There is, we might say, more technique than craft in his work, real technique which is, in his own words, 'a spiritual quality, a condition of mind, or an ability to invoke a particular condition of mind...a method of getting at life', but his technique has to be continuously renewed, as if previous achievements and failures added up to nothing in the way of self-knowledge or self-criticism of his own capacities as a maker. There is very little 'parnassian' in Kavanagh, very little sense of his deploying for a second time round technical discoveries originally made while delivering a poem of the first intensity out of its labour.

*

To begin, then, with the first such poem we meet in the *Collected Poems*, 'Inniskeen Road, July Evening':

> The bicycles go by in twos and threes —
> There's a dance in Billy Brennan's barn to-night,
> And there's a half-talk code of mysteries
> And the wink-and-elbow language of delight.
> Half-past eight and there is not a spot
> Upon a mile of road, no shadow thrown
> That might turn out a man or woman, not
> A footfall tapping secrecies of stone.
>
> I have what every poet hates in spite
> Of all the solemn talk of contemplation.
> O Alexander Selkirk knew the plight

> Of being king and government and nation.
> A road, a mile of kingdom, I am king
> Of banks and stones and every blooming thing.

The title names place and time, which is all-important in the world of early Kavanagh. Loved places are important places, and the right names 'snatch out of time the passionate transitory'. Inniskeen is the poet's birthplace where he lived on the family farm for more than thirty years, and it would seem that this poem comes towards the end of his sojourn for although it contemplates the scene in the present, there is a feeling of valediction about it. By the end, the experience has almost attained the status of memory, a regal distance intervenes, and impatience vies with affection in the ambiguous 'blooming'. The poet's stance becomes Wordsworth's over Tintern Abbey, attached by present feelings but conscious that the real value of the moment lies in its potential flowering, its blooming, in the imagination. Indeed, the poem could carry a Wordsworth subtitle, 'or, Solitude'.

There are two solitudes, the solitude of the road and the solitude of the poet, and the road's is an objective correlative of the poet's. The second quatrain has a curious double effect: the road has become still, there is neither sound nor shadow, and yet the negatives of 'no shadow thrown' and 'not a footfall' do not entirely rob the scene of its life. The power of the negated phrases, 'turn out a man or woman' and (especially) 'a footfall tapping secrecies of stone', works against the solitude and establishes a ghostly populous atmosphere, and this prepares us for the poet's double-edged feelings in the sestet of being at once marooned and in possession. I suppose the basic theme of the poem is the penalty of consciousness, the unease generated when a milieu becomes material. It is a love poem to a place written towards the end of the affair and it is also one of the earliest and most successful of Kavanagh's many poems about the nature of the poetic life. I have dwelt on it in some detail in order to show something that I believe even Kavanagh's admirers do not sufficiently realize, that he is a technician of considerable suppleness. I take great pleasure in that 'not' at the end of the seventh line, for example: the bag of flour has almost toppled him but that 'not' does not unbalance, it lands us instead on the lovely thawing floe of 'A footfall tapping secrecies of stone'.

Of course it would be wrong to insist too strongly on Kavanagh as a weaver of verbal textures. There is a feeling of prospector's luck — which may be deliberately achieved, but I don't think so — about many of his best effects. We need only compare the nice lift of a Kavanagh stanza with its inspired wobble:

> Cassiopeia was over
> Cassidy's hanging hill,
> I looked and three whin bushes rode across

> The horizon – the Three Wise Kings
> ('A Christmas Childhood')

with lines by a wordsmith like Hopkins:

> Look at the stars! look, look up at the skies!
> O look at all the fire-folk sitting in the air!

to see that the attitudes towards form and language are completely
different. Hopkins is a maker, Kavanagh a taker of verses, a grabber of
them. He is not so much interested in the inscape of things as in their
instress. He is, as it were, the Van Gogh rather than the Cézanne of
Monaghan. The 'ineluctible modality of the visual' does not seek to
transpose itself into aural or verbal patterning. The poem is more a con-
ductor than a crucible. It seeks 'weightlessness' – a quality he praised
in one of his own stanzas – rather than density: which is not to say that
it abjures the concrete. On the contrary, the poetry is most successful
when it is earthed in the actual where 'the light that might be mystic or
a fraud' can strike and be contained.

Which brings us back to *Plowman*. I have seen this book described as
Georgian but the lyrics are closer to Blake's *Songs of Innocence* than to
any such attending to natural surfaces. Most of them aspire to visionary
statement – statement, not evocation or description – as in 'To a
Child', the first stanza of which was the one that pleased its author by
its 'weightlessness':

> Child do not go
> Into the dark places of the soul,
> For there the grey wolves whine,
> The lean grey wolves.
>
> I have been down
> Among the unholy ones who tear
> Beauty's white robe and clothe her
> In rags of prayer.
>
> Child there is light somewhere
> Under a star,
> Sometime it will be for you
> A window that looks
> Inward to God.

Well, maybe so. But the whole thing's weightless enough to float past
you. The trouble is that romantic clichés like 'dark places of the soul'
and 'Beauty's white robe' may be counters for genuine insight but we
miss the experience even if we get the meaning. Yet implicit in the 'I'
of the poem, in this man who has come through (whatever), this seer in
the pristine sense, is the 'comic' Kavanagh of the later poems. The
persona in most of these apprentice pieces has a notion of 'the main
purpose / Which is to be / Passive, observing with a steady eye'. In the
last stanza of 'To a Blackbird', for example, the wise passiveness of the
Canal Bank sonnets is rehearsed:

We dream as Earth's sad children
Go slowly by
Pleading for our conversion
With the Most High.

But it is only when this ethereal literary voice incarnates itself in the imagery of the actual world that its messages of transcendence become credible. When the poet stands at the centre of his world, speaking as king or exile, instead of meting and mincing out his voice through the ventriloquist's doll of a mystical exquisite, he does indeed 'find a star-lovely art / In the dark sod.'

Those lines could stand as commentary on the much anthologized lyrics of Kavanagh's early Monaghan period, of which 'Shancoduff', 'A Christmas Childhood', 'Spraying the Potatoes' and the verses 'from *Tarry Flynn*' are the most outstanding. All of these make the home territory 'a theme for kings', 'part of no earthly estate', turn the black hills into 'Alps'. Their kingmaking explorations make possible the regal authority of the later 'Epic' which is their magnificent coda and represents Kavanagh's comprehension of his early achievement. They give body to the assertion in 'Art McCooey' that poetry is shaped 'awkwardly but alive in the unmeasured womb', a womb which is the equivalent of what he called elsewhere 'the unconscious fog'. What we have in these poems are matter-of-fact landscapes, literally presented, but contemplated from such a point of view and with such intensity that they become 'a prospect of the mind'. They are not poems about 'roots' — *The Green Fool* (1938), his first autobiography where he mediates between his audience and his territory with a knowing sociological wink, has more of that kind of selfconsciousness — any more than Wordsworth's 'spots of time' in *The Prelude* are about 'roots': their concern is, indeed, the growth of a poet's mind.

It is significant the way the word 'poet' keeps turning up in these poems, used with certainty, to dramatize the speaker in an absolute way. 'A poet' owns the hungry hills of Shancoduff, 'poet' is lost to potato-fields in the spraying poem, a 'child-poet' picks out letters in 'A Christmas Childhood', and on each occasion the word slews the poem towards a resolution. If we compare such usages, and the 'poet' of 'Inniskeen Road', with earlier *Plowman* lyrics — 'O pagan poet you / And I are one' ('To a Blackbird') and 'Her name was poet's grief' ('Mary') — we can see a new authority and boldness. There he was a postulant, full of uninitiated piety towards the office, now he has taken orders, has ordained himself and stands up in Monaghan as the celebrant of his own mysteries. The word is used as the sign of the imagination, a fiat and an amen. Kavanagh's Monaghan is his pastoral care in the sacerdotal as much as in the literary sense.

Yet his destiny was to become a mendicant rather than a parish priest, called from his 'important places' in Monaghan to consecrate new ground for himself on the banks of the Grand Canal in Dublin, to end up, not like his own 'Father Mat', 'a part of the place, / Natural as a round stone in a grass field', but as an embittered guru. *Tarry Flynn* (1948) is his delightful realization of the call to leave, the pivot and centre of Kavanagh's work, an autobiographical fiction full of affection for and impatience with his parish. This book brings to fruition the valediction to 'every blooming thing' promised in 'Inniskeen Road' and in it Kavanagh achieves his first and fullest articulation of his comic vision, that view from Parnassus which was the one sustaining myth or doctrine he forged completely for himself. Towards the end of the novel there is an account of Tarry retreating to his upstairs room to compose verse, which is at once an account of the novel's genesis and an explication of Kavanagh's subsequent insistence on the poet's detachment, his duty merely 'to state the position':

> This corner was his Parnassus, the constant point above time. Winter and summer since his early boyhood he had sat here and the lumps of candle-grease on the scaly table of the old machine told a story. . .
>
> The net of earthly intrigue could not catch him here. He was on a level with the horizon – and it was a level on which there was laughter. Looking down at his own misfortunes he thought them funny now. From this height he could even see himself losing his temper with the Finnegans and the Carlins and hating his neighbours and he moved the figures on the landscape, made them speak, and was filled with joy in his own power.

Still, despite this celebration of detachment, much of Kavanagh's poetry is born out of a quarrel between 'the grip of the little fields' and 'the City of Kings / Where art, music, letters are the real things'. In *A Soul for Sale* (1947), besides the lyrics of unconscious joy, there are poems of greater emotional complexity, more sombre in tone, more meditative than lyric, the best of which are 'Bluebells for Love' and 'Advent', poems which attempt to renew in the face of experience an insouciance that has been diminished and endangered by too much 'tasting and testing'. And there is a sonnet sequence – how often, by the way, Kavanagh finds the discipline of this form a releasing one – called 'Temptation in Harvest' where the last four sections beautifully and wistfully annotate what the poet was later to describe somewhat melodramatically as 'the worst mistake of my life', his move to Dublin in 1939. This was in retrospect: in the verse, his departure appears as simple obedience to his muse:

> Now I turn
> Away from the ricks, the sheds, the cabbage garden,
> The stones of the street, the thrush song in the tree,
> The potato-pits, the flaggers in the swamp;
> From the country heart that hardly learned to harden,

From the spotlight of an old-fashioned kitchen lamp
I go to follow her who winked at me.

Kavanagh's most celebrated poem, however, is about a man who did not follow the hints of his imagination. *The Great Hunger*, first published in 1942 and collected in *A Soul for Sale*, is Kavanagh's rage against the dying of the light, a kind of elegy in a country farmyard, informed not by heraldic notions of seasonal decline and mortal dust but by an intimacy with actual clay and a desperate sense that life in the secluded spot is no book of pastoral hours but an enervating round of labour and lethargy. The poem comes across initially with great documentary force, so that one might be inclined to agree with Kavanagh's characterization of it as being 'concerned with the woes of the poor' as the whole story but that is only part of the truth, though admittedly the larger part of it.

Nevertheless, the art of the poem is replete with fulfilments and insights for which the protagonist is famished. It is written in a voice urgent and opulent as 'the mill-race heavy with the Lammas floods curving over the weir', (weightiness rather than weightlessness is the virtue here), in a verse that can 'invoke a particular condition of mind' and discovers 'a method of getting at life'. It is the nearest Kavanagh ever gets to a grand style, one that seeks not a continuous decorum but a mixture of modes, of high and low, to accommodate his double perspective, the tragic and the emerging comic. It modulates from open to stanzaic forms, and manages to differentiate nicely between the authentic direct speech of the characters and its own narrative voice which is a selection and heightening of that very speech. Kavanagh's technical achievement here is to find an Irish note that is not dependent on backward looks towards the Irish tradition, not an artful retrieval of poetic strategies from another tongue but a ritualistic drawing out of patterns of run and stress in the English language as it is spoken in this country. It is as if the 'stony grey soil of Monaghan' suddenly became vocal. 'Clay is the word and clay is the flesh.'

The poem is the obverse of Kavanagh's *bildungsroman, Tarry Flynn.* It is not about growing up and away but about growing down and in. Its symbol is the potato rather than the potato blossom, its elements are water and earth rather than fire and air, its theme is consciousness moulded in and to the dark rather than opening to the light. It is significant, for example, how Stephen Dedalus's metaphor of nets ('When the soul of a man is born in this country there are nets flung at it to hold it back from flight. You talk to me of nationality, language,

religion. I shall try to fly by those nets') is repeated and revised in
Kavanagh's presentation of Patrick Maguire:

> The drills slipped by and the days slipped by
> And he trembled his head away and ran free from the world's halter,
> And thought himself wiser than any man in the townland
> When he laughed over pints of porter
> Of how he came free from every net spread
> In the gaps of experience. He shook a knowing head. . .

The nets that Maguire eludes are those very experiences whose reality
Stephen Dedalus goes 'to encounter for the millionth time'. Maguire's
running free of the world's halter involves an evasion of those chances
'to err, to fall' which Stephen embraces. His 'knowing head' looks out
from under the meshes of family and church ties. Where Stephen dis-
obeyed his mother and defied her pious devotion, fearful of the
deleterious 'chemistry' that such obeisance might set up in his soul,
Maguire succumbs to 'the lie that is a woman's screen / Around a
conscience where soft thighs are spread'. When she told him to 'go to
Mass and pray and confess your sins / And you'll have all the luck', 'her
son took it as literal truth'. His sexual timidity is continuously related
to his failure to achieve any fullness of personality: when he 'makes the
field his bride' he settles for 'that metaphysical land / Where flesh was
a thought more spiritual than music'.

But not only does the poem refract the Joycean motif, it consciously rejects the Yeatsian 'dream of the noble and the beggarman'. It
is a rebuke to the idea of the peasant as noble savage and a drama-
tization of what its author called 'the usual barbaric life of the Irish
country poor'. Against the paternalistic magnificence of

> John Synge, I and Augusta Gregory, thought
> All that we did, all that we said or sang
> Must come from contact with the soil, from that
> Contact everything Antaeus-like grew strong —

against this we must set Section XII of the Kavanagh poem which
answers it with a vision of 'the peasant ploughman who is half a vege-
table', 'a sick horse nosing around the meadow for a clean place to die'.

Yet while these twists help us to see *The Great Hunger*'s place in
modern Irish literature, what gives it its essential impetus is not the
literary context but its appetite for the living realities of Patrick Maguire's
world, and the feeling generated by the disparity between Maguire's and
Kavanagh's response to that world. What would be present to Maguire
as work and weather, for example, is transformed by the poetry into
matters of love and celebration:

> The fields were bleached white,
> The wooden tubs full of water
> Were white in the winds
> That blew through Brannagan's Gap on their way from Siberia;

> The cows on the grassless heights
> Followed the hay that had wings —
> The February fodder that hung itself on the black branches
> Of the hilltop hedge.
> A man stood beside a potato-pit
> And clapped his arms
> And pranced on the crisp roots
> And shouted to warm himself.

In the words of a later poem, 'naming these things is the love-act and its pledge', and despite the poem's overt anatomy of barrenness, there is a conjugal relationship between its language and its world which conveys a sense of abundance. If Maguire's satisfaction is to masturbate over the ashes, Kavanagh's is to allow the imagination to roam stud-like in the cold fields. The poem accumulates a number of incidents in which the fallow/fertile and the repression/fulfilment contrasts are dramatized, and simultaneously it establishes the prevailing atmosphere of futility in which these incidents occur:

> A wonderful night, we had. Duffy's place
> Is very convenient. Is that a ghost or a tree?
> And so they go home with dragging feet
> And their voices rumble like lade carts.
> And they are happy as the dead or sleeping. . .
> I should have led that ace of hearts.

If Maguire is blamed, he is also explained — 'the poet merely states the position' — and the position is that Maguire's soul is never born. The self he achieves is one dressed to fit the constricting circumstances of home, community and church. His sexuality is dammed or leaked at the hearth or harnessed to 'probe in the insensitive hair' of the potato crop; his sense of wonder is calloused by habit so he misses the chance to find 'health and wealth and love' in 'bits and pieces of Everyday'; the pinnacle of his intellectual ambitions is determined by the community, to rise to a 'professorship' like

> the pig-gelder Nallon whose knowledge was amazing.
> 'A treble, full multiple odds. . .That's flat porter. . .
> My turnips are destroyed with the blackguardly crows. . .'

and his religious sensibilities atrophy, to be replaced by 'an old judge's pose: / Respectability and righteousness'.

But there is no condescension in this. It is a loving portrait which Kavanagh was to reject because 'it lacks the nobility and repose of poetry'. It is true that there are strident moments, especially at the end when

> The hungry fiend
> Screams the apocalypse of clay
> In every corner of this land,

yet I do not feel that the apostrophizing of the Imagination at the beginning and the end involves a loss of repose. One can see that the

poem's fundamentally tragic note is subsumed into the comic vision of *Tarry Flynn* and that it is a step on the way to that vision, yet if *The Great Hunger* did not exist, a greater hunger would, the hunger of a culture for its own image and expression. It is a poem of its own place and time, transposing the griefs of the past — its title conventionally refers to the Great Famine of the 1840s — into the distresses of the present, as significant in the Irish context as Hardy's novels were in the English, socially committed but also committed to a larger, more numinous concept of love whose function he decreed was not to look back but 'to look on'.

*

While the phrase 'socially committed' would have been repellent to Kavanagh, it does remind us that he was a child of the thirties, as depressed and more repressed in Ireland than elsewhere. And while he abjured, in his prose of the 1950s and 1960s, any 'messianic impulse', he was always as concerned in his own way as Yeats was about 'unity of culture' and 'unity of being'. His acute sense of the need to discriminate between 'parochial' and 'provincial' mentalities, his reaction against the romantic nationalist revival of Synge and Yeats as 'a thoroughgoing English-bred lie', his refusal to allow social and religious differences within the country to be glossed over in a souped-up 'buckleppin' idiom, his almost Arnoldian concern for touchstones of excellence — *Ulysses, Moby Dick* — and his search for an art that would be an Olympian 'criticism of life', all this surfaces in his essays from an over-all concern for the 'quality of life' in the country, especially the literary life:

> I am beginning to think there may be such a thing as a Celtic mind which lives on no sustained diet, but on day-to-day journalism. On reflection, I begin to see that this unfaith is not local to Ireland. Yeats, for all his emphasis on Ireland, was the last great Victorian poet. His work was born within the safety of that large, smug, certain world where no one questioned how much was being taken for granted.
>
> Whatever be the reason, it appears to me that we cannot go on much longer without finding an underlying faith upon which to build our world of letters.
>
> Because of their absence of faith, the anger of men like O'Connor and O'Casey is worthless and even pitiful.

('Poetry and Pietism')

The essays of the 1950s and the 1960s are full of such sweeping remarks. In Dublin he seems to have been pulled in two directions: to be the poet as outsider, as parishioner of Monaghan, and the criticism in *Kavanagh's Weekly* (1952) as well as the satire of *Come Dance with Kitty Stobling* (1960) is generated by this desire to be on the one hand the parochial precursor in provincial Dublin; yet on the other hand there is an implicit wish to be a parishioner of Ireland, to be the poet as integral part of a whole parochial culture. Much of what he says is a plea for an ideal national culture but it is premised on the rejection of nationality as a category in cultural life. In Dublin his Monaghan sceptre becomes a forked stick, that only occasionally works as a divining rod, as on the banks of the Grand Canal or in the environs of 'The Chest Hospital'. In the end he finds himself at bay in that new parish which he called his 'Pembrokeshire', a domain that was again 'part of no earthly estate', centring around Baggot Street Bridge. Over and over again he reverts to his experience of a poetic rebirth in these surroundings:

> I have been thinking of making my grove on the banks of the Grand Canal near Baggot Street Bridge where in recent days I rediscovered my roots. My hegira was to the Grand Canal bank where again I saw the beauty of water and green grass and the magic of light. It was the same emotion I had known when I stood on a sharp slope in Monaghan. . .

It should be said that this shift or tremor that released his new sense of his powers was occasioned by considerable emotional and physical distress. In 1952 he had been the victim of a notorious profile in a magazine called *The Leader* and had conducted an unsuccessful libel action against the magazine, during which his cross-questioning in the witness-box became something of a spectator sport for Dubliners. That was in 1954 and shortly afterwards he underwent an operation for lung cancer. So the Parnassian calm which he conjures in these first redemptive sonnets represents both aesthetic and spiritual resourcefulness:

> I learned, I learned — when one might be inclined
> To think, too late, you cannot recover your losses —
> I learned something of the nature of God's mind,
> Not the abstract Creator but He who caresses
> The daily and nightly earth; He who refuses
> To take failure for an answer till again and again is worn.

('Miss Universe')

Still, despite the generous epiphanies represented by the best work of his last decade, Kavanagh's face inclines to set like Maguire's in a judicial pose. Despite the accuracy and serious implications of his critical *aperçus*, despite the continuous vaunting of the comic point of view, the over-all impression to be got from reading the second half of the *Collected Poems* is of a man who knows he can do the real thing but much of the time straining and failing. He should not simply be taken at his own word on the superiority of his comic vision, the supremacy of 'not caring' as a philosophy of life. When it serves as a myth for entrancement or Franciscan acceptance, and approaches the condition of charity, as it does in the Canal Bank sonnets and in meditations like 'Intimate Parnassus', or when it is guaranteed by the purgatorial experiences on which it is based as in 'The Chest Hospital', 'Miss

Universe', 'Prelude', 'Auditors in', 'If Ever You Go to Dublin Town' and in a song like 'On Raglan Road', or when it is offered as a poetic with the rhythmic heave of 'Yellow Vestment', then Kavanagh is 'embodying' rather than 'knowing' the truth of it, and the old sense of a man at once marooned and in possession, impatient and in love, pervades the verse; and the verse itself is supplied with energy from below and beyond its occasion.

But too often the doctrine that 'poetry is a mystical thing and a dangerous thing' was used as a petrified stick to beat the world with. Too much of the satire in *Come Dance with Kitty Stobling* remains doggerel ensnared in the environment which it purports to disdain. The pleasures to be derived from 'Adventures in the Bohemian Jungle' or 'The Christmas Mummers' are those of a ringside seat at a cockpit where the fight is lively but untidy and ends without a kill. And as for squibs like 'Irish Stew', 'Spring Day', 'Who Killed James Joyce?' and 'Portrait of the Artist', they simply represent an inelegant opportunism:

> Did you get money
> For your Joycean knowledge?
> I got a scholarship
> To Trinity College.
>
> I made the pilgrimage
> In the Bloomsday swelter
> From the Martello Tower
> To the cabby's shelter.

('Who Killed James Joyce?')

If my memory is right, one of the best known photographs of Kavanagh is with Brian O'Nolan on a Bloomsday outing.

Paradoxically, such poems contribute to an idea of the poet that Kavanagh was at pains to disassociate himself from in his essay on 'The Irish Tradition': 'One of the Irish ideas of the poet is of the uproarious clown. I have hardly ever heard an Irish admirer of Gaelic or any other poetry speaking of the poet that he didn't give the impression that he thought it all a great joke.' Unfortunately, Kavanagh's spirited living out of his idea of the autocracy of the personality often furnished fuel for such an attitude, and a performance like 'Sensational Disclosures! (Kavanagh Tells All)' treads a very dangerous line between exploiting and excoriating it. When he formulated the mood of such regenerative poems as 'Canal Bank Walk' into the desire 'to play a true note on a dead slack string' he too often ended up, as the *Collected Poems* end up, 'In Blinking Blankness', making an aesthetic out of self-pity, formally cornered, so that doggerel seemed the only appropriate mode for an exploration of the self, a form not very conducive to 'nobility and repose'.

Kavanagh's achievement lies in the valency of a body of individual poems which establish the purity, authority and authenticity of his voice rather than in any plotted cumulative force of the opus as a whole. It could be said of him (as Thomas Kinsella has said of Austin Clarke) that his *Selected Poems* would be the marvellous book, more cogent and coherent than the *Collected*. If I feel that the man who suffered was not fully recompensed by the man who created, Kavanagh felt it too. Without myth, without masters, 'No System, no Plan', he lived from hand to mouth and unceremoniously where Yeats — and Sidney — fed deliberately and ritually, in the heart's rag-and-bone shop. And one might say that when he had consumed the roughage of his Monaghan experience, he ate his heart out.

Alan Warner's enthusiastic and thorough Clay is the Word: Patrick Kavanagh 1904-67 *(Dolmen, 1973) contains a 'Checklist' of writing by and about Kavanagh. Ed.*

Searching the Darkness:
Richard Murphy, Thomas Kinsella, John Montague and James Simmons
by Edna Longley

IT MAY be that the twentieth-century poet in any country no longer needs to feel himself significantly in touch with a particular tradition. Thomas Kinsella has generalized the situation of the contemporary Irish writer in relation to the whole spectrum of his Gaelic and Anglo-Irish inheritance as universally representative: 'every writer in the modern world. . .is the inheritor of a gapped, discontinuous, polyglot tradition'.[1] I suspect that there is a difference between the effects on the individual artist of a fragmented tradition, and one now felt to be in fragments: an incomplete jigsaw is more tantalizing than one put back in the box, a half-built house more haunting than a ruin, especially when the foundations and conditions exist for finishing the job. The fact that the critic of Irish literature, like the political and social commentator, soon finds himself speaking of 'traditions' rather than 'tradition', points to the unique possibilities of synthesis still open to the Irish poet (and the equal chance of falling between several stools). Yeats of course provides the great, but not necessarily definitive, model for such a synthesis, for the fusion of a plural inheritance within the single framework from which it ultimately derives, or which it may anticipate ('an Ireland / The poets have imagined'). As Professor Sean Lucy implies, 'the story of Anglo-Irish poetry' is a continuing one, 'the story on the one hand of a complex and developing relationship between two traditions, two cultures, two languages; and on the other it is the story of a search: it is part of the quest of the English-speaking Irish for an identity, the reshaping of English to express the Irish experience'.[2] Both Lucy's analysis and Kinsella's surely rather exceptional sense of fragmentation suggest that Irish poets up till now have found themselves in an essentially Romantic situation. The fact that the legendary pioneers have done their work, established certain outposts and frontiers,

does not mean that the subjective 'search' is over. Life may indeed be
more difficult for the settlers who follow:

> . . .Now the extraordinary hour of calm
> And day of limitation.
> The soft grasses stir
> Where unfinished dreams
> Are buried with the Fianna
> In that remote rock cave.
>
> Who today asks for more
> — Smoke of battle blown aside —
> Than the struggle with casual
> Graceless unheroic things
> The greater task of swimming
> Against a slackening tide?

> (John Montague, 'Speech for an Ideal Irish Election')

For the poet the 'task' is that of finding new forms of expression for
new states of mind. And if Montague in this early poem did not under-
estimate its magnitude, he has perhaps, like other poets and critics,
done so retrospectively: 'And then, in the late Fifties, Irish poets began
to write, without strain, a poetry that was indisputably Irish (in the
sense that it was influenced by the country they came from, its climate,
history and language) but also modern'.[3] Maurice Harmon associates the
poetry of Montague, Kinsella and Richard Murphy with the spirit of
(premature) optimism about change and liberation from the past which
existed in the Republic at that period:

> Where the previous generation had sought protection from outside influences
> in the areas of culture and commerce, the new generation looked outward to
> Europe and to America and were consciously part of the cosmopolitan, post-war
> era. The high-point of this profound reversal in national policy came in 1958
> when the Irish Government adopted Mr. T. K. Whitaker's revolutionary
> economic programme. Under his initiative, as T. P. Coogan has pointed out,
> 'planning' and 'growth-rates' were to replace 'civil war', 'oath', and 'partition'
> in the national vocabulary.[4]

Just as the political optimism of the fifties has boomeranged to some
extent, so the achievement of the poets who began to publish during
that decade may have been too readily taken for granted. Were complex
issues lying beneath the surface? Was Irish poetry too hastily packaged
for export? If Ireland's poetic tradition is not yet fully evolved, neither
is its critical — although the major writers have of course received their
due both at home and abroad. Kinsella and Montague have been the
first to appeal to internationalized standards, as well as for an internationalized aesthetic, but have hardly been judged by them in the
domestic market, where quantitative rather than qualitative criteria still
sometimes prevail. With the standing army of poets, as Patrick Kavanagh
has said, 'never less than ten thousand', there tends to be an easy confidence in the existence of at least one major-general. Dublin can still

peculiarly combine provincial insulation with metropolitan complacency. Also, both the English and American audiences often over-indulge the Irish poet, when they do not ignore him. The poets with whom I am concerned have scored some remarkable successes, constructed a crucially important bridge for those who come after them, but in my view reveal as much as resolve the difficulties of taking Irish poetry forward from their great predecessors. They mark a point of transition rather than of arrival. I shall question Montague's 'without strain', believing that the indispensable growth has left some stretch-marks.

Montague's implied awareness of himself in 'Speech for an Ideal Irish Election' as a kind of middleman between 'Romantic Ireland' and the prose of the present, perhaps between 'Romantic' Irish poetry and something else, points to a Romantic selfconsciousness as a continuing or intensified characteristic of the new poetry. Particular manifestations of such selfconsciousness will be examined later, but it has its origins in what looks more like an anxiety to assert, than automatic entry into, new freedoms. And the impression of clothes not yet fully adjusted to the figure is borne out by the way these poets see or place themselves in relation to the 'traditions' of which I have spoken, with their implications of cultural as well as aesthetic alignment. Montague, for instance, with some support from Kinsella, has more and more insisted on the necessity for the Irish poet to obtain membership of a sort of global village of poets without relinquishing his green passport. I find his skit 'Regionalism, or Portrait of the Artist as a Model Farmer' — 'This potato I plant deep / In my candid garden heap / And like a sympathetic farmer / Shield her from all might harm her, / Foreign beetles and exotic weeds, / Complicated continental breeds' — more persuasive on this point than some of his recent pronouncements which seem to recommend the wholesale importation of 'foreign beetles and exotic weeds' without a judicious quarantine period. His lecture 'The Impact of International Modern Poetry on Irish Writing'[5] begins 'with a simple geographical fact. Ireland is an island off the coast of Europe, facing, across three thousand miles of ocean, towards America'. The notable omission in Montague's geography, closer than 'three thousand miles' away, is fairly obvious. 'The English question' surely remains a major fact of Irish literature as of Irish history. (This may be truer of poetry than of the novel, a form that more readily crosses frontiers.) It is understandable that Montague and Kinsella should be in a hurry to declare their creative independence of England, to appeal over its head to a United Nations of poets —

> Now the unsmiling Saxon, surprised
> And diffident, greets an equal
> As, exemplary in the Congo,
> Rational in the U.N.,

We prospect the lands beyond
Kipling's setting sun.

(Montague, 'The Rough Field')

They embrace, even more eagerly than some contemporary English poets, with a touch of sadism rather than masochism, the notion that 'the centre of energy has shifted to America'. I agree that 'an Irish writer has a better chance of being a European than an Englishman',[6] perhaps of feeling at home with American poetry, but Montague's over-playing of his hand, his aversion to the Liverpool boat in favour of direct flights to Paris and California, lead him into absurdity: 'there is also the significant fact that [Yeats] is very little read in Europe'[7] (significant for Europe or Yeats?); 'so far as I know, Louis MacNeice has rarely been translated into another language, and even in America, his reputation has never been high'.[8] Again, the suspect values of the export-market, and not being translated could have something to do with untranslatability, generally held to be a virtue. As well as 'equating international travel and international poetry'[9] (to which he pleads guilty), Montague also dubiously equates internationalism and modernism (good) set against regionalism/nationalism and traditionalism (bad): an approach which boosts the minor Denis Devlin over the head of MacNeice betrays its own fragility and wish-fulfilment. In fact Montague's poetry in practice exhibits considerably more of the latter elements than of the former, and the whole thesis may be an attempt to justify some of his more recent procedures.

But his very holding of such a thesis is itself an interesting phenomenon. His ideas, and Kinsella's concept of tradition, perhaps mark the point at which the revolution of Pound and Eliot became relevant to Ireland. Montague has indeed criticized some of his younger contemporaries for neo-Georgian formalism, and the parallel may indicate a few strange features in the relationship between Irish and English poetry. It is a relationship, like other Anglo-Irish relationships, in which time-scales do not necessarily synchronize. Is the relative traditionalism of poets like Seamus Heaney and Derek Mahon an outcrop of the Movement or a gesture backwards to Yeats and MacNeice, or does it confirm as peculiarly Irish Yeats's instinct that 'ancient salt is best packing'? Was their 'eye on the object' approach brought into being by the kind of forces that shaped the best of the original Georgians or does it belong spiritually to some even earlier phase of English poetry? Or does their whole stance denote the entry of Irish poetry into certain classical assurances? These younger poets also seem to have remained in closer contact with English writing, whatever their other affinities and affiliations. This contact may epitomize a relaxation of barriers or simply have been easier for poets domiciled in Ulster during a creatively formative period than for their Southern compeers (perhaps an unexpected benefit of Union, or new kind of Anglo-Irishness). The fact that all of these poets have looked to London rather than to Dublin for publication, Heaney's deep digestion of R. S. Thomas and Ted Hughes, as well as of Kavanagh and Montague, points in the same direction. It is of course a two-way traffic. In 'A New Song', Heaney virtually makes a reverse take-over bid for the English language as 'planted' in Ulster:

> But now our river tongues must rise
> From licking deep in native haunts
> To flood, with vowelling embrace,
> Demesnes staked out in consonants.

This is one of a whole series of poems in his third collection, *Wintering Out*, which explores the linguistic aspect of the 'relationship' and 'search' that Lucy has described. Despite the aggressiveness of 'flood' (rather than ignoring conquest Heaney seeks to pay it back in its own coin) 'embrace' suggests a fruitful fusion. But what is or has been right for Heaney may be wrong for Montague. (Lucy's wise observation: 'Typically, we seem to feel that there is a right and a wrong to it instead of a free range of choice' should be a framed text for Irish critics of Irish poetry.) Yet Montague has paradoxically been perhaps the most successful of his generation in assimilating English influences. He admits that Auden 'was the liberating example',[10] and his name will recur in my attempts to show how the individual poets I am concerned with have drawn on the various possible sources in forging their own modes and idiom.

All the poets considered in this essay were born between 1927 and 1933. Montague's first important collection, *Poisoned Lands* (1961), and Murphy's *Sailing to an Island* (1963) followed closely on the landmark of Kinsella's *Another September* (1958), while the youngest poet, James Simmons, suitably brought up the rear with *Late but in Earnest* (1967). My opening remarks, as will have been evident, apply more directly to Kinsella and Montague, both of whom fall between Murphy's modified Anglo-Irish inclinations, and Simmons's genuinely free-wheeling tendency to bypass authorities, national and international, for the authenticities of popular art (' "I ain't got no diplomas", said Satchmo / "I look into my heart and blow" '). There may be a pattern in this, as in the fact that Murphy's reaction against an Ascendancy heritage, and Simmons's against the restraints of Ulster Protestant culture — he once gave a poetry-reading that emptied Bangor town hall — frames the equally disparate experience that Kinsella brings to his poetry from Southern Catholic and Montague from Northern Catholic origins. And although Murphy, Kinsella and Montague have been so often linked together, the qualities of their poetry are in fact very different — Kinsella refers to 'a scattering of incoherent lives'[11] — and it is perhaps permissible to associate all four precisely in terms of such individual or Romantic separateness, with the varying degrees of self-consciousness it involves about being Irish, being a poet, or both. What comes over strongly from the work of these poets is the sense of isolated imaginations, seeking on various levels for structures in which to lodge themselves. The first person or a first-person persona features prominently, together with myths and metaphors of lonely questing. *Sailing to an Island* fully exploits, indeed almost exhausts, the symbolic implications of its title, while imagery of the voyage, the sea and its hazards is less obtrusive but fundamental in *Late but in Earnest.* Murphy and Simmons display a similar anxiety properly to maintain and steer the ship of poetry, with its cargo of the individual spirit and wider responsibilities: 'And in memory's hands this hooker was restored. / Old men my instructors, and with all new gear / May I handle her well down tomorrow's sea-road' (Murphy); 'Only luck / And our skill can help us, and will or won't / Preserve the vessel, warm and afloat, / And aiming somewhere still, / Late but in earnest' (Simmons). Kinsella has only recently added to this genre, catching the boat with *Finistère* (1972). Possibly for profound ethnic reasons, his questing, and Montague's, generally takes place on land or along inland waters —

> The West a fiery complex, the East a pearl,
>   We gave our frail skiff to the hungry stream. . .

This is the opening of 'Downstream'; 'A Country Walk' also partially follows the course of a river, but more representatively, like 'Baggot Street Deserta', 'Nightwalker', 'Phoenix Park', employs the roads and streets of Ireland to express a disturbed search of the solitary consciousness for contact and integration. The first signals are sent out from the poet's window in 'Baggot Street Deserta':

> Fingers cold against the sill
> Feel, below the stress of flight,
> The slow implosion of my pulse
> In a wrist with poet's cramp, a tight
> Beat tapping out endless calls
> Into the dark. . .

Montague too goes for several walks in his poems. His most recent publication, *The Rough Field*, begins with a bus-drive and ends with a car-drive, while the whole sequence articulates and temporarily completes a characteristic 'circling' over personal and Irish circumstance:

> Harsh landscape that haunts me,
> well and stone, in the bleak moors of dream,
> with all my circling a failure to return. . .

Such myths, methods and moods can of course be paralleled elsewhere, but the sustained and explicit nature of the different journeys, all this 'searching the darkness for a landing place' (Kinsella, 'Downstream'), the 'aiming somewhere still', seems to me emblematic of the selfconsciousness, uncertainties and ambitions which I have suggested these poets share. They are at sea because of doubts regarding both their starting-point and their destination. In so far as both are Ireland, there is still a choice of stances on that 'quaking sod', as Montague suggests in *The Rough Field:* 'From the Glen of the Hazels / To the Golden Stone may be / The longest journey / I have ever gone.' The connection between 'Irish Poetry and Irish Nationalism', or Ireland's development as a nation, is investigated elsewhere in this volume (pp. 4—22), and an Irish poet evidently finds less firm ground than an English poet, as soon as he steps out beyond the purely personal: unformed or unstable institutions, the minefield of the past. Since his own past may be partially moulded by such circumstances, the journey outwards can legitimately coincide with the journey inwards, as it does with exactitude in the poetry of Seamus Heaney. But in addition to the extra-personal dimension latent in the pursuit of 'identity' the creative malleability of such a melting-pot brings with it other special potentialities. The spectrum of choice among literary traditions reflects the multiplicity of ways in which Ireland presents itself as a physical and metaphysical entity. It can therefore fulfil from the outset the conditions of a poetic image or myth, as the polarities of its qualities do the conditions of a realistic or tragic art. There are the overlapping contours of nationalism and regionalism — the ideological, social and political scope suggested by the former, the rooting particularities afforded by the latter. There is the nexus supplied by the interpenetration of past and present — Murphy's 'The past is happening today', Montague's 'Once again, it happens' — a nexus woven of social as well as political threads in the intersecting perspectives of rural and urban Ireland. The Irish poet may inhabit imaginatively, as the majority of his countrymen do unimaginatively, 1690, 1798, 1916 or even 1975, and find relevance in pre-history or Gaelic civilization. Ireland too can look different from Dublin, Belfast, Derry, Galway, Tyrone and Monaghan. Patrick Kavanagh's disappointed pilgrimage to Dublin dramatized many distances. The unfinished business of history, the Irish ability to 'preserve' things, impedes progress but advances art: Seamus Heaney's 'Bogland' registers the advantages as well as the disadvantages of a retentive racial memory:

> Butter sunk under
> More than a hundred years
> Was recovered salty and white. . .

One such advantage, the 'salt' of a well-preserved folk-culture, valuably flavours the artistic and linguistic stock of the Irish Poet. It may be a base for take-off (Kavanagh) or touchdown (Yeats) in that cultural counterpoint which makes the origins of one poet another's destination.

Finally, there are the microcosmic possibilities of a country big

enough to be a nation, 'small enough / To be still thought of with a
family feeling', for the strands of national life to be intimately connected.
MacNeice's further dream: 'that on this tiny stage with luck a man /
Might see the end of one particular action' may be undercut, but the
notion of the 'tiny stage' survives his disillusioned sense of the drama
likely to be enacted. The Irish poet then has the chance of putting himself in touch with a fusion of landscape, geography, history, society and
politics which can wear a variety of mythological colouring – one poet's
myth is another's 'poisoned lands' – enabling him to express not only
Ireland and himself but human life with unusual completeness. The
poetry of Yeats, Kavanagh and MacNeice demonstrates how a stance
in relation to Ireland can generate or feed an imaginative stance of rich
complexity. Yeats's hawk's eye-view becomes the foundation of a cosmic and comprehensive vision, Kavanagh's effort to bring 'The Hidden
Ireland' to the 'light of imagination' imparts a new tension and intensity
to certain Romantic themes, while the sideways step of exile, as well as
his awareness of Ireland's contradictions, seems to have nourished the
objectivity, scepticism and flexibility of MacNeice's whole approach:
'Time and place – our bridgeheads into reality / But also its conceal-
ment!' ('Carrick Revisited'), the trajectory of his departures and returns
matching the trajectory of his poetry from 'the Particular' to 'All other
possible bird's-eye views'. I would now like to consider how Murphy,
Kinsella, Montague and Simmons have separately exploited the natural
resources I have listed; where they stand in relation to the more Anglo-
Irish and Protestant perspectives of embracing/rejecting the totality
of Ireland and the more native and Catholic compulsion to excavate,
articulate and exorcize the buried centuries (the two approaches are not
mutually exclusive); and, most important of all, how their chosen angle
of vision transmutes the raw materials within the complete refinery of
their art.

Yeats's 'September 1913' in pronouncing that 'Romantic Ireland's
dead and gone' also wrote the epitaph of a certain kind of Romantic
Irish poetry. At one of its extremes John Montague's viewpoint continues that tradition which includes the scornful thunderbolts of Yeats,
the 'anguish and anger' of Joyce, the unsatisfied hunger of Kavanagh,
the astringency of MacNeice:

> Ancient Ireland, indeed! I was reared by her bedside,
> The rune and the chant, evil eye and averted head,
> Formorian fierceness of family and local feud.

– an outburst which echoes and complements MacNeice's:

> The land of scholars and saints:
> Scholars and saints my eye, the land of ambush,
> Purblind manifestos, never-ending complaints. . .

> (*Autumn Journal*, XVI)

Yet MacNeice's 'odi atque amo' points to the persistence of an imaginative as well as political deadlock. The characters in Montague's poem ('Like Dolmens round My Childhood, the Old People') are subsequently defined as 'Gaunt figures of fear and of friendliness', 'their shadows pass / Into that dark permanence of ancient forms'.

Post-Yeatsian Ireland seems to have contributed a new element to this tension. Kinsella's condemnation in 'A Country Walk' of the worshippers at the Easter shrine, 'that have exchanged / A trenchcoat playground for a gombeen jungle' not only updates Yeats's repudiation of Paudeen, but implies a search for new gods. The often-quoted lines which follow —

> Around the corner, in an open square,
> I came upon the sombre monuments
> That bear their names: MacDonagh & McBride,
> Merchants; Connolly's Commercial Arms. . .

strike me more ambiguously than they do Maurice Harmon, for whom they constitute 'Kinsella's deflation of names once glorified by Yeats'.[12] It seems to me that both poets mix glorification and deflation in about equal parts — are MacDonagh, McBride and Connolly degraded by their present context, or is their present context degraded by them? What is really new is the depressive note, the passing of even Yeats's post-revolutionary exhilaration: (' "This is not", I say, / "The dead Ireland of my youth, but an Ireland / The poets have imagined, terrible and gay" '). The Ireland that Kinsella imagines may not be dead but appears only half-alive, or caught between two lives, suffering along with the poet the inevitable withdrawal symptoms of heady intoxications. What at its worst is a limbo, at its best 'the extraordinary hour of calm' (uncanny prescience), seems to have impelled poets to draw up a balance sheet (Montague's 'Hymn to the New Omagh Road' partially takes this form), reckoning profit and loss and future prospects. Relaxation from history enables them to digest its ironies, pick over confused debris and close the gap between past and present:

> Who owns the land where musket-balls are buried
> In blackthorn roots on the eskar, the drained bogs
> Where sheep browse, and credal war miscarried?
> Names in the rival churches are written on plaques.
>
> Behind the dog-rose ditch, defended with pikes,
> A tractor sprays a rood of flowering potatoes:
> Morning fog is lifting, and summer hikers
> Bathe in a stream passed by cavalry traitors.
>
> A Celtic cross by the road commemorates no battle
> But someone killed in a car, Minister of Agriculture.
> Dairy lorries on the fast trunk-route rattle:
> A girl cycles along the lane to meet her lover. . .

These are the opening stanzas of Richard Murphy's long lyrical

sequence 'The Battle of Aughrim' (published in the book of that title
in 1968) and Murphy is the poet who has most obsessively engaged in
this kind of accountancy, tackling the theme of 'Ireland' in an even
more head-on fashion than the equally involved Montague. Murphy's
obsessiveness, his concern with the external facts of history, may be
explained by an anxiety not only to digest Ireland but that Ireland
should digest him:

> Huddled among boulders were those whose ancestors had lost the pitiless
> struggle for the land which ours had won. . . They were truly Irish, and that is
> what my brother and I wanted to be. They seemed sharper, freer, more cun-
> ning than we were. Stones, salmon-falls, rain-clouds and drownings had entered
> and shaped their minds, loaded with ancestral bias. . . They seemed most
> mysterious and imaginative to us.[13]

In seeking a 'truly Irish' identity Murphy also seeks absolution from
Ascendancy guilts. His persona in *Sailing to an Island* suggests the ex-
landlord whose isolation or Absentee-ism has now turned against himself, returning to his ruined and lost possessions, with their legacy of
human ruin, to attempt expiation and a revitalizing contact with the
natives. The title-poem dramatizes the difficulties of such a pilgrimage:
'There are hills of sea between us and land, / Between our hopes and
the island harbour'. At the start of the voyage the poet's cheek is 'kissed
and rejected, kissed, as the gaff sways / A tangent,' later 'Ropes lash
my cheeks'. There are in fact two islands, two Irelands, in the poem.
Clare Island, the 'chosen' destination, 'its crags purpled by legend' as
they might have been by the early Yeats, proves as inaccessible as the
'mirage' and 'dreams' it evokes. And it has to be exchanged for the dis-
enchanting actualities of contemporary Inishbofin towards which the
tide runs more favourably, and where the poet eventually finds a 'bed'.
Even this harbour, attained after he has exiled himself from the pub
chatter, is shadowed by the ambiguity — 'the moon stares / Cobwebbed
through the window' — which has characterized the whole journey with
its sense of obstacles to be overcome or screens to be penetrated. The
heavy seas off the cliffs of Clare Island, the boat with its 'rotten hull'
'bucking' as if to throw off its passengers, symbolize the racial experience which divides the visitor from true sailors and islanders. Such
experience may be mimetically recreated 'in holiday fashion', or in a
poem, but can it ever be truly 'known' or shared?

> Am I jealous of these courteous fishermen
> Who hand us ashore, for knowing the sea
> Intimately, for respecting the storm
> That took five of their men on one bad night
> And five from Rossadillisk in this very boat?

The answer is almost certainly 'yes', despite an apparently penitential
episode on Inishbofin: 'I slip outside, fall among stones and nettles', and
the next two poems in *Sailing to an Island,* closely linked with the first,

explore more positive means of atonement, in its primary as well as its secondary sense. 'The Last Galway Hooker' also carries the freight of history, but its wounds are healed as the poet takes over from its second-last owner, the 'best of the boatsmen from Inishbofin', and the co-operation he has received from craftsmen who 'picked up the tools of their interrupted work' seals his own imaginative 'reconstruction' in the poem. The double reconstruction restores more than a boat. This time the poet can make and follow through an almost Yeatsian 'choice'.

> So I chose to renew her, to rebuild, to prolong
> For a while the spliced yards of yesterday. . .

by which he asserts his rights in the ship and their concomitant responsibilities (possibly a redefinition of the neglected obligations of his caste). In 'The Cleggan Disaster' the ambivalences of 'Sailing to an Island' (being on boat and island but not of them), are resolved by the alternative method of empathy. Though apparently keeping himself out of the picture, the poet may be seeking identity through identification, as by an objective narrative technique, moving in its restraints, he implies the dimensions of the tragedy:

> There was a king of the Mayo fishermen
> Drawn from the sea in the chain of his own nets.
> Of those who survived, a young one was seen
> Walking at noon in the fields, clutching a bailer.

Several poems in the second section of *Sailing to an Island* veer in a contrary but complementary direction, backwards to Murphy's Anglo-Irish origins and the 'legacy' they have bequeathed him. These poems centre on the death of the poet's grandmother and the selling off, through 'time's auctioneers', of the house where 'she in the long ascendancy of rain / Served biscuits on a tray with ginger wine'. They literally catalogue the furniture of an Anglo-Irish heritage in the context of its disposal and dispersal:

> The pistol that lost an ancestor's duel,
> The hoof of the horse that carried him home
> To be stretched on chairs in the drawing-room,
> Hung by the Rangoon prints and the Crimean medal.

> Lever and Lover, Somerville and Ross
> Have fed the same worm as Blackstone and Gibbon,
> The mildew has spotted *Clarissa*'s spine
> And soiled the *Despatches of Wellington*.

Despite its obsolescence such furniture is as lovingly polished by the poetry as it is cherished by the poet: 'Time can never relax like this again', 'They walked through pergolas / And planted well, so that we might do better'. But if Murphy values the personal and cultural aspects of his inheritance, he is unforgiving towards — perhaps cannot forgive himself for — their political and military corollaries:

> The battle cause, a hand grenade
> Lobbed in a playground, the king's viciousness
> With slaves succumbing to his rod and kiss,
> Has a beginning in my blood.

Cromwell receives an unfavourable mention in 'The Cleggan Disaster', and the Battle of Aughrim, 'the last decisive battle in Irish history', whose consequences − the Penal Laws − turned the screw of oppression even tighter, eventually became the focus for all that Murphy repudiates. The quatrain quoted above concludes 'Now', the first section of the sequence, which employs an archaeological strategy and stratification whereby the past is conjured up by means of its scars and relics in the present. Starting from 'the land where musket-balls are buried', Murphy moves on to a woman who 'reads from an old lesson' 'Aughrim's great disaster / Made him two hundred years my penal master', and finally 'brings me from Knock shrine / John Kennedy's head on a china dish'. The third poem finds the past alive, if sick, and living in Belfast:

> Apprentices uplift their banner
> True blue-dyed with 'No Surrender!'
> Claiming Aughrim as if they'd won
> Last year, not 1691.

In the fifth section the poet 'drives to a symposium / On Ireland's Jacobite war' and discovers the sort of paradox Yeats found on the walls of the Municipal Gallery: 'Once an imperial garrison / Drank here to a king: / Today's toast is republican, / We sing "A Soldier's Song".' The sixth recounts the adventures of a piece of slate through twelve centuries: 'This week I paved my garden path / With slate St Colman nailed on lath'. The seventh ('Left a Cromwellian demesne / My kinsman. . .') continues the movement towards the personal and familiar which is completed by a Copperfieldian recall of the poet's christening, and the more plausible recollection of his schooldays which begins 'One morning of arrested growth'. This variety of stance and image is well-maintained in the rendering of the battle and its aftermath. Murphy quotes the address of the Marquis of St Ruth, the leader imposed by Louis XIV on the Irish army, and versifies the conclusion of the Reverend George Story's *An Impartial History*, 'This war has ended happily for us: / The people now must learn to be industrious'.

Elsewhere we are given the perspective of the Planter ('Slow sigh of the garden yews / Forty years planted. / May the God of battle / Give us this day our land'); and of the Gael, the Irish rank and file locked in a different blood-relationship with the land:

> At the whirr of a snipe each can disappear
>
> Terrified as a bird in a gorse-bush fire,
> To delve like a mole or mingle like a nightjar
> Into the earth, into the air, into the water.

Parts of the sequence demonstrate that Romantic Ireland lives: the whole poem is up to a point an epic starring Patrick Sarsfield. 'Cavalier, / You feathered with the wild geese our despair' brings us back full circle to 'September 1913'.

It is hard to fault 'The Battle of Aughrim' on its many-faceted adjustment of history to poetry, on humane intention, historical conscience and emotional accuracy, on precision of detail and image. But something programmatic in its design and designs (the poem was commissioned by the B.B.C. Third Programme)[14] stands in the way of total subjection to the offered experience: sometimes it's like attending 'a symposium / On Ireland's Jacobite war'. I have indicated the flexibilities which soften the hard-edged pattern of 'Now', 'Before', 'During' and 'After' but the determined confrontation of History (compare Geoffrey Hill's 'Funeral Music' launched under similar auspices) must involve a certain exteriority, the jettisoning of concerns which lie outside or inside that part of the self defined in terms of race and family. Despite the concreteness and power of individual scenes Murphy rings the changes on a rather limited number of components: the tensions, ironies and paradoxes of history, present set against past, violence against landscape — all adumbrated in the very first poem. The sequence itself is drawn up in battle-lines. It could be argued that the sea-poems (not the house-poems) in *Sailing to an Island* exhibit the same exteriority, coupled with a more monotonously documentary approach — the boat-lore ceases to grip — and louder gear-changing into the symbolic. The fact that the poetry goes so much more than halfway to meet the critic who is himself questing for 'Irishness' may arouse suspicion.

Harmon calls Murphy's first poetic venture, *Archaeology of Love* (1955), 'steeped in Mediterranean and classical culture';[15] a poem in *Sailing to an Island,* 'The Netting' (of a Greek vase) exaggerates and thus draws attention to his attraction towards heraldic stylization, a caressing of antique objects, costumes and décor and of words with similar appeal: 'credal', 'eskar', 'catafalque', his demeanour that of a loving archaeologist before the regalia of the past:

> I have learnt to restore
> From dust each room
> The earthquakes lowered
> In that doomed spring,
> To piece beyond the fire
> The cypress court
> With gryphons basking. . .

Here as elsewhere the archaeology, the exteriority, the deliberate 'tasting of vintage terror' (also less ironic than it should be in the 'symposium' poem), the combination of search and research, seems indeed to result from Murphy's excessive consciousness of being an outsider, of needing to work his passage and establish credentials for naturalization. The three richest poems in *Sailing to an Island* are portraits of the artist (Roethke, a poet) or thinker (Wittgenstein at Rosroe) as an outsider. 'The Progress of a Painter' comes almost too near the bone, but in doing so 'escapes' what it probes:

> Barred aviaries of birds that never flew
> But hopped about his hierophantic mind
> With lacquered plumes gaudier than pheasants grow,
> Escaped at last through water, sedge and wind.

Such a consciousness, including that of eighteenth-century literary forebears, may also have shaped the cool and detached tone of Murphy's style. However, in this sphere too he strains at times after attachment, is the outsider trying to get inside his (predetermined) subject. In the first two stanzas of 'The Last Galway Hooker' we are perhaps too aware of the attempt to inject a dramatic rhythm into descriptive and narrative material:

> Where the Corrib river chops through the Claddagh
> To sink in the tide-race its rattling chain
> The boatwright's hammer chipped across the water
>
> Ribbing this hooker, while a reckless gun
> Shook the limestone quay-wall, after the Treaty
> Had brought civil war to this fisherman's town.

Again, the need to 'place' the boat in landscape and history, to orbit a whole context around an essentially static centre of gravity, puts pressure on the resources of relatives, demonstratives and verbs: 'where', 'while', the proliferation of 'the' and duplication of 'this', the indicative mood in present, past and pluperfect tenses, an infinitive and present participle. This illustration could be multiplied from both Murphy's books, and perhaps the labour-pangs of his syntax signal the whole difficulty of discovering a contour and a continuum which will hold past and present, fact and feeling. He pieces together his poetry as carefully as a shattered vase, but the joins are occasionally visible, the set pieces not quite set: 'The sea *became* a dance. . . / *Now* he was dancing round the siege of Death: / *Now* he was Death' ('The Cleggan Disaster', my italics). However such analysis and emphasis does less than justice to the respectable, if not golden, mean achieved by this level style. Murphy is again liable to rise above a sound position in the batting averages, burst through self-imposed straitjackets, when he is evoking precisely such a release —

> He broke prisons, beginning with words,
> And at last tamed, by talking, wild birds

> (Wittgenstein)

Or alternatively when a really tight form elicits a genuinely Augustan astringency: 'This week I paved my garden path / With slate St Colman nailed on lath' — a couplet sharpened for maximum penetration by an unusually dense texture of alliteration and assonance which hinges on the chiasmus of n, a, 1 sounds. A similar pointing achieves a different purpose in the lines about the native Irish quoted above: the declension of the off-rhymed endings, 'fire', 'nightjar', 'water', profoundly dramatizes meaning (elsewhere off-rhyme, like enjambment, sometimes seems a reflex, an overdriven vehicle), as does the 'mingling' of sounds in the penultimate line. Another book from Murphy is overdue:* perhaps his relative silence covers a recognition that the next sea-road, which must surely lead inwards, requires different gear.

If Murphy's language wears the hairshirt of puritanical, possibly penitential restraints, Thomas Kinsella's offers a cavalier richness. While both are conspicuously occupied with the need to deploy a variety of stylistic effects, Murphy is the more liable to be caught steering, Kinsella floundering. In an earlier essay on Kinsella's poetry[16] I noticed his ambitious and important effort to assimilate the stylistic and formal achievements of the best modern poets with, nevertheless, a failure to absorb such influences into the modulations of his own voice: 'His native village, vaguely honoured / And confused by stories newly arriving, / Would have a little of minor value to add' (Auden), 'Interpreting the old mistakes / And discords in a work of Art' (Eliot). It is difficult to hear the same poet in these quotations, or to relate their qualities to what appears to be Kinsella's most natural and native note, in *Another September,* a bardic rhetoric tending towards mythic formulations:

> Soft, to your places, animals,
> Your legendary duty calls.
>   It is, to be
> Lucky for my love and me.
>   *And yet we have seen that all's*
>   *A fiction that is heard of love's difficulty. . .*

The touch of Yeats in the last two lines encumbers but cannot detract from the sinuous beauty of the first four, 'soft' and 'legendary' licensed by and pivoting on the audacious simplicity of 'It is, to be'. However, such harmony and precision are by no means invariable in *Another September* where the elements of Kinsella's more evolved style at times make as strange bedfellows as his influences. One linguistic family takes its origin from the mythological-decorative impulse of the book, the trappings that inevitably accompany heraldic beasts, 'propitious creatures of the wood', 'deer' (not all that common in Ireland), numinous goddesses and heroes as they go about their 'legendary duty'. A more transcendental décor and vocabulary is associated with the

* *High Island* (Faber) appeared in Autumn 1974. Ed.

cosmic backdrop against which several of the poems take place: the
younger Kinsella embroiders the cloths of heaven as assiduously as the
younger Yeats: 'the lunar curtain', 'a crawling arch of stars', 'the
figured void'. Words like 'epic', 'elegiac', 'heroic' and 'tragic' (several
times) complete this particular spectrum and denote its aspirations.
Tougher abstractions at once conflict with and fail to modify the effect
of embroidery, import an Audenesque colour without an Audenesque
intellectual grasp: 'A masochism gasped and flew / Gladly into the
shared air', 'Much as calamities do, she took / Her station near the heart'.
'The superficies / Of windy disaster', 'Her rectitude in every season /
Centres in the rigour of the winter'. 'The Travelling Companion', in
which Kinsella invents his own animal and attempts to create a moral
emblem, illustrates the collision between the two kinds of language and
the failure to lodge them in the colloquial and concrete:

> Yet balanced, snarling, on claws, a fertile tension
> Stretched its brightening muscles, sniffed and made
>   Off in a carnal wonder, prowled with the hungry,
> Panicked with alert deer, preyed in the sky,
> Skittered brilliantly across a still glade.

In *Downstream* (1962), Kinsella seems to be aiming at 'a more
thoughtful and quiet power'. A welcome note of intimacy, and an
emergence from a solipsistic universe in 'A Lady of Quality' is confirmed by a series of social poems and poems about people. Kinsella
still however displays an anxiety to escape from the particular to the
general, to mythologize and moralize. 'Thinking of Mr. D.' (in *Another
September*) he comes up with 'A barren Dante leaving us for hell'. What
such flourishes dissipate is a truly observed, truly felt situation which
roots and controls all the perspectives. Too many poems are neither
descriptive nor metaphysical nor mythological, but a confused blend of
these approaches. The elegy 'Cover Her Face' comes closest to organic
success but collapses at several points into a familiar rhetoric:

> . . .Such gossamers as hold
> Friends, family – all fortuitous conjunction –
> Sever with bitter whispers; with untold
> Peace shrivel to their anchors in extinction.
> There, newly trembling, others grope for function.

Gossamers may sever (though hardly 'with bitter whispers'), shrivel but
not to 'anchors', 'tremble' but not 'grope'. Enjambment does not make
'untold / Peace' any less of a cliché. That the polysyllabic rhymes are
all abstractions simply compounds their crime. An equivalent stanza in
Philip Larkin's 'Ambulances', the one beginning 'For borne away in
deadened air. . .', may be equally abstract but the tension between
coherence and disintegration is much more gradually and subtly mimed
by the shutting-off syntax. 'Sever' and 'shrivel' look melodramatic beside

'the sudden shut of loss'. The suggestiveness of 'something nearly at an end, / And what cohered in it' shows up 'all fortuitous conjunction' as simply a fortuitous conjunction. And Larkin leaves his metaphors unmixed or latent.

From *Downstream* onwards there is an alarming increase in the proportion of poems which discover the poet brooding among seasonal landscapes or embarking on lengthy symbolic walks by night and day. Form simultaneously becomes more meandering. It is hard to see how 'Nightwalker' (1968) advances on the more ordered 'rage for order' in 'Baggot Street Deserta'.:

> The foot of the tower. An angle where the darkness
> Is complete. The parapet is empty.
> A backdrop of constellations, crudely done
> And mainly unfamiliar; they are arranged
> To suggest a chart of the brain. Music far off.
> In the part of the little harbour that can be seen
> The moon is reflected in low water.
> Beyond, the lamps on the terrace.
> > The music fades.
> > Snuggle into the skull.
> Total darkness wanders among my bones.
> Lung-tips flutter. Wavelets lap the shingle.
> From the vest's darkness, smell of my body:
> > Chalk dust and flowers. . .
> Faint brutality. Shoes creak in peace.
> Brother Burke flattens his soutane
> Against the desk.

We find the same 'backdrop', that 'suggestion' of parallelism between the physiological and cosmic systems, and opposition between light and darkness. But the strong rhythmic 'pulse' which, despite local failings, holds the earlier poem together has been exchanged for Eliotish discontinuities smacking of stage directions rather than of necessary points on the current of meditation. For instance, 'Music far off', 'The music fades', 'arranged', or the obviousness of the jump from 'smell of my body' to the *recherche du temps perdu*: 'Faint brutality'. Repetition of 'the', 'is' and 'darkness' exposes the creaking nature of the whole mechanism. Harmon calls 'Nightwalker' 'closely similar in method to *The Waste Land*'[17] and it's certainly not for want of trying. Again, I suppose, one has to admire Kinsella's ambition and read the poem as a deeper diagnosis of the cultural and perhaps aesthetic predicament outlined in 'A Country Walk'.

'Nightwalker' begins: 'I only know things seem and are not good' and ends 'I think this is the Sea of Disappointment'. Adrift in the Dublin suburbs the poet muses on the past, the Famine, the supression of the Irish language and 'national spirit', the extent to which the people themselves have connived with this process or the new commercial imperialism, and questions, before his 'lost soul' 'turns for home', whether anything new will be found in the future: 'A seamew passes over, / Whingeing: / *Eire, Eire. . .is there none / To hear? Is all lost?'* Significantly he looks to Joyce's tower, not Yeats's, for a guidance which may be mystically and implicitly received. In any case, Kinsella is perhaps not wholly responsible for the limbo which the poem presents or even the limbo which it is. Yet the movement from the personal to the national seems strained, and the exclusion of the latter element from 'Notes from the Land of the Dead' (the first poem in *New Poems 1973*) makes this a more coherent and successful excursion into the wasteland. The establishing of a particular and neurotic persona provides a context for surrealistic effects: 'Many a time / I have risen from my gnawed books / And prowled about. . .'

The poem does, however, slip from time to time into marshy portentousness: 'Falling. / Mind darkening. / Toward a ring of mouths. / Flushed. / Time, distance, / Meaning nothing'; 'A thick tunnel stench / rose to meet me. Frightful. Dark nutrient waves. / And I knew no more'. 'Frightful' and 'meaning nothing' about sum this up. Kinsella's Eliotesque, Dantesque trips to the underworld, the 'Pit', the 'basement of the self' might carry more complete conviction if the hinted horrors were less nameless.

But Kinsella's later poetry does not consist entirely of nightmares, daydreams and selfconscious introversion. In *New Poems 1973* his ability to pierce to the bone when confronted by actual sickness and death ('A Lady of Quality', 'Cover Her Face') is proved again in 'Tear', a poem about his dying grandmother. No posturing apparatus intrudes between emotion and word, sight and insight:

> I was sent in to see her.
> A fringe of jet drops
> chattered at my ear
> as I went through the hangings.
>
> I was swallowed in chambery dusk.
> My heart shrank
> at the smell of disused
> organs and sour kidney. . .

This is a journey into a real pit, real darkness: 'I couldn't stir at first, nor wished to, / for fear she might turn and tempt me / (my own father's mother) / with open mouth'. The sequence 'Hen Woman', which may owe something to an intelligent reading of Seamus Heaney, displays a new tangibility of texture:

> As I watched, the mystery completed.
> The black zero of the orifice
> closed to a point
> and the white zero of the egg hung free,
> flecked with greenish brown oils.

A few hammy stage props linger on: 'and time stood still', 'A mutter of thunder far off'. I could do without the section which frankly admits its metaphysical straining to suck as much meat as possible from the egg: 'I feed upon it still, as you see; / there is no end to that which, / not understood, may yet be noted / and hoarded in the imagination' (syntactical strain too). Kinsella's habitual insensitivity to the possible cliché appears in 'The brooding silence seemed to say "Hush. . ." ' and 'her face dark with anger', to the real nature of dramatic rhythm in 'gathered the hen up jerking / languidly. Her hand fumbled. / Too late. Too late.' He has always relied too much on the *content* of the verb alone to supply vigour – *fumble, stumble, mumble,* proliferate in *Finistère* – or of the adverb to qualify its effect ('Tear' has 'shuddered tiredly'). It may be that we have to accept all Kinsella's œuvre, like this egg-poem, as being good in parts: brilliant passages robbed of their resonance and context by over-anxious manipulation, by a lack of instinct for what makes a poem, by uncertainty where to start or when to stop. Kinsella's poetry cries out for an Ezra Pound to differentiate between what belongs in the wasteland and what in the wastepaper basket.

Paradoxically then, with all his superior qualifications for feeling at home in Ireland and the world, Kinsella, to a more radical extent than Murphy, writes the displaced poetry of a displaced person. His consciousness of 'a gapped, discontinuous, polyglot tradition' results in 'gapped, discontinuous, polyglot' poems confused as to their true focus, form and tongue. Harmon's observation that 'the typical movement' in the work of poets of this generation 'was an initial outward trend and then the return to Ireland'[18] does not apply literally to Kinsella – he has lived in America but has never adopted either the exile stance or noticeably un-Irish subject-matter – yet can be metaphorically adjusted to his apparent feeling that Ireland has left him. In 'A Country Walk' and 'Nightwalker', and with glancing references in other poems, he reaches out from his solitude to the nation, as he does to the universe, only to retreat dissatisfied into his shell.

The recent signs of a more lasting return or commitment are not all good. In taking on the 'legendary duty' of translating from the Gaelic the Ulster epic, *The Tain,* Kinsella must have fertilized his own poetic roots as well as putting Ireland and Irish literature deeply in his debt. But *Butcher's Dozen,* his response to the events of Bloody Sunday, constitutes a more dubious arousal of the heroic passions of the past. Into the mouths of rather gruesomely evoked phantoms of the dead victims he puts a fascist hysteria unqualified by any words of his own:

'You came, you saw, you conquered. . .So.
You gorged – and it was time to go.
Good riddance. We'd forget – released –

> But for the rubbish of your feast,
> The slops and scraps that fell to earth
> And sprang to arms in dragon birth. . .'

A pamphlet called *Kinsella's Oversight,* issued by the British and Irish Communist Organization, has supplied a political corrective to the attitudes of the poem, but it is alarming that Kinsella's search for meaning and an inspiring cause in contemporary Ireland should find expression in a backward- rather than forward-looking emotion, in language on every level so uncontrolled. Lacking all along John Montague's enthusiasm for 'swimming / Against a slackening tide', he seems readier to be swept off course by the resurgence of old currents.

That Montague should have been better prepared imaginatively than Kinsella for the Northern Irish troubles is of course understandable, but none the less creditable. The seeds of them are on view — and were obviously left unviewed — in *Poisoned Lands* and the growth of *The Rough Field* (1972), which contains poems from *Poisoned Lands* as well as from subsequent volumes, seems to have proceeded in step with events: 'Continual operation on the body of the past / Brings final meaning to its birth at last'. These lines have gained in 'meaning' since Montague wrote them. In *Poisoned Lands* he is, up to a point, performing an autopsy. But he recognizes that he may be still surgeon as well as coroner, that the patient may be only anaesthetized:

> . . . We are afraid, as the hints pile up, of disaster
> Enlarged as a dinosaur, rising from the salt flats,
> The webbed marshes of history, making the hand tremble
> Hardly knowing why.

(The last line is given retrospective point by the fact that world turmoil seems the primary fear.) In so far as he is opening up a corpse, Montague not unexpectedly finds putrefaction and petrification — rigor. The former imagery predominates in the title poem (where it takes its origin from the rural practice of putting out poisoned meat for predators): 'a clinging stench / Gutting the substances of earth and air', and in 'Charnel Houses' (after Eluard); the latter kind of imagery in 'Like Dolmens round My Childhood, the Old People', this very title and first line archaically hewn. 'The Sean Bhean Vocht', closer to 'Old Gummy Granny' than to Yeats's girl with 'the walk of a queen', combines the two: 'A doll's head mouthing under stained rafters', 'Eyes rheumy with racial memory; / Fragments of bread soaked in brown tea / And eased between shrunken gums. / Her clothes stank like summer flax. . .' This poem also contains the recurrent images of primitive superstition and malignancy, of blood and death — a well plausibly rusted and polluted by a legendary battle.

Montague's vision of 'poisoned' or 'shadowed lands' is rounded out by a chillingly detached parable of the cycle of violence, 'Wild Sports of the West', which follows ironically Yeats's instructions to 'sing the peasantry, and then / Hard-riding country gentlemen': 'Evening brings the huntsman home, / Blood of pheasants in a bag: / Beside a turfrick the cackling peasant / Cleanses his ancient weapon with a rag.' As Montague moves south, the long shadows of the past blur into those of the present, where disinfectant may purge life as well as germs ('Slum Clearance'), old moulds be too suddenly broken as they are for 'Murphy in Manchester':

> . . .Soon the whistling factory
> Will lock him in:
> Half-stirred memories and regrets
> Drowning in that iron din.

One quality which distinguishes any regret on Montague's part for the changing face of Ireland from Kinsella's, in addition to a more positive acceptance of the inevitable, is its social compassion, also extended to the older victims of history and circumstance: his characters are real people as well as emblems or dolmens.

The possibility that the past may be vanishing, fossilizing or crystallizing — a dinosaur, 'Old Mythologies', 'The transfigured heroes assume / Grey proportions of statuary' — also permits Montague to capture 'ancient forms' more affirmatively; and to imagine Tara, whether 'Gaelic Acropolis or smoky hovel', 'wolf-skinned warriors', wolfhounds, 'an impossibly epic morning'; or find value in monastic ruins or a Yeatsian 'manor' (Woodtown): 'Here the delicate dance of silence. . .' His apparent celebration of roots in 'Prodigal Son' stretches to embrace the whole island in 'Incantation in Time of Peace':

> At times on this island, at the sheltered edge of Europe
> The last flowering garden of prayer and pretence,
> Green enclosure of monks and quiet poetry,
> Where the rivers move, without haste, to a restless sea,
> And the rain shifts like a woven veil
> Over headland and sleeping plain. . .

The MacNeice-like zeugma, 'prayer and pretence' stiffens and validates the softer images. This too is the poem and stanza in which the dinosaur is latent, a syntactical web corresponding to the historical, and which ends on a vista of clouds 'banking / For a yet more ominous day'. However unspecific this prophecy, it seems to be the dark Northern undertow in *Poisoned Lands* which strangely rescues Montague from the different limbos that Murphy and Kinsella inhabit, and makes the past more alive in him than in the former, makes him more alive in the present than the latter. Montague's instinct that 'the extraordinary hour of calm' may be simply a remission in a long disease, that propitiatory incantations are necessary, gives his rendering of Irish historical, social and political material a greater urgency.

Montague's more complete sense of Ireland, his conflicting Northern and Southern, regional and national, urban and rural perspectives, must also have helped him to become a more complex poet than the others. Despite its relatively high concentration on Irish subject-matter, *Poisoned Lands* is a more varied collection than either *Another September* or *Sailing to an Island.* It includes, for instance, poems more particularly engaged with childhood experience in the countryside — poems which anticipate, and may have influenced Seamus Heaney's more consistent use of this approach in *Death of a Naturalist.* 'The Water Carrier' may ultimately symbolize the poet's relation to his larger subject (one bucket for 'rust-tinged', the other for 'spring water'), but the immediate texture of the experience is primary: 'Inhaling the musty smell of unpicked berries, / That heavy greenness fostered by water'. Subsequently, however, the poem moves into less Heaneyish areas:

> Recovering the scene I had hoped to stylize it,
> Like the portrait of an Egyptian water-carrier:
> Yet halt, entranced by slight but memoried life.

All this a Heaney poem takes for granted. Although both poets often draw water from the same source, Montague tends to remind us of the presence of the buckets, to make explicit in a poem the attitude from which he writes it. Similarly, 'The Mummer Speaks', strikingly similar in imagery and implication to Heaney's 'The Last Mummer', includes this distancing or detachment: 'A scene in farmhouse darkness, / Two wearing decades ago'. This need not be a qualitative distinction, but rather emphasizes a contrast in stance which could be referred to the ten-year generation gap. Looking for a pattern underlying the variety of *Poisoned Lands,* and picking up Montague's hint that 'the decisive influence was Auden', we notice that the influence in his case goes beyond verbal and rhythmical echoes, though it includes them: 'Now the extraordinary hour of calm / And day of limitation', 'At times on this island', 'At times, we turn in most ordinary weakness', 'The city had lost interest and / Even his chosen friends' ('The Quest').

Montague's concern with line, outline and all kinds of architecture, noticeable chiselling of word and image, and the willingness to generalize implied by a vocabulary which contains 'Ireland', 'mythology', 'legend', 'history' and 'memory' as well as more local abstraction can all be paralleled in Auden, and suggest in particular that he is adopting Auden's 1930s role of cultural diagnostician, analyst and therapist. A compulsion to 'stylize' and schematize experience, to set the 'scene', appears at its most universal in 'Musée Imaginaire' which begins 'Consider here the various ways of man' and proceeds to consider them in terms of 'conflicting [artistic] modes', just as in other poems he lays out for our inspection rooms in the museum of Irish history. It seems to me that Montague makes a much better job of being Ireland's Auden than Kinsella does of being Ireland's Eliot. The accent is so entirely

Irish that the correspondence has been little noted. He also displays something of Auden's gift for deft encapsulation, zipping up the Zeitgeist, hence the extent to which he is quoted in this essay and by *Irish Times* leader writers.

This role carries with it some attendant risks, held at bay in *Poisoned Lands*, but looming larger in *The Rough Field:* confusion of the surgery with the pulpit, debilitating abstraction and externality. Montague sometimes uses the word 'sensual' where Heaney invites it (again perhaps merely a difference in stance).But the non-Irish poems in *Poisoned Lands* illustrate how fruitfully Montague has absorbed Auden, and Auden as modified by the Movement, grafted him on to Irish sources of inspiration, and let all ladders fall away as he carves out his own idiom. 'The Quest' (for the minotaur) ends:

> With torch and toughened hands
> Well equipped:
> Layer after layer of the darkness
> He then stripped.
>
> And came at last, with harsh surprise,
> To where in breathing darkness lay
> A lonely monster with almost human terror
> In its lilac eyes.

If the final stanza illustrates Montague's (Audenesque) dependence on the precisely defining adjective, the whole rhythm is similarly precise. Possibly an allegory of his 'equipment' to probe his Irish sources, the poem draws on them to establish a further mastery.

At its best Montague's next book of poems, *A Chosen Light* (1967), lives up to the aesthetic suggested by one of its best poems, 'A Bright Day':

> At times I see it, present
> As a bright day, or a hill,
> The only way of saying something
> Luminously as possible.
>
> Not the accumulated richness
> Of an old historical language —
> That musk-deep odour!
> But a slow exactness
>
> Which recreates experience
> By ritualizing its details —
> Pale web of curtain, width
> Of deal table, till all
>
> Takes on a witch-bright glow
> And even the clock on the mantel
> Moves its hands in a fierce delight
> Of so, and so, and so.

In so far as this is an altered aesthetic, it follows the poet's liberation from the darkness and 'odour' of *Poisoned Lands* into the 'light' of a

Parisian exile. And it implies that Montague is in the process of adapting the contours which gave shape to his shaping Irish experience to more intimate subject-matter. One untribal ritual explored in this volume is that of love:

> All legendary obstacles lay between
> Us, the long imaginary plain,
> The monstrous ruck of mountains
> And, swinging across the night,
> Flooding the Sacramento, San Joaquin,
> The hissing drift of winter rain. . .

The 'exactness' of reference and rhythm which opens up the severing vistas of plain, mountain and rain not only licenses but validates 'legendary'. 'The Siege of Mullingar' — best known for another of Montague's encapsulations, *'Puritan Ireland's dead and gone, / A myth of O'Connor and O'Faolain'* — similarly achieves the kind of pattern it asserts:

> . . .We saw a pair, a cob and his pen,
> Most nobly linked. Everything then
> In our casual morning vision
> Seemed to flow in one direction,
> Line simple as a song:
> *Puritan Ireland's* etc.

But not all the poems in *A Chosen Light* attain such 'line', nor do they 'flow in one direction' to the same extent as the poems in *Poisoned Lands*. Along with the necessary diversification of scene and theme goes some dilution of the rich linguistic mix which gave *Poisoned Lands* its most fundamental coherence. The further coherence supplied by a central cluster of images is replaced by a more deliberate mounting of 'chosen' objects for illumination:

> In that stillness — soft but luminously exact,
> A chosen light — I notice that
> The tips of the lately grafted cherry-tree
>
> Are a firm and lacquered black.

> ('Il rue Daguerre')

Similarly 'Enclosure', 'Paris, April 1961' and 'Vigil' end on rather arbitrarily resolving images of a chandelier, a rainbow, the 'All Clear' after 'a warning exercise'. This technique is also apparent in *Poisoned Lands* and plenty of poems still end in darkness or on a dying fall, but the more pronounced effort to establish a 'luminous, exact ritual' (all these words recur in *A Chosen Light*) can appear mannered when applied to smaller scale material. A poet's second book is of course more likely to be the result of various 'choices' than his first, nourished on natural imaginative compost, and *A Chosen Light* is unified up to a point by its exploration of the decisions of maturity in the double limbo of personal and cultural liberation.

It has taken exile to create for Montague the vacuum which root-lessness presents to Murphy and contemporary Ireland to Kinsella. It is, however, not a point of arrival around which his concerns now regroup and revolve, but a planting of his flag on the further shore already implicit in *Poisoned Lands*. Roaming between these poles the poet often figures as tourist, visitor or revenant, passing a French château or 'Wayside Crucifix', entering Irish cottages as an outsider, coming home to see his 'former / self saunter up the garden path'. Montague's concern in his Irish poems is now not to exorcise but to re-enter the past. Family poems about his father and uncle (who have also served their time in exile) attempt to close the generation gap, and the gap between his two selves, as the love poems do the spaces between people. Occasionally he strives too frantically to connect: in 'Back to School' a Second World War internment camp near Dungannon is recalled when 'years later, I saw another camp — / Rudshofen in the fragrant Vosges'; in 'Wayside Crucifix' the French road rather ponderously conjures up a run from Dublin to Belfast, — 'My wife's tense / Face blurs into an earlier / Image'.

The 'ritualizing' procedures of *A Chosen Light* may be in part a typical lifebelt of exile, like taking the Irish newspapers, and *Tides* (1970) which finds Montague attached to no particular shore, retrospectively confirms their supportive value. This is his real limbo book: experiment with Black Mountain and possibly French techniques has produced a predominant short syllabic line which possesses the monotonously levelling quality of waves and engulfs much of Montague's distinctiveness and distinctness. Not only do his rituals and rhythms need more room to manoeuvre, but a form which may be appropriate to the diminuendos of dying: 'the moon in her / last phase, caring / only for herself' (is it significant that *all* these poets have written poems about a dying or dead grandmother?), or the ebb and flow of love-making, appears artificially imposed in other contexts. For instance when the poet returns, as a seagull, to his home ground: 'the ivy strangled / O'Neill Tower only // a warm shelter to / come to roost if / crows don't land // first. . .' Montague's mimicry of sea-rhythms in 'Sea Changes', a sequence of poems for engravings by William Hayter, perhaps places the whole collection as a transitional attempt to exchange the sculptural, hard-edged character of his earlier writing for a more sinuous, wavering line.

But tides can turn, or pull in unexpected directions. The very layout of *The Rough Field* (1972), with its ten sections and numbered poems, adapted sixteenth-century woodcuts, marginal glosses and inserted background matter, indicates that the old patterning habit, like the old themes, has returned with a vengeance. The sequence is in part a rearranged anthology of Montague's Northern Irish, and some of his Irish poems which have now come home — to roost, perhaps: 'as the

Ulster crisis broke, I felt as if I had been stirring a witch's cauldron'. In a sense Montague is taking up the thread where Peter Douglas, hero of his short story 'The Cry'[19] had left it. Peter, now a journalist, returns to his Catholic family in the rural North, becomes indignant when an I.R.A. suspect is apparently beaten up by the police, and drafts an article designed to bring this sort of situation home to a wider audience. But Peter lets go his chance of being the earliest correspondent into Northern Ireland as he sees that the rights and wrongs of the situation are less simple and less simply resolved than he had supposed. 'Two peoples linked and locked for eternity'[20] conspire to expel his intrusive interest. Montague now treads with considered and fastidious steps along the path beaten by subsequent 'Nosy Parkers' to the Field in which he was first. D. E. S. Maxwell has framed one of the highest estimates of his achievement, calling *The Rough Field* 'Mr.Montague's most elaborately mounted poem, varied and sure in structure and verse. Its viewpoints are attractive and humane, passionate at times, never strident. The sequence brings under firm control the traffic of past and present; scene, feeling, idea and their precipitation into symbol.'[21]

For me there is some disharmony between the 'elaborate mounting', 'firm control' and the natural or evolved rhythms of the sequence, between real and imposed structure. The opening section, 'Home Again', concludes with two older pieces, the poem about the *émigré* uncle who 'played the fiddle — more elegantly, the violin' ('A rural art silenced in the discord of Brooklyn') and 'Like Dolmens round My Childhood, the Old People'. The first three poems, however, sometimes suggest a programmed itinerary. The bus-ride from Belfast generates some splendid encapsulations and perceptions: ' "God is Love", chalked on a grimy wall / Mocks a culture where constraint is all'; later: 'No Wordsworthian dream enchants me here / With glint of glacial corry, totemic mountain' (a characteristic 'balancing' of perspectives). But the 'cultural' relevance of other details is more ploddingly pinned down: Victoria Street station is 'symbol of Belfast in its iron bleakness', 'Lisburn, Lurgan, Portadown' are 'solid British towns, lacking local grace'. There is perhaps too an over-deployment of the (atmospherically) defining adjective: *narrow, stern, dour, despoiled, gaunt, plaintive, pale, harsh, bleak.* The next poem has *desolate, chill, pale, dark* (all right, we know you're disenchanted).

In both cases the tactics of *A Chosen Light* supply an over-obvious corrective: 'the evening star, which saw me home', 'Hands now strive to kindle / That once leaping fire' — indeed they do. The third poem, one suspects very much according to plan, fills in details of the family home and tree and their roots in history. The use of a daguerrotype of the poet's grandparents, and the transition from it, 'Such posed / Conceit recalls post Famine years', draws attention, like 'symbol of Belfast in its iron bleakness' to the posing of Montague's own conceits. Later poems begin 'All around, shards of a lost tradition' (an abstract echo of 'Like Dolmens. . .'), 'The gloomy images of a provincial catholicism', 'Symbolic depth-charge of music / Releases a national dream'. (A dangerous extreme has been reached when the rituals of poetry itself are pressed into service.) The second and third sections comprise a paradigm of the strengths and weakness of the poem. The former is a loving tribute to his grandmother, organically developed from the poem in *Tides*, in which 'the pressed herbs / of your least memory' 'exude' a greater poetic 'sweetness' than Montague's more forced entries into racial memory. In contrast 'The Bread God', subtitled 'A Collage of Religious Misunderstandings', exhibits all the fragmentation to be expected from such an intention. Vignettes of Catholics going to mass or communion in country churches are interspersed with extracts from extremist Protestant propaganda. Some beautiful images, however, redeem the laboured irony: 'A few flowers / Wither on the altar, so I melt a ball of snow / From the hedge into their rusty tin before I go' ('Penal Rock/ Altamuskin').

Montague's intentions also obtrude in 'A Severed Head' and 'Hymn to the New Omagh Road'. His potted history of the O'Neills, the 'itemizing' of a landscape of change, recall, as does the wider rendering of 'credal war', the strategies of *The Battle of Aughrim*. Montague is no less and no more successful than Murphy in such endeavours, but they disappoint hopes his poetry had previously encouraged. Other signs of strain or will may be detected in the inferior working of old preoccupations: 'Once again, with creased forehead / and trembling hands, my father calls / me from stifling darkness' and the transplantation of images from earlier poems to more symbolic soil where they can function as leitmotifs: the fault, shards, all too obviously geared to the inclusive symbolism of the Field itself. More convincing as poems are the meditative pieces where the solitary poet works out or walks out, the complexities of his relationship with his roots, the always vividly evoked detail of the countryside supporting generalization. It is a pity that 'A New Siege' which brings the story up to date in Derry 1969 should fall for the inevitable temptation of barren historical collage.

> London's Derry!
>   METHOUGHT I SAW
> DIDOE'S COLONY
>   BUILDING OF CARTHAGE
> culverin and saker
>   line strong walls
> but local chiefs
>   come raging in
> O'Cahan, O'Doherty

                    (a Ferrara sword
                   his visiting card)
                      a New Plantation
                  a new mythology
                     Lundy slides
                  down a peartree
                      as drum and fife
                  trill ORANJE BOVEN!

We meet again the 'posed conceit': 'symbol of Ulster / these sloping
streets / blackened walls', most pervasively in the shape of a heavily
ritualized refrain which begins almost half the stanzas: 'Lines of
history / lines of power', 'Lines of defiance / lines of discord' / 'Lines of
leaving / lines of returning'. Despite some redeeming and redemptive
images: 'the loneliness of Lir's white daughter's / ice crusted wings /
forever spread / at the harbour mouth', and pungent political formulations, the poem seems too conscious of its synthesizing position in
relation to events and to the sequence as a whole: 'the emerging order /
of the poem invaded / by cries, protestations / a people's pain'. There is
a sort of desperate lassooing not only of the historical context, but of
reiterated symbols and universal relevance: 'streets of Berlin / Paris,
Chicago / seismic waves / zigzagging through / a faulty world'.

    It is hard to say why *The Rough Field,* for all its compendiousness,
does not entirely constitute Montague's finest hour as cultural analyst.
Perhaps the situation is simply too tailormade, perhaps he has said it all
before, perhaps the surprising 'permanence of ancient forms' has stifled
some of his outward-looking and future-looking vitality. He is mournfully exhuming what *Poisoned Lands* had apparently exorcized. There is
ultimately no halfway house between the poles of Montague's vision —
home and exile, 'the webbed marshes of history' and the isolated
individual — or his dual stances of attachment and detachment, partici-
pant and observer. If he is the first poet of one line, he is the last of
another, Ireland's Auden and, like the fiddler who plays a 'Lament for
the O'Neills', laureate of 'what is already going, / going / GONE',
'assuaging like a bardic poem, / our tribal pain'. Douglas Dunn observes:
'Realism and mysticism are [Montague's] extremes. He is torn between
the past and the present, between blood and breath, and it is in this way
that his poems enact a fundamental Irish impasse.'[22] But the very
enactment and articulation of the impasse, the willingness to assume
inherited responsibilities which finally links the roles of coroner and
mourner, the selfconsciousness of meaning and method which may
deny Montague's own art some of its natural fulfilment, have liberated
Irish people and Irish poets into a new consciousness which they probably
take too much for granted. His poetry is indeed

                    a net of energies
                  crossing patterns

> weaving towards
> a new order
> a new anarchy

even if it has recently become rather too aware of itself as such. Poetry may be selfconscious about everything except itself.

Since Dunn displays an English impatience* with 'Montague's simplistic refusal to come to terms with the nature of modern societies', his 'finally lost dream of man at home in a rural setting'[23] (this dream, for obvious reasons, has a longer history in English poetry), it is surprising that he is not more sympathetic to the poetry of James Simmons, much more 'at home' in urban surroundings than his contemporaries, as well as the freest from all Irish umbilical cords. (Montague's Paris is another matter, because exotic.) Until recently it has been Ulster 'Protestant' poets who have most successfully come to terms with the city, perhaps because 'Catholic' poets have refused to let the iron of the gantries enter their souls, or because the racial myth of the former is garrisoned walls industriously manned, that of the former countryside encroaching like a guerrilla fighter. And Belfast is still the only city in Ireland with an industrial *tradition.*

Just as MacNeice rescued the city from Eliot's deadening fog and made it a vital poetic symbol, so Simmons has taken up the cudgels in a sequence entitled *No Land is Waste, Dr. Eliot* (1972):

> What roots? What stony rubbish? What rats? Where?
> Visions of horror conjured out of air,
> the spiritual D.T.s. The pompous swine. . .
> that man's not hollow, he's a mate of mine. . .

The first poem in *Late but in Earnest* includes a MacNeicean celebration of love in the city:

> . . .Her amber pint of beer, tobacco shreds,
> This atmosphere of this, her morning,
> Are on speaking terms with my head.
> Outside the crippled houses respond
> To the continual miracle of sun and dust.
> Roofs, railings and the time of year
> Walk beautifully together because they must.

The second, 'Ode to Blenheim Square', has this beautifully cadenced image: 'The blemishes don't show / At sunset either, / Or under snow'. My three quotations also illustrate the opening out towards life which is most deeply characteristic of Simmons's poetry, a generous democracy of response which appreciates 'blemishes', day-to-dayness, the most ordinary people and activities. Dunn refers to his 'suburbanly bed-

---

* Mr Dunn meant his impatience as 'critical', not English, which he is not. John Montague's sentiment would have been described, in George Liechtheim's phrase, as 'agrarian romanticism', had I known it at the time. A negative attitude towards the City in *The Rough Field* encouraged my remark. Ed.

roomised vision',[24] and these may be two a penny in English poetry —
though I suspect with less zest and colour — but coming to Simmons
after Murphy, Kinsella and Montague one becomes aware of all that
they have excluded. Whether or not Simmons has equally suffered the
nightmare of history, his social and domestic scenes certainly represent
a healthy awakening to the normalities of the living present. After the
austerities of Montague's physical and emotional landscapes, the somewhat heraldic postures of even his lovers — only 'at the Fleadh Cheoil
in Mullingar' does 'puritan Ireland' seem truly 'dead and gone' — the
visions of horror all three poets have conjured out of air, life rushes in,
almost wilfully exposing warts and all: 'She is scarred like a soldier, /
She droops like a jelly, / There are three distinct ridges / Of fat on her
belly. / There are varicose veins / on her legs, at the back. / Her vagina is
more / A crevasse than a crack. . .' ('Macushla, Machree').

If this poem sets the scene for a host of later domestic dramas, its
humour, like that of No Land is Waste, Dr. Eliot introduces another
life-enjoying, life-enhancing element often missing in the introspective
struggle of Irish poetry from the national to the personal.

The fact that Simmons is also a song and ballad writer, more
attracted towards Jazz and Tin Pan Alley than lamentations for the
O'Neills, fertilizes his poetry with a fresh aspect of the thirties aesthetic,
'the whole delightful world of cliché and refrain'. Simmons's delight in
the life of language makes the very act of writing seem more like fun
than a 'legendary duty'. The salute to Jazz which begins his most recent
collection, The Long Summer Still to Come (1973),* expresses and
enacts the anti-mandarin view of art implied in No Land is Waste, this
time by importing two of the mandarin's phrases into a surprising
context:

> . . .the word of life, if such a thing existed,
> was there on record among the rubbish listed
> in the catalogues of Brunswick and H.M.V.,
> healing the split in sensibility.
> Tough reasonableness and lyric grace
> together, in poor man's dialect.
> Something that no one taught us to expect.
> Profundity without the po-face
> of court and bourgeois modes. This I could use
> to live and die with. Jazz. Blues.

Simmons also wishes his 'word of life' to find a live and lively
response in other people. His poetry addresses individuals, the conscience he tries to create, or consciousness he wishes to change, is not
that of the race: 'I wait to hear my songs used / or rejected, alive in the
throats of singers / or laughed off the stage: alive / in the minds of old
uncontroversial / men and the girls who half listen. . .' Just as his poems

*Mr Simmons has since published West Strand Visions (Blackstaff Press). Ed.

exhibit the thirties fascination with the apparently vulgar, recognize with Auden that 'the pious fable and the dirty story / Share in the total literary glory', they display a similar ambition to entertain, to reach out towards the reader in the street. Since Simmons falls far short of pop appeal, the effect of the intention on the nature of his poetry is more significant than its actual ratings' success. He outlines his imagined audience in the manifesto which prefaces the first issue of *The Honest Ulsterman,* the literary magazine he founded in May 1968 and edited for a year and a half: 'I hope this magazine gets into the hands of school children and the so-called man in the street, people who think a dull life is inevitable, normal'.

Simmons of course excludes something too. The staple of his poetry is statement, by Auden, out of the Movement, and apparently unfiltered through the Irish sieves' that give Montague's use of this approach such a special texture. In releasing himself with one bound from hereditary shackles, he refuses hereditary riches, takes a style from off the peg and thus accepts technical restrictions at odds with his philosophy. A Simmons poem shapes a well-defined situation, subject or standpoint: 'Marital Sonnets', 'Protestant Courts Catholic', 'Drowning Puppies', 'On Gardens', 'Photographs', 'To a Jealous Friend', 'A Reformer to His Father', 'To Certain Communist Friends'. Poetry tends towards parable: 'If God treats the human race like my father / Treats customers we needn't worry' ('The Publican'), morals adorn tales or inform emblems:

> For every year of life we light
> A candle on your cake
> To mark the simple sort of progress
> Anyone can make,
> And then, to test your nerve or give
> A proper view of death,
> You're asked to blow each light, each year,
> Out with your own breath.

('A Birthday Poem')

He is attracted towards epigram: 'Now that my faculties give in / I see the need for discipline' and the couplet-form generally: 'Discs are turning. Needles touch the rings / Of dark rainbows. Judy Garland sings'. Simmons's formalism does not always establish the delicate counterpoint with a regularly iambic and rhyming base evident in 'A Birthday Poem' and 'In Memoriam: Judy Garland'. Like Murphy's decorums or Montague's ritualism, it can appear an archaically limiting straitjacket. But if Simmons's technical reflexes sometimes twitch pointlessly or trivially: 'The night I found you first with Bill / was in a bar / where you had emptied many a gill, / he, many a jar', if pattern degenerates into a patness 'Obstacles stop us, not dead belief. / Spaces don't make us afraid, / Nor the long time we'll be dead, / Worn out with joy and grief', he displays a compensating ambition to turn his moralities into myth. The sea, for instance, often loosens his rhythms or releases imagery from the bondage of statement:

> Now men who never saw
> the sea cannot forget,
> thanks to ancestral memory,
> the shape of an inlet
> where long-boats scraped
> ashore, the look of a cape
> round which is Durban.

('The Straight Line and the Circle')

This is the spirit of exploration speaking, and a sequence in *In the Wilderness* (1969), based on *King Lear,* and 'Stephano Remembers' in *Energy to Burn* (1971) show how much Simmons's poetry benefits from symbolic and dramatic nourishment:

> . . .Oh, Caliban,
> You thought I'd take your twisted master's life;
> but a drunk butler's slower with a knife
> than your fine courtiers, your dukes, your kings.
> We were distracted by too many things. . .
> the wine, the jokes, the music, fancy gowns.
> We were no good as murderers, we were clowns.

He has defended himself against critics who feel that he has fallen into the domestic/confessional rut by claiming *all* his poems are dramatic in essence. An early poem, 'Written, Directed by and Starring' places him as a compulsive script-writer for himself. It all depends on the quality and variety of the scripts. Slice-of-life naturalism, frankness of sexual situation and language palls, and Dunn does have a point in finding the setting too often a 'crumpled bed', 'a soiled conscience / And a sore head':

> . . .And there's no end now to my new screen-plays,
> They just go on from scene to scene to scene.

But even this aspect of Simmons's poetry is partially redeemed by the tone of voice which projects some life into the flattest pieces and ultimately gives a distinctive personality to all his statements. The angle of vision implied by the voice also redeems some of the poems from 'commonplace confession' (Simmons is aware of the hazards), a routine moan about middle age and marriage. If with less penetration than Larkin, he does explore 'the long perspectives / Open at each instant of our lives', adding footnotes to Larkin as he covers some of the same ground from the point of view of Arnold in 'Self's the Man', finding a solving degree of beauty in both infidelities and fidelities, and making 'while trying to tell no lies, / a noise to go with love':

> . . .A disappointed spirit with meal-time for a cock,
> I start back as the bells say six o'clock

> to the nicest woman I have ever met,
> where my bed is made and tea-table set.

Simmons's poems chart, in a more pronounced fashion than most contemporary English poetry, the fluctuating reactions of an individual to the fluctuating circumstances of life. If he is more of a libertine than an agnostic, more bent on being honest about than faithful to his experience, not only individual but selfconsciously individualistic, he complements and extends by his exaggerations the other kinds of self-consciousness I have been noting. His example already seems to have made younger Northern poets freer to be themselves.

What does the free individual or individualist do at a time of mass movements and mass emotions? Always naturally on the side of Caliban or a 'hollow man' against the forces that exploit or patronize them — Prosperoism in politics and poetry — Simmons's more explicit development of an anti-authoritarian ideology, or anti-ideology ideology, in recent years must have something to do with the resumption of tribal pressures. He tells 'Certain Communist Friends':

> Social reform by revolution
> is the morning's great pollution.
> In new disguise, trying to infect
> my infant liberty, I see a sect
> of hateful puritans. Hate! Hate!
> is the only hope they contemplate.

'Sect', 'puritans', the phrase 'infant liberty', like the imitation of Blake, are probably not accidental. I am not entirely happy with Simmons's prose and verse appearances as a rather homespun philosopher of rather simplistic libertarian ideas. Nevertheless, his poetry has been profoundly shaped by reaction against the 'puritanism', the spiritual coercion, enforced by Irish politics as well as by Irish society.

'Ulster Today', somewhat pointedly dedicated to John Montague, brings Simmons's attitudes into the open and up to date:

> Sitting at my desk among papers
> I wonder nothing that troubles the TV news
> moves me to write. . .
>   I have nothing to add:
> the stones hurt, the smiling boys are boys,
> the farcical and painful history of Ireland
> is with us, unchanged. If the next bomb
> kills *me* it will still be irrelevant. . .

Dunn dislikes the disengagement of this, finds Simmons 'disrespectful. . . to anything larger than he is', like Irish history.[25] Although the poem hardly summons one to its aesthetic defence (Simmons is often over-hasty with catch-all adjectives of condemnation like 'irrelevant' and 'silly'), its stance may perhaps be condoned in terms of racial ennui, the unusual candour with which the poet reserves his real passion for the

shop ('Whereas / the silly reviews in *The Irish Times* / have driven me
mad!'), or explained in terms of the reluctance of the sensitive Protestant who has never discriminated against anybody to see what all the
fuss is about. Detachment or moderation are also perhaps the only
options available to such a man or poet. Unlike the Southern Anglo-
Irishman (Murphy) having rejected one commitment he is usually unable
to embrace another (a Joycean syndrome of losing one's faith but not
one's self-respect).

Simmons may also have found himself in another kind of dilemma
after October 1969. On *his* return to Ireland, after four years in Nigeria,
he made for the first time a 'conscious' effort both to put down roots
and to change things. The launching and the name of *The Honest
Ulsterman* betoken this decision. But having started 'a handbook for a
revolution', he found a totally different revolution on his hands to the
one he had anticipated. Yet Simmons has of course been much more
deeply 'moved to write' about the Northern situation than the drop-out
negativism of 'Ulster Today' led one to expect. That he was adopting a
posture of deliberate over-reaction became clear when he read the poem
in the teeth of a T.V. camera zooming greedily in on 'The Arts and the
Troubles'. His song 'Claudy' has probably brought home to more people
the personal cost of violence than any other piece of topical writing,
(a different end of the telescope from 'A New Siege'):

> . . .And Mrs. McLaughlin is scrubbing her floor,
> and Artie Hone's crossing the street to a door,
> and Mrs. Brown, looking around for her cat,
> goes off up an entry — what's strange about that?

> Not much — but before she comes back to the road
> that strange car parked outside her door will explode,
> and all of the people I've mentioned, outside,
> will be waiting to die, or already have died. . .

In founding *The Honest Ulsterman* Simmons curiously echoed the
cultural aspect of Thomas Davis's intentions in founding *The Nation:*

> I look to a new flowering when not only men and women but towns and coun-
> tries will assume their real, unique personalities. Ulster education, politics and
> architecture will be as distinctive as our police force [*with hind-sight, a couple
> of unlucky lapses there*]. A new knowledge of our own history will give us new
> interest and pleasure in all the names and places we come across, unless our
> unfortunate history has completely estranged us from our past.[26]

Although Simmons could equate regionalism with individualism,
he could not of course graft on to his dream either the old Republican
nationalism or the new Craigite variety. But the magazine, like his
poetry, continues, in a significant historical polarity with *The Nation*,
to bear witness to the possibility of the *real* revolution taking place:

> . . .and Fats Waller, the scholar-clown of song
> who sang, *Until the Real Thing Comes Along.*

> Here was the risen people, their feet
> dancing, not out to murder the élite. . .

It might be going too far to call Simmons 'the scholar-clown' of Irish poetry, but the freedoms he claims, for himself and for his art, including the liberty to 'play his guitar while Derry burns',[27] are those which the other three poets adumbrate. On the socio-political level alone they have given new and coalescing contours to the Irish experience, Murphy formally introducing Anglo-Ireland to the Hidden Ireland, Kinsella suffering the traumas of an adolescent nation as it takes charge of its own fate, Montague drawing on his knowledge of an Ireland still more deeply hidden to produce one of the broadest imaginative surveys, both geological and aerial, ever made of the country. *The Rough Field*, for all its flaws — *with* all its flaws — is perhaps the most characteristic and significant achievement of a generation. But even if all these poets, including Simmons, have partially committed elsewhere energies which might have been dedicated to purely artistic goals, their importance by no means rests on subject-matter. Just as in times of division the poet cannot afford to mortgage the complete humanity of his imagination to a cause or programme, can only take up a constructive stance or Auden's cry for 'new styles of architecture, a change of heart', so it is by virtue not of anything they 'say', but of the changing architecture of their own hearts and art that Murphy, Kinsella, Montague and Simmons have altered the map. Their bold outlines are already being shaded in.

NOTES

1. 'The Divided Mind' by Thomas Kinsella, in *Irish Poets in English*, ed. Sean Lucy, Mercier Press, Cork, 1973, pp. 216-17.

2. ibid., Introduction, p. 15.

3. 'The Impact of International Modern Poetry on Irish Writing', ibid., pp. 154-5.

4. 'New Voices in the Fifties', ibid., p. 186.

5. ibid., p. 144.

6. ibid., p. 150.

7. ibid., p. 146.

8. ibid., p. 147.

9. ibid., p. 156.

10. ibid., p. 155.

11. 'The Irish Writer' in *Davis, Mangan, Ferguson? Tradition and the Irish Writer*, ed. by Roger McHugh, Dublin, 1970, p. 57.

12. *Irish Poets in English*, p. 187.

13. 'The Pleasure Ground', *Listener*, LXX, 1794 (15 August 1963), p. 237. Quoted by Harmon, in *Irish Poets in English*, p. 197.

14. Available as a gramophone record (Claddagh Records, Dublin).

15. *Irish Poets in English*, p. 205.

16. 'The Heroic Agenda: the Poetry of Thomas Kinsella', *The Dublin Magazine*,

V, 2 (summer 1966), pp. 61-78.

17. *Irish Poets in English*, p. 193.

18. ibid., p. 205

19. Included in the fine collection, *Death of a Chieftain,* London, 1964, pp. 61-87.

20. ibid., p. 86.

21. 'The Poetry of John Montague', *Critical Quarterly*, XV, 2 (summer 1973), p. 185.

22. 'The Speckled Hill, the Plover's Shore: Northern Irish Poetry Today', *Encounter*, XLI, 6 (December 1973), p. 72.

23. ibid., p. 71.

24. ibid., p. 74.

25. ibid.

26. *The Honest Ulsterman,* 1 (May 1968), Editorial, p. 6.

27. See Michael Longley, 'Letter to James Simmons', in *An Exploded View,* London, 1973, p. 33.

The Contemporary Situation in Irish Poetry
by Michael Smith

Some days past I have found a curious confirmation of the fact that what is truly native can and often does dispense with local colour; I found this confirmation in Gibbon's *Decline and Fall of the Roman Empire*. Gibbon observes that in the Arabian book *par excellence*, in the Koran, there are no camels; I believe if there were any doubts as to the authenticity of the Koran, that this absence of camels would be sufficient to prove it is an Arabian work. It was written by Mohammed, and Mohammed, as an Arab, had no reason to know that camels were especially Arabian; for him they were part of reality, he had no reason to emphasize them; on the other hand, the first thing a falsifier, a tourist, an Arab nationalist would do is to have a surfeit of camels, caravans of camels, on every page; but Mohammed, as an Arab, was unconcerned: he knew he could be an Arab without camels.

(Jorge Luis Borges, 'The Argentine Writer and Tradition', *Labyrinths*, Penguin, 1970.)

I

I THINK IT is true to say that outside Ireland there is little or no interest in contemporary Irish poetry. From time to time a British or American publisher produces a kind of curiosity-anthology of Irish verse; and from time to time an American scholar of Anglo-Irish literature leaves aside his Joyce or his Yeats or his Synge and conducts an invariably superficial inquiry into recent Irish verse — a kind of mooching around in what he presumes are the shadows of the Great Men.

And in Ireland the situation is not very different. A mere handful of people take any serious interest. The standard of reviewing in the papers is symptomatically low. There is no regularly appearing literary magazine of any value. The publishing of poetry is carried out by a few enthusiasts who can do little more than make gestures in the form of slim pamphlets and very limited editions. A Dublin literary salon, if such a thing existed, might be described as a few slim-pamphlet poets and would-be journalists swapping gossip and dirty yarns over sloppy pints in a pub.

But before commencing any dissection of the *corpus poetarum Hibernorum*, a few words on values and intentions. I take my understanding of modern poetry from Baudelaire: the poet's function is to explore life and consciousness, confronting, with passionate self-honesty and with the wisdom of his own insights, the chaos of reality within and without; to discover the light in the dark; to wrest some significance for the individual in a universe that seems to take no account of him; to be his own priest/philosopher in his investigations into good and evil, the mode of these investigations, for the poet as poet, being language.

II

The Irish poet Thomas Kinsella, in the course of an essay considering his own relationship as an Irish poet to his Irish forebears, finds little affinity with those who have gone before him. Ireland has produced no Metaphysicals, no Blake, no Wordsworth. Kinsella is right. Ireland has produced nothing *if* one is looking for a Donne or a Blake. But how serious is that? What had the Chilean Neruda, the Argentinian Borges, the Peruvian Vallejo? What they had, what they *all* had, was the conviction of the importance of poetry which Baudelaire expressed when he wrote, 'Literature must come before everything else, before food and pleasure, before even my mother.'

It is the urgency and seriousness that lie behind this statement of Baudelaire's that I take as the keynote of modern poetry. The question of how the modern poet relates to the past, literary or otherwise, is a question that every poet must work out for himself. The dangers to the individual that beset any general prescription are obvious. The best of modern poetry is personal, and it is only whatever of the past that can be assimilated personally that can be used in the writing of poetry. The rest is a matter of history and general knowledge. The literature of Europe was as much Eliot's as anyone's, is as much Borges' as anyone's.

In this process of assimilating and relating to the past, nationality may or may not be important. It depends on the individual, on the nature of his needs. The more confidence he has in his own abilities, the less will be his dependence on local precedents, on his national past. To the self-confident poet, a national past may be important but he will not be essentially dependent on it. What counts for him is his own talent and the state of the language in which he finds himself. The modern poet is primarily concerned with the relationship, or the lack of one between himself and the world of his experience; and if his experience is confined to his own backyard, so much the worse for him

F

as a poet. (I do not, of course, see the poet as a geographer: the world of experience is not found in an atlas.) Regrettably, Irish poetry of this century, to go no further back, is, with a few notable exceptions, a poetry of the parish pump. And herein lies the explanation for the lack of interest in it that one finds abroad.

In 1934, when considering 'Recent Irish Poetry', Samuel Beckett arrived at a similar conclusion. As Beckett saw it, the common failure of the Irish poets – the failure that led to the production of parish pump poetry – was their 'flight from self-awareness,' which, Beckett adds, 'might perhaps better be described as a convenience';· and he damningly continues:

> What further interest can attach to such assumptions as those on which the convenience has for so long taken its ease, namely, that the first condition of any poem is an accredited theme, and that in self-perception there is no theme, but at best sufficient *vis a tergo* to land the practioner into the correct scenery, where the self is either most happily obliterated or else so improved and enlarged that it can be mistaken for part of the *décor*? None but the academic.

There it is. The most perceptive analysis of Irish poetry ever penned! And in 1934! And almost as true today!

The reasons for this fatal limitation of Irish poetry – its failure to develop – are more complex than can be dealt with briefly here. Obviously they connect with the economic and general cultural retardation of Irish society under the yoke of British imperialism. The Irish poet's passport to success in London has always been his provision of local interest or colour; a regional voice, essentially diversionary. Not, certainly, an individual and personal voice.

That, at any rate, is how the present writer sees 'the Irish situation'. On examination he finds that he himself as a poet can more meaningfully and creatively relate to Antonio Machado than to, say, Austin Clarke; more to Pablo Neruda than to, say, Patrick Kavanagh. It is a question of relationships that are productive and liberating, and those which are confined and repetitive. What matters is poetry, not whether it is homegrown or imported. This latter question is the concern of nostalgia, sentimentality and tourism. Healthy cultures are hybrid.

I am aware that all this is contrary to the views of many influential Irish poets, critics and literary journalists. So be it. If, as I seem to be saying, there really is no such thing as Irish poetry that is at the same time poetry, the thing now to consider is whether there are any Irish poets, men or women born and reared here who have written good poems, who have understood the Baudelairean stance, who have been able to distinguish between the *human* and the Irish condition. I believe there are some such Irish poets. They are the notable exceptions to the poets of the parish pump. Constituting a radical threat they have been either ignored or their achievements have been demeaned by those who have a stake in the poetry of the shamrock patent.

III

Leaving aside Yeats who belongs unquestionably to world literature, the first modern Irish poet one comes upon is Thomas MacGreevy. MacGreevy left Ireland first for London and then, drawn by Joyce, who later became his close friend, for Paris where he encountered the most advanced literature then being written. He studied it, absorbed it and brilliantly wrote about it. But the modernity of MacGreevy, in the consideration of him as an Irish poet, is to be found in a note to his *Poems* of 1934:

> It is scarcely necessary to give detailed references to the echoes from the Greek Anthology, Virgil, Shakespeare, O'Rahilly, Flecker, Prophets and Evangelists, Catholic hymn writers, operatic and musical comedy librettists, nursery rhymers, etc., that occur throughout the poem [Crón Tráth na nDéithe] ; or, since it is obvious, finally to acknowledge the debt, so far as form is concerned, to modern French and Spanish writers of the eclectic school, as also to Mr Joyce and the one or two writers in English who have successfully adapted the technique of *Ulysses* to their own literary purposes. . .As a matter of fact I think the mode in which a writer strings words together is of secondary importance. The influences he has allowed to act on his mind seem to me of much more consequence. In my own case the profane influences that matter are most probably Pierre Corneille, Giorgio Barbarelli and Franz Schubert.

However, I am not suggesting that MacGreevy was never selfconsciously Irish (he describes himself in one of his poems, 'Homage to Vercingetorix', as 'an Irish-Irishman'); but when it came to the writing of poetry he never shirked his own personal individuality, in the formation of which, he was prepared to admit, his reading of Corneille mattered more than the whole of Anglo-Irish literature.

MacGreevy's poetry owes something to Eliot, more to the imagists and most to Joyce's idea of the *epiphany* of which Ellman tells us:

> The epiphany was the sudden 'revelation of the whatness of a thing', the moment in which 'the soul of the commonest object. . .seems to us radiant.' The artist, he felt, was charged with such revelations, and must look for them not among gods but among men, in casual, unostentatious, even unpleasant moments. He might find 'a sudden spiritual manifestation' either 'in the vulgarity of speech or of gesture or in a memorable phase of the mind itself'.

This description of *epiphany* serves perfectly to describe also what MacGreevy was aiming for in his poetry. Beckett must surely have seen this when he wrote: 'It is in virtue of [their] quality of inevitable unveiling that his poems may be called elucidations, the vision without the dip.' It is the casual moment which, even without invitation, suddenly unloads its riches, that MacGreevy's poems record. The impact of just such a moment is the point of 'Homage to Li Po':

> I fought the fever,
> I made a poem,
> I thought I had got this too adolescent heart in hand —
> One must be classical.
>
> Then I set out, serene,
> To enjoy the bright day.
> But I met you again.
>
> I am a sick man again.

And in another poem, 'Recessional', the actual epiphanic process is beautifully rendered:

> In the bright broad Swiss glare I stand listening
> To the outrageous roars
> Of the Engelbergeraa
> As it swirls down the gorge
> And I think I am thinking
> Of Roderick Hudson.
> But, as I stand,
> Time closes over sight,
> And sound
> Is drowned
> By a long silvery roar
> From the far ends of memory
> Of a world I have left
> And I find I am thinking:
> Supposing I drown now,
> This tired, tiresome body,
> Before flesh creases further,
> Might, recovered, go, fair,
> To be laid in Saint Lachtin's,
> Near where once,
> In tender, less glaring, island days
> And ways
> I could hear —
> Where listeners still hear —
> That far-away, dear
> Roar
> The long, silvery roar
> Of Mal Bay.

MacGreevy's friend, Wallace Stevens, responded to this particular poem with a poem of his own, 'Our Stars Come from Ireland':

> Out of him I made Mal Bay
> And not a bald and tasselled saint.
> What would the water have been,
> Without that that he makes of it?
>
> . . . .
>
> The sound of him
> Comes from a great distance and is heard.

Apart from the actual achievements of his poetry, MacGreevy has another importance in the Irish context. Despite the paucity of his output, he stands as a possible father figure for young Irish poets; a pointer and an influence rare in the Irish context, that is towards modernity, towards that dangerous commitment to the writing of personal poetry traditionally shunned by, or thought impossible for Irish verse-writers.

MacGreevy is already a seminal influence in modern Irish poetry. It was from him, and from Joyce *through* him, that both Denis Devlin and Brian Coffey, the two best Irish poets after MacGreevy, took their example. Beckett himself fits into this picture, both as MacGreevy's intimate friend and in virtue of his sharing Joyce's friendship with MacGreevy. More than this, MacGreevy and Beckett shared the same views on poetry as is evident in the fact that both their signatures are appended to the manifesto 'Poetry is Vertical' (reprinted in Mac-Greevy's *Collected Poems,* New Writers' Press, Dublin, 1971).

Devlin and Coffey are both fine modern poets. The poetry of both is complex and has a surface obscurity, lacking what John Montague calls 'primary readability'. This has made its acceptance (by non-poets) in Ireland extremely difficult. Even now, many years after Devlin's death and the publication of his *Collected Poems,* Devlin is not widely appreciated (and when he is, it is often as a kind of maverick poet, a kind of poet he most certainly was not). Coffey is hardly appreciated at all (he is not included in either the *Penguin Book of Irish Verse* or the *Sphere* anthology, and seemingly barely made it into the recent *Faber Book of Irish Verse* with part of the part of a poem). There are the customary Irish reasons for this state of affairs. Both poets, but especially Coffey, are intensely personal and therefore unacceptably unIrish.

Coffey's poetry is stringently investigative. Its real complexity derives from the fact that its language and techniques (learned from the French Symbolists) are forms of knowing, not receptacles of poetically *a priori* experience — the norm of Irish poetry. But to lend more meaning to these merely suggestive comments, some points from the manifesto 'Poetry is Vertical' (already referred to) will be useful:

> The reality of depth can be conquered by a voluntary mediumistic conjuration, by a stupor which proceeds from the irrational to a world beyond a world.
>
> The transcendental 'I' with its multiple stratifications reaching back millions of years is related to the entire history of mankind, past and present, and is brought to the surface with the hallucinatory irruption of images in the dream, the daydream, the mystic-gnostic trance, and even the psychiatric condition.
>
> The final disintegration of the 'I' in the creative act is made possible by the use of a language which is a mantic instrument, and which does not hesitate to adopt a revolutionary attitude toward word and syntax, going even so far as to invent a hermetic language, if necessary.
>
> Poetry builds a nexus between the 'I' and the you' by leading the emotions

of the sunken, telluric depths upward toward the illumination of a collective reality and a totalistic universe.

These statements are almost in the nature of essential directives for the reader of Coffey's poetry. They constitute a fruitful point of departure towards the tracing of the complex interactions between the 'I' and the 'Other' that are Coffey's central preoccupation.

Denis Devlin, having absorbed an incredible range of European influences both of the past and present, set himself the task of exploring the possibilities of spiritual and religious salvation in the modern world. What is generally overlooked in Devlin's work is the extent to which it is socially concerned. There is, for example, a strong satirical motivation at work in a great many of the poems, although it is never explicit. Although he repudiated the aims of the British 1930s, Devlin shared something with them. The difference, drawing him closer to Eliot and away from early Auden, lies in the religious nature of his perspectives.

IV

It is only now that Devlin and Coffey have begun to be accepted in their rightful place in the critical hierarchy of Irish poets. To those young writers who emerged during the 1960s and 1970s they were, at best, great shadowy figures looming on the edge of awareness, at worst, unknown. For the majority of this latest generation of Irish poets the only alternative poetic to a moribund Celtic Twilight was that received from Kavanagh via James Liddy: honest self-revelation and a minimum of preoccupation with form.

It is those poets who, from this naïve beginning, developed and refined a poetry similar in many ways to that of Coffey, Devlin, etc., and who have now begun to look back to them as progenitors. They seem to me to be producing work which can stand beside the best, not just of Irish poetry, but of that poetry which by virtue of its exploration of the human spirit, dispenses with nationalistic props.

To the present writer Trevor Joyce is the most important Irish poet, north or south of the Border, under thirty-five. He is important from the point of view of intelligence and the range and depth of his knowledge and sensitivity. Though he has produced little, he dwarfs everyone of his own generation and many of his poems can be more than favourably compared with anything produced by his seniors, Kinsella and Montague. There is such control and omniscience in Joyce's handling of an experience, to put it bluntly, that the reader feels he is in the presence of a major writer. For a similar feeling when reading an Irish poet one has to go to the work of Devlin or Coffey.

And yet Joyce is little known even in Ireland. To explain that, one must consider the fact that Joyce is published by a very small poetry press with consequently poor distribution. Moreover, his poetry is so far ahead of the backward poetry reading public in Ireland (in so far as any poetry reading public can be said to exist in Ireland) that it is almost incomprehensible to them. As regards publication in anthologies, the modern sections in anthologies of Irish verse are traditionally a personal matter: the editors generally know so little about poetry that discriminating among the work of young poets without reputation usually ends up as a matter of *personal* likes and dislikes; and Joyce is not in that game.

Convinced that so much poetry could be written in Ireland, and so little of it be considerable, only through a facile attitude to the language and forms of poetry, Joyce attempted to evolve a more honest and intelligent approach to these. But he was not content with the *naïveté* of the Kavanagh/Liddy notion of sincerity and self-revelation. He found it necessary to locate and define the self in its multiple manifestations and in its fundamental role as determining the forms through which experience is received and the social forms through which it may be given to others. Thus, to refer to Kavanagh, technique became a means of being honest, and language and form reflected on themselves.

Joyce's world is solipsistic, but tensely so, since the poetry, with great beauty and power, also intimates a non-self world, a world that for Joyce is often, initially, sad and meaningless, the movement of the poem being that of establishing a relationship with this world whereby the potential for redemption within both is mutually revealed. The vital centre of the poetry is in that relationship. Its ambience does not glibly correspond with the phenomenal world of common sense. What we have are fragments of that world of which Joyce struggles to make sense; in that struggle an apparently trivial insight can have far-reaching consequences because Joyce's real preoccupation is with ultimate questions, especially that of time.

Here is a representative poem of his:

Christchurch. Helix. 9th Month

Passages of labyrinth repeat;
the crypt gives vellum thighs to the dead,
mark our return in this way;
again we hollow dust-caves, ankle-deep.

Paths are furrowed by rats' feet,
scribbled as cryptic schemes, motifs
of death and propagation;
here the fruit of death dilates.

Arid courses interplay, rivers of dust,
graphs wrought in frost, dust-falls interpret sunlight.
A cat plays knucklebones with something grey
and we move into daylight:

for mornings the roads are chrome
and the sun is a citron stain on a limed wall.

The poem's progress is mimetic of the state of consciousness which it represents. Repetitive circling through references to writing ('passages', 'vellum', 'graphs', etc.) suddenly reveals itself through confrontation with mortality as turns on a helix, and poem and consciousness simultaneously rise to birth in a world of illumination.

After Joyce, both in achievement and promise, comes Michael Hartnett. There can have been few poets who began writing so promisingly. Take this poem which he wrote when he was about seventeen:

Sickroom

Regularly I visited
since your sickness
you in the black bedroom
with the gauze of death
around you like your sheets.

Now I must be frank:
these are not roses beside you,
    nor are these grapes,
        and this is no portrait
            of your father's friend.

I know you cannot rise.
You are unable to move.
But I can see your fear,
for two wet mice
            dart
cornered in the hollows
of your head.

Hartnett's first period, his poetry until he was about twenty-one, achieves, through accurately worked images, a delicate delineation of intimately personal experience. The poems of that period are his best. From the beginning Hartnett had a highly developed sense of control over language and imagery, a sense of control that now seems to have become restrictive. In those early poems, however, he chose just the right kind of experience to write about, experience that did not interfere with his sense of technical control, his ability to create beautiful and compact forms. But something has gone wrong for Hartnett. Something perhaps he had in mind when writing the following:

I have exhausted the delighted range
of small birds, and now, a new end to pain
makes a mirage of what I wished my life.
Torture, immediate to me, is strange:
all that is left of the organs remains
in an anaesthetic of unbelief.

Hartnett's early work promised that he would develop into a poet considerable by any standards; but something went wrong. What Hartnett brought to poetry and what enabled him to avoid the conventional pitfalls of Irish versifying was a precision of language and image which could examine experience as deftly as a scalpel. But when he approached areas where depth of experience was lacking, or extra-poetic factors inhibited its examination, the poetry devolved into a decorative preciosity. Perhaps Hartnett's method of writing a poem was perfected too early. Once it had used up the experience in the context of which it had been fashioned, it became constricting. Hartnett began as a poet with a definite style and in the end the style dominated and jailed the man. His notion of himself as a poet depended on that style. He has been left with the style and for years he has been looking around for something to do with it, in the meantime producing rather trivial work. Recently he has turned to translation, but the emancipation that could be won through this exercise has merely led to a consolidation of his style since he has chosen to translate only those poets — for example, Lorca — whose work easily accommodates it. His versions of Lorca are superb, but it is Hartnett the poet, not the translator, who is our concern here.

There are others about whose poetry, either because they have not a sufficient body of published work, or because they have not subscribed to any explicit poetic, it would be spurious to make any judgement more extensive than that implied by placing them in the context of those writers I have examined above. But since it is perhaps at this stage of his development that a poet can most benefit from any sympathetic critical attention, I will make of that my apology for noting their existence by at least quoting from their work.

Gerard Smyth is a young Dublin poet. He writes a poetry of intense emotionalism that is generally neither naïve nor escapist. Some of the discernible influences are Kenneth Patchen's reverberating simplicity of statement and Trakl's wide-netting expressionism.

Always and Forever

Tonight frost sucks the air.
My words are loud but don't ring echoes,
only strains that snap the hoar-frost
from some neighbour's window.

More sad to say:
my words do not bring answers, only
sighs that rattle too softly to survive
the cut of this glass-edged air.

What more to say
except goodbye, in a tone that's almost mute
for fear that it might be for
always and forever.

Goodbye turns a lonely key that locks
a door cemented with this season's ice.

Augustus Young is a Cork poet in whose work the language of medicine and the natural sciences provides a precision whose unfamiliarity is sometimes so exploited as to seem surrealistic. He much admires some of the contemporary east European poets and has done versions from the Czech for which his stark and functional style peculiarly qualifies him.

Lab. Animals

Devouring what you give birth,
determined to die-out,
my rice-rats from the swamps,

Complan in your teeth, chew
cancers. I know your feed (
my father died of it),

Beasts to be put away.
The door bangs, a clean thought.
Wind dismisses my key,

double-locks with a gust.

Secured by the strange, old
bodies assured of death.

Other young poets whose work deserves attention but who can only be named here are: Paul Durcan, Brian Lynch, Paul Murray, Macdara Woods and Geoffrey Squires.

V

The tradition to which all these poets contribute was first established in Ireland in the thirties, and of that founding generation Brian Coffey is still writing poetry, which confirms the richness and genuineness of that tradition. There are, however, others who, while not perhaps quite so venerable, have carried down that poetic to those among us who are only now elaborating it. Pearse Hutchinson, Anthony Cronin, James Liddy and Patrick Galvin, though very different writers, share passionate and honest intelligence, that refusal to fly from self-awareness which Beckett commended. But these four are poets who have given much of a lifetime to their art, and whom it would be presumptuous to try to evaluate within the scope of one brief article. Their work may be seen as the compensatory reward for the risks involved in that tradition and that art. Perhaps the greatest of those risks of too passionate investigation, and one not threatening those who consider that 'in self-perception there is no theme', was adumbrated by MacGreevy. . .

You thought she had left you alone,
She of the Second Gift,
Save for belief in her.

You thought she had left you alone
When, the struggle at end,
The god went, silent, away
Through the flames that leaped and sang.

You thought she had left you alone
When, his piping over,
The shepherd waited
The silence that waited his silence.

It is because of this danger of final impotence from too much passion that it is inappropriate to speak now of a new movement or of a revival in Irish poetry. Those poets now emerging would benefit more from a parallel development of an intelligent and sympathetic criticism than by a world of hack reviewing, hack anthologies and misplaced nationalism.

SOME BOOKS

Samuel Beckett, *Poems in English*, Calder & Boyars, London, 1961.
Eiléan ní Chuilleanáin, *Acts and Monuments*, Gallery Books, Dublin, 1973.
Brian Coffey, *Selected Poems*, New Writers' Press, 1971.
–– *Irish University Review,* Special Brian Coffey Issue, Dublin, spring 1975.
Anthony Cronin, *Collected Poems*, New Writers' Press, Dublin, 1973.
Denis Devlin, *Collected Poems*, Dolmen Press, Dublin, 1964.
Paul Durcan, *Endsville*, New Writers' Press, Dublin, 1967 (shared with Brian Lynch).
Patrick Galvin, *The Wood-Burners*, New Writers' Press, Dublin, 1973.
Michael Hartnett, *Selected Poems*, New Writers' Press, Dublin, 1970.
Pearse Hutchinson, *Tongue without Hands*, Dolmen Press, Dublin, 1963.
    –– *Expansions*, Dolmen Press, Dublin, 1969.
    –– *Watching the Morning Grow*, Gallery Books, Dublin, 1972.
John Jordan, *Patrician Studies,* New Writers' Press, Dublin, 1971.
Trevor Joyce, *Pentahedron*, New Writers' Press, Dublin, 1972.
James Liddy, *In a Blue Smoke*, Dolmen Press, Dublin, 1966.
    –– *Blue Mountain*, Dolmen Press, Dublin, 1968.
Brian Lynch, *Endsville*, New Writers' Press, Dublin, 1967 (shared with Paul Durcan).
Thomas MacGreevy, *Collected Poems*, New Writers' Press, Dublin, 1971.
Michael Smith, *Times & Locations*, Dolmen Press, Dublin, 1972.
Gerard Smyth, *Twenty Poems*, New Writers' Press, Dublin, 1970.
    –– *Orchestra of Silence*, Gallery Books, Dublin, 1971.
Geoffrey Squires, *Drowned Stones,* New Writers' Press, Dublin, 1975.
Macdara Woods, *Early Morning Matins*, Gallery Books, Dublin, 1972.
Augustus Young, *On Loaning Hill*, New Writers' Press, Dublin, 1972.

Contemporary Poetry in the North of Ireland
by D. E. S. Maxwell

I

A. E. SAID THAT, 'A literary movement consists of half a dozen writers living in the same city who cordially detest one another.' Northern Ireland now has more than its half dozen. This essay concentrates on three, but the reason is editorial and carries no overtones from A. E.'s remark. Seamus Heaney, Michael Longley and Derek Mahon are among the first group of Ulster poets to have won international recognition both as an identifiably regional group and as individuals. The statement is not intended to demean earlier writers from the North of Ireland; the names of John Hewitt, W. R. Rodgers and Louis MacNeice would be an immediate refutation. Its purpose is to suggest a unique – in Ulster – combination of talents, a school yet a school of individuals, with its origins concentrated at quite a precise point in time. A near analogy for such an emerging chorus of new voices might be Auden, Day Lewis, MacNeice and Spender in the 1930s.

The regional affiliation of these younger Irish poets is too emphatic to be ignored. It is important because its accent is insistent, though only one strain in a register of inflections, Irish and other, to which these poets have listened and variously given their own character.

A basic issue is what, in the process, they had to work from locally. Did Heaney and the rest have to subdue to poetic statement for themselves the singularities of their province, and their lives within it; or was there some existing literary *argot* on which they might draw? One thinks, in this connection, of Louis MacNeice's comment on English woods:

> they are assured
> Of their place by men; reprieved from the neolithic night
> By gamekeepers or by Herrick's girls at play: . . .

given, in fact, a stylized location, unlike – in MacNeice's poem – 'the wilds of Mayo'; or of Ulster. Was there an Ulster literary tradition to which these poets might accommodate themselves; or was it all to be done with an ear to the English literary voice, a Northern Irish scene and intonation to be personally achieved?

II

Northern Harvest, an anthology of Northern Irish writing, appeared in 1944. Its poetry section included poems by John Hewitt, W. R. Rodgers, Roy McFadden and Robert Greacen, the editor of this volume. Roughly contemporary issues of *Lagan,* a Northern periodical edited by John Boyd, carried poems by the same writers: in its first issue by Rodgers, Hewitt, McFadden and Greacen; again in the second number, as well as a review of recent publications by the last three; and in 1946 by Louis MacNeice.

Poems appeared from many other hands. The above names, however — though MacNeice was at the time infrequently thought of as an Ulster writer — were those that, it seemed headily possible, were establishing and consolidating an 'Ulster literary renaissance'. Robert Greacen was more persuaded of its reality than John Boyd. Introducing the second *Lagan* collection, the latter recalled its editors' earlier disagreement 'with the theory that we were experiencing a renaissance in Ulster. Looking back, we have had no reason to regret our caution.'

'Naissance' might in any case have been more accurately the word in dispute. There was no body of regional literature to be re-born. For the present subject, however, a pertinent question may be how far the Northern poets of the sixties and seventies could usefully look for local example to their predecessors of the thirties and forties. The inheritance offered is certainly in many ways a strange one. Its creators were urgent for an utterance distinctively of Ulster, which for Greacen meant the six counties so named after the historic province. Their peculiar qualities — reserve, taciturnity, lack of display — abruptly perished, according to Greacen, at the border to their south and west. The aim of *Northern Harvest,* however, was not to foster a reading public in Ulster, or even Ireland at large, but to 'win a sympathetic audience in Great Britain'.

There is, in short, an ambiguity, and for Greacen's own poetry it seems a disabling one, between the Ulster allegiance and the solicitude for a British *imprimatur.* The formula would appear unlikely to satisfy the prospectus of *Lagan* which, although there is still a certain defensiveness, saw Ulster in less restrictive connotations and made firm literary demands of its writers. In his first editorial, John Boyd asked that the Ulster writer should 'train his ears to catch the unique swing of our speech; train his eyes to note the natural beauty of our hills and the unnatural ugliness of our towns: above all, he must study the subtle psychology of our people'. He had in mind, no doubt, something more fully possessed of its subjects than the 'dialect verse' of Richard

Rowley and W. F. Marshall, though the latter's is not to be dispraised.

A number of Roy McFadden's early poems do communicate fluently with a tension between the plains and hills of Down, 'stone on stone, blocking the downward tremble / Of the breaking wave', or with a Belfast 'patient in its hates'. The scene takes on a presence, at its best, in crisp particulars, deployed in a controlled run of the verse line:

> Evening moves like a blessing on this island,
> And on the sea a sudden turn of wings; . . .

('Evening in Donegal')

> From the cupped peace of these aloof
> Uncertain hills, a quiet hint
> Of a corner-lurking past.

('Letter from the Mournes')

But Dylan Thomas's New Apocalypse seduced McFadden, as it did Greacen, from his virtues. Landscapes improvidently launch themselves into modish phantasmagoria; feeling and observation sink beneath an overload of words: the poems are Apocalyptic with nothing in them to be apocalyptic about.

McFadden has none the less a genuine poetic substance. He wrote in 'The Journey Home', more plainly than was his custom then, of the shock of the familiar scene altered by time —

> He marks each innovation, facing betrayal,
> All his bridges blown and the boats burned,
> Having only a name, his accent wrong.

In his own later poetry, McFadden has found a clearer tongue and an acuter and less distracted perception of his 'clabbered clout of ground'. He has turned his attention, as Michael Longley has remarked, to the real, or imagined-real, people of his world, to Clutey Gibson of Belfast, Tom Hunter of Lisburn. With his new economy, and often an elegant wit —

> You trembled after
>
> The gun's colon:
> When wings declined
> In a misprint of commas,
> Sentenced to stop. —

McFadden has, indeed, re-made himself, and speaks now in concert with his younger contemporaries.

Louis MacNeice has, in a sense, been welcomed home by the new generation of Ulster poets.* They see in him much more than the literary con-man of much English critical opinion: the plain man's glib guide to a world never beyond matter-of-fact understanding, where frivolous wit ('the bald-at-thirty Englishmen whose polished / Foreheads

*See Michael Longley's article on MacNeice, pp. 98–104.

are the tombs of record sales') gets the better of responsible vision. There may, in the search to redress the balance, be some over-compensation. MacNeice undeniably is comic, in the best possible ways. It would be wrong to present him as characteristically sombre.

W. R. Rodgers would be perhaps a more dangerous guide. Where MacNeice may at times be slick with words, Rodgers can be manic: 'the loops and balloons of bloom / Bobbing'; 'chutes of stilled chatter'; 'in the nick and nook of time'. Alliteration, assonance, pun, internal rhyme, all beckoned with every prospect of acknowledgement: 'the daft words proliferate in me like laughter'. The exuberance is not a quality associated with Ulster speech, whose verbal dexterity is more often terse than eloquent: its virtue is aphorism not embroidery, more prolific in an invective than in any lyric mode. Rodgers is then the more to be welcomed, a kind of Presbyterian Hopkins (whom Rodgers had in fact not read), willing to 'chance the lucky dip' of words.

There is in Rodgers, however, a core of bonier language. 'Home Thoughts from Abroad' dedicates to Ian Paisley and his 'borborygmic roars / Of rhetoric',

> this contraceptive pill
> Of poetry to his unborn followers.
> And I place
> This bunch of beget-me-nots on his grave.

'Journeys,' for Rodgers, 'are always curly.' Linguistically, they take in the fascinations of elaborately orchestrating words and of tuning them to a more colloquial pitch. In his sequence 'Resurrection' we have, 'This was a rough death, there was nothing tidy about it,' to set against,

> Only the windows of his wounds
> Were wide open, and the red curtains of blood
> Blew out into the storm, torn to ribbons.

Of the two manners, the latter is the more instinctive to Rodgers. In his longer poems it tends to dilute the matter of feeling and circumstance. His poems leave the impression of a response, often triumphant, to words, not to experience. Thus in a later poem, 'Lament for an Educated Hole in the Road', he is remarking less his introduction to American life than, with gusto, to American idiom: 'Los Angelically speaking'. Rodgers has the gift of a splendid gab, not always under control. When it is, as in 'A Last Word', his requiem for Louis MacNeice, it united word and sentiment:

> Under the highly improbable sky,
> Needlessly blue,
> He piles the cold clay. It is all,
> You might say, so dead true.

John Hewitt has half-disclaimed his reputation as a nature poet. He draws attention to the equally relevant circumstances that he is 'an

Irishman of planter stock, by profession an art-gallery man, politically
a man of the Left'. Of the three, the first is the most pressing in Hewitt's
work. Because of it, his 'nature poems' are not descriptive merely. The
scenes are emblems of a complex fate of conquest, tenure, alienation,
the invader possessed by the land he indifferently subdued. Habit and
the land, intimate with one another, bind the planter to his new soil —
as in 'The Colony', ostensibly about the Roman occupation of Britain:

> the use, the pace, the patient years of labour,
> the rain against the lips, the changing light,
> the heavy clay-sucked stride, have altered us.

Hewitt does not sentimentalize his scene. It is 'a bare place',
'narrow and brown', 'barren', 'harsh', a 'mad island crammed with
bloody ghosts'. Its living inhabitants occupy in one perspective 'the
squalid focus of their huxter life'; and the poet recalls in his Belfast
childhood intimidating an errand-boy 'Repeatedly to curse the Pope of
Rome'. Yet that poem, 'The Green Shoot', moves to an earlier, tender
reminiscence, of carol-singers in the street 'singing a song I liked until I
saw / my mother's lashes were all bright with tears'. Both exterior and
interior scenes — somewhat in the manner of Lawrence's 'Piano' — are
precisely realized. The poet, in this admirably poised lyric, is caught
between 'ready sentiment' and 'flinty violence': 'a green shoot asking
for the flower'.

Hewitt's terrain, then, human and physical, is not all bleak. Warmer
hues, moments of companionship, 'with song and sap astir', are part of
its grain. As the frictions of the scene, however, afflict the man, so their
accommodation to words challenges the poet. Ireland as a country has
its being in small towns, villages, townlands, not cities. It was from a
city-rearing that Hewitt

> ...opened eyes and found both tongue and feet.
> Its windows and its walls, its doors and stones
> have tailored this close flesh upon my bones...

So, having 'followed a trade / three generations now',

> How far an acre spreads I scarcely guess;
> no crop's yield offers sign I may assess.

The countryside's lore and 'vocabulary of skill' are to be won at second-
hand. The reward is an identity and a definition, for

> talk of weather is also talk of life,
> and life is man and place and these have names.

The quotations in this note may exemplify Hewitt's achievement in
such an intentioned 'naming of parts'. The scene, and the sustained
attention to the scene, supply and control the words, usually in quite
traditional poetic forms. Unlike Rodgers's, the words do not tumble
away from the properties they represent. Hewitt's poem, 'Homestead',

refers closely and persuasively to what Seamus Heaney has called 'an almost Augustan poise and directness, married to an elegiac, inward note'. The homestead is literally a house. It becomes a home not only for the poet's friends. Through him it makes place for their counterparts in the Irish past. It is 'a dwelling, and yet an outcrop, part of the place'; and, in its acquiring character, a metaphor of the search for a personal idiom that will conflate scene, feeling, thought and image:

> There is nothing for it but to build right here
> in roughcut stone and spread a roof of *scraws*.

Making his own way, Hewitt has written a poetry both 'an outcrop, part of the place', and accessible beyond its locality.

III

By the early fifties, John Montague and James Simmons had published work. They are, in their very different ways, distinguished poets, and are considered elsewhere in this collection. Heaney, Longley and Mahon began to publish in the sixties. What is first striking in their poetry, especially when it is compared with most of what appeared in the thirties and forties in Ulster, is its remarkable self-possession; and this is in part an inheritance from the three poets discussed above.

Seamus Heaney now has three collections: *Death of a Naturalist* (1966), *Door into the Dark* (1969), and *Wintering Out* (1972).* Critics are supposed to be clamorous that a poet should develop — as MacNeice sardonically observed, such critics, to observe any development, 'need something deeper than a well and wider than a church-door'. Its publishers claimed for *Wintering Out* 'a noticeable widening of his poetic landscape'. The opinion, though disputed in some reviews of the volume, is well founded. *Wintering Out* draws out previous themes into new alignments; it takes up fresh verbal and imaginative ambits; it consistently implies from its sense-impressions, still robustly present, a mosaic of thought and feeling. The poems of his first volume are concerned, primarily, to register the energies of a scene in its physical being. There is certainly an emotional response to what is being observed; and a coalescing towards symbol; but sensuous observation is in command.

The habitat is rural, entered at one level, it seems, assured of kinship:

> By God, the old man could handle a spade.
> Just like his old man.
>
> Snug on our bellies behind a rise of dead whins
>
> The long grey tapes of roads that bind and loose
> Villages and fields in casual marriage.

The scenes, bred into the bone from childhood years, can riot in luxuriant growth and colour, like the 'glossy purple clot' of the first

* Seamus Heaney has since published *North* (Faber, 1975). Ed.

blackberry, its flesh 'sweet / like thickened wine'; the seasonal tasks reassuring and familiar, churning day or a potato digging:

> The rough bark of humus erupts
> knots of potatoes (a clean birth).

The kinship is fragile and misleading; Heaney's country life is neither glossy nor Arcadian. The influence of natural objects can be as often as not to inspire fear, revulsion, disillusionment. The naturalist whose 'death' gives the volume its title progresses from an uninstructed fascination with 'the warm thick slobber / Of frogspawn' in the flax-dam where bluebottles 'Wove a strong gauze of sound around the smell.' Later, coming on the 'gross-bellied frogs', croaking in multitude, 'The slap and plop were obscene threats. . .'

> . . .gathered there for vengeance and I knew
> That if I dipped my hand the spawn would clutch it.

The blackberries betray their beauty, 'A rat-grey fungus, glutting on our cache'; churning is hard graft, blistering hands, souring the house; there is a routine, but to the child frightening, violence, when Dan Taggart drowned kittens, 'Or with a sickening tug, pulled old hens' necks'. 'Sickening': a recurrent word.

The conclusion is throwaway — pests have no place on a farm. The poet establishes 'a dreaded / Bridgehead', as when in 'An Advancement of Learning', he stares out the rats he loathes. The uncomely is to be assimilated too: violence, menace, are inherent in the land, whether in its daily occupations, or in a heritage of blood. In 'At a Potato Digging', 'Fingers go dead in the cold', and memories stir of other, earlier deaths:

> Live skulls, blind-eyed, balanced on
> wild higgledy skeletons
> scoured the land in forty-five
> wolfed the blighted root and died.

The next poem, 'For the Commander of the *Eliza*', is a mordant narrative of an incident recorded in Cecil Woodham-Smith's *The Great Hunger*. Past and present run together in a chiaroscuro of experience; the collection initiates the poet's design, 'to set the darkness echoing'.

There is a tension, in Heaney, between the farm life natural to his childhood, and the recognition that he has abandoned his father's ways, belonging and not belonging:

> Between my finger and my thumb
> The squat pen rests.
> I'll dig with it.

His diction, in a way, reflects the tension. It draws, discreetly, on a vein of 'country words': 'slabber', 'muck', 'crocks', 'creel', 'clabber'; and it complements them with a delicately sophisticated imagery: a river 'wearing / A transfer of gables and sky'; 'Sky a tense diaphragm'. Heaney controls an exceptional variety of words, and of line. Knowing his background as his father does, he disturbs in it also more distant echoes and reflections. *Door into the Dark* consolidates his statement.

Tangible reality does not lose its tenure. 'The Outlaw' celebrates the workmanlike servicing performed by an unlicensed bull. 'The Wife's Tale' — Frost-like in a way — intimates in a harvest incident a domestic relationship bound to the 'here and now' of daily life. Even the poems where the exteriors do not hazard their density, though, are commonly elegies for occupations, observances, crafts, past or fated to pass: an abandoned stable, a blacksmith remembering hoofs on the street outside his forge, a thatcher recollected from the palmy days of his skill. Surfaces increasingly contrive underlayers of meaning: loss and continuity, the cycle of birth and death, the sexual antithesis.

Thus 'Rite of Spring' represents a water pump, thawed out from its frozen angle at the end of winter, in a kind of orgasmic release: 'Her entrance was wet, and she came.' The voice of the speaker in 'Mother' working at a pump, conceives of her chore in sexual references. The stream in 'Undine' is a metaphor — 'he dug a spade deep in my flank / And took me to him' — of the 'subtle increase and reflection' of female response. These emblems of human encounters participate in the seasonal rhythms of salmon and eel (notably in 'A Lough Neagh Sequence'). Their most moving expression is in 'Elegy for a Still-Born Child', where the narrating voice moves at the end from the 'wreath of small clothes, a memorial pram', to a journey whose imagery may question its desolation:

> Past mountain fields, full to the brim with cloud,
> White waves riding home on a wintry lough.

There are shadows in the apparent clarities of Robert Frost that we may recognize in Heaney. 'The Plantation', towards the end of this volume, has the same kind of suggestiveness as 'Passing by Woods on a Snowy Evening'. It is a fable of a threatening wood, 'birch trees / Ghosting your bearings', deceptive, yet enticing 'Past the picnickers' belt'. Within earshot of the road, it is beyond the road's definitions, offering as it perplexes the chance of discovery, 'To be pilot and stray — witch, / Hansel and Gretel in one.' The more literal landscapes of other poems fall into such equivocations, their contours dissolving. The seascape of 'Girls Bathing', endlessly consuming itself, is like the flux of the years. In 'The Peninsula', 'horizons drink down sea and hill, / The ploughed field swallows the whitewashed gable'. The poem's final sequence, in an intricately managed sentence, frames a stanza of close visualization within the cryptic interpretation of it:

> Now recall

> The glazed foreshore and silhouetted log,
> That rock where breakers shredded into rags,

> The leggy birds stilted on their own legs,
> Islands riding themselves out into the fog
>
> And drive back home, still with nothing to say
> Except that now you will encode all landscapes
> By this: things founded clean on their own shapes,
> Water and ground in their extremity.

The final poem, 'Bogland', is like 'The Plantation', a compression of paradoxes which Heaney has placed in Ireland, though they are omnipresent: deep loughs which kill and preserve; an island looking outward to sea, and inexhaustibly in upon itself; a journey within that leads to common habitations:

> Every layer they strip
> Seems camped on before.
> The bogholes might be Atlantic seepage.
> The wet centre is bottomless.

Wintering Out takes as its Preface a poem from a sequence ('Whatever you say, say nothing') published in the *Listener,* expressly about the Northern Irish violence. The point of the Preface, and of the exclusion of its companion pieces, is that the collection is to be read with the present horrors as one of its loci; but only as one, and, it may be, not a major one. The 'common sound effect' of gelignite (a phrase from the *Listener* sequence) has a buried life in poems seemingly apart from it. 'The Last Mummer', for example, portrays this representative of his dying art parading the suburbs, angry with frustration, and throwing stones at the houses. Heaney comments, 'I didn't mean this to be a poem about Northern Ireland, but in some way I think it is.'

In 'A Northern Hoard', five poems in Part I of *Wintering Out,* the detail of riot, tribal hatreds, the 'smeared doorstep' and the 'lumpy dead', directly, though intermittently, surfaces. For Heaney, the mindless violence, eroding even personal love, means exile, ears stopped to the mandrake-shriek of roots torn up. 'I deserted': but the defection is inconclusive, broken by fitful returns, neither return nor absence satisfying. The private torment shelves into and out from public views, each powerfully augmenting the other, of a fragmented society, hard and ravenous:

> flint and iron,
> Cast-offs, scraps, nail, canine.

The vistas of *Wintering Out* open directly on the present Northern violence. If the volume has a central question, it is that of Shakespeare's MacMorris, 'What ish my nation?', turning for its answers to circumstances of which the present troubles are only one instance. Repeatedly here, Heaney invokes the rights and rites of language, in places whose names, English and not-English, pronounce a domicile: '*Anahorish*, soft gradient / of consonant, vowel-meadow'; 'the tawny guttural water / spells itself: Moyola'; 'Demesnes staked out in consonants'. Language is divisive too: in Broagh, the final '*gh* the strangers found / difficult to pronounce'; a Protestant neighbour, with a biblical image, speaks a 'tongue of chosen people'; McCracken's hanged body is 'a swinging tongue'. So language draws in a host of other memorials to a troubled inheritance of 'vowels and history', where heir and outcast dispute their roles: 'man-killing parishes'.

The phrase is from 'The Tollund Man', where Heaney finds outside Ireland an archetype of ceremonial dispossession. The preserved, sacrificial corpse is a 'saint's kept body', germinal, an ancestor of

> The scattered ambushed
> Flesh of labourers,
> Stockinged corpses
> Laid out in the farmyards.

The Tollund Man assumes in death a 'sad freedom'. Visiting his homeland, though 'Not knowing their tongue', the poet would confirm a kinship:

> I will feel lost,
> Unhappy and at home.

The theme unifies the collection, glancing, for instance, into three related poems which are allegories of love and rejection, selfish, tender, destructive: 'Maighdean Mara' (the mermaid), 'Limbo' and 'Bye-Child'. Formally, the poems move within a starker diction of 'stones', 'stubble', 'rock', more elusive rhymes, manners of declaration whose design is to solicit inference. If, as Brian Friel suggests, every writer has one tune to sing, Heaney's orchestrations of his have progressively enriched it.

A review in *Hibernia* of Michael Longley's second collection, *An Exploded View*, found fault in an emotional coldness, a lack of 'commitment to the subject itself', a 'stand-offishness'. The verdict is a bizarre one, if only in view of a poem like 'Wounds', which movingly associates memories of the poet's father in the First World War with the manifold atrocities of Belfast. Delicate, brutal, it memorializes a legion of dead,

> as heavy guns put out
> The night-light in the nursery for ever; . . .

The complaint might be more plausibly (though still wrongly) directed against Longley's first collection, *No Continuing City*. It could be argued that there one is first made conscious less of the pulse of life than of a delight in superior impersonations. Auden is present, but as a guest, not a gate-crasher, as in the tightly controlled verse of 'Epithalamium' (see, in Auden, 'A Summer Night 1933'). Longley also has MacNeice's trick of subverting a cliché: 'I take the words out of their mouths'; 'heartbreaks play into my hands'. This, however, is to draw attention to major virtues: he has Auden's hold over intrepid stanza/

sentence relationships; and MacNeice's sense of the moment that can resurrect a phrase pronounced dead.

These are qualities of a remarkable technical command which is important not only in itself. It suggests the primacy Longley gives to the act of composition, the poetic shaping which is, so to speak, its own experience. In Dr Johnson's phrase, it brings realities to mind, but operates on autonomous rules and logic. Several of the poems seem to be devising what may be various parables of the traffic, and its fascinations, between reality and artifice, masquerade, the metamorphoses of art. 'A Questionnaire for Walter Mitty' interrogates its hero as one might the claims of the artist: 'Could it be truth you carry, lies you spend?'; 'Do you employ deceit or just disguise?' The end, in a dramatically abrupt transition, carries the enquiry into the myths of a God in life:

> how would you define
> The water-walker who made the water wine —
> Was it Christ the God? was it Christ the man?

'Graffiti' wittily puts a case for the sterotypes of confounding an art of stereotypes. In advertising posters, as in 'all good fairy tales', wishing has made it so:

> One kiss and, in the twinkling of any eye,
> The Calibans accepted, warts and all,
> At long last resurrected from the sty,
> So blond, so beautiful, and six feet tall.

The deodorized images invite an (equally stylized) appeal to things as they more or less are:

> these who decorate her lovely crotch
> With pubic shrubbery and with a notch,
> Unwittingly imply a sort of spring.

Finally, the stuffed birds of 'The Ornithological Section', though frozen in a make-believe life, excite images of their former 'gay trajectories', and even, 'By some deep need of ours conveyed', propose a future. A human being, too, may look for the meaning of an individual life in a death given the significance of form, 'our actions thus defined / By that repose in which they end'. Movement finds its liveliest expression in the fixities of art. So Emily Dickinson, in the poem which takes her name as its title, enshrines life 'By christening the world'.

It is presumably poems of this kind that madden *The Honest Ulsterman,* the irreverent periodical founded by James Simmons, for which Heaney, Longley and Mahon are 'the Tight Assed Trio'. The desired alternative might be conveyed in S. J. Perelman's injunction, 'Open up your bowels and let the sunlight in'. What is admired is something taken to be earthier, easier of access, and less worked — though *The Honest Ulsterman* has also been censorious with writers who take 'the troubles' as subject — fiddling 'while Belfast and Derry burn'. In fact, Longley's consideration of what art may contrive from life implicates life itself. The poems about the, as it were, readymade characters of classical legend — Circe, Nausicaa, Persephone, Narcissus — release them from the stock associations of their legends into landscapes identifiable with those of real places and people of other poems. Circe would be at home on the Inishmore of 'Leaving Inishmore'. The physical scene of light and heat occupies the poem, until a turn at the end shifts to 'a January idiom' — 'the curriculum/vitae of sailors and the sick at heart'.

'A Personal Statement', on the synthesis of mind, body and experience, is untypical in having to strain after words. The idea first stated, there is nothing more to do but repeat it over twelve stanzas of ingenious but thinning wordplay and the cliché game: 'Follow my nose', 'points of contact', 'alarms and excursions', 'raise your sights', 'believe my eyes'.

By contrast — and representatively — 'The Hebrides' both creates a scene and at once begins to populate it with ideas of the kind that 'Personal Statement' dissipates. The islands are with literal appropriateness, 'last balconies', and though desolate ('granite', 'orphaned stone', 'ling and bracken'), vibrant in other than city ways with life: gulls, the osprey, salmon. The scenery parallels a scenery of the mind and feelings: balconies, breakwaters, wind and wave; and in the self (the theme is a central one), flux and poise, the precedents of a housebroken normality and the challenge of displacement:

> Granting the trawlers far below their stance,
>   Their anchorage,
> I fight all the way for balance —
>   In the mountain's shadow
> Losing foothold, covet the privilege
>   Of vertigo.

Words here are resonant with the feeling that brings them together.

The case for Longley as more than a cute artificer is most obviously made — if made it needs to be — by his love poems — 'Epithalamium', 'No Continuing City' — or by the affectionate recollection of his father, 'In Memoriam'. These speak for themselves. They do so because they avoid the adolescent premiss that commonplace experiences, being new to oneself, will be universally fascinating; and consequently work to govern the tempting gush of confessional. Longley's first volume insists, directly and convincingly, on the capacity of art to renew the life it draws on.

'We are trying,' says the epigraph to An Exploded View, 'to make ourselves heard'. One subject not given any extended hearing in No Continuing City asserts itself in this second volume: Ireland, and in particular its violently renascent discontents. Like 'Skara Brae's' 'exploded view / Through middens, through lives', exposing the strata of the past under the present, Longley's contemplation of his native country and province enters it amongst the other co-ordinates of the world he maps. It is often a disquieting one, its parts fragmenting. Words like 'splintered', 'fractured', 'detonates', 'splintering', 'lesions', 'dispersals', 'elisions', 'exploded', 'scatter' most obviously state the motif. They run through not only poems about the violence, though that is their home base.

There is a touch of Grand Guignol in the grotesques of 'The Adulterer', 'Confessions of an Irish Ether-Drinker', 'Nightmare'; 'The Fairground''s various monsters spirit 'the solitary spectator' into their company and kind. 'Caravan' too projects reality into uneasy, menacing, possibilities. A gypsy caravan suggests a family companionship, which in the poet's mind becomes his own. Watched ('tiny, barely in focus') by — his wife? — he imagines riding off through a blizzard to buy food:

> Or to be gone for good
> Having drawn across my eyes
> Like a curtain all that light
> And the snow, my history
> Stiffening with the tea towels
> Hung outside the door to dry.

Episodes like these are disquieting, but not depressing, partly because they have contrary aspects. There are poems of union, of a solacing perfection caught in some balancing of objects: when a lake's

> surface seems tilted to receive
> The sun perfectly, the mare and her foal,
> The heron, all such special visitors.

More important, however, whatever afflictions he observes, the poet keeps his head, not aloof but composed. The poems addressed 'To Three Irish Poets' reflect within 'The stereophonic nightmare / Of the Shankill and the Falls', on personal friendships, on memories of places and people which assemble to

> Claim this my country, though today
> *Timor mortis conturbat me.*

The urbane octosyllabics, by turns strictly and irregularly rhymed, respond to the varying pitch of feeling:

> Blood on the kerbstones, and my mind
> Dividing like a pavement,
> Cracked by the weeds, by the green grass
> That covers our necropolis,
> The pit, terror. . . What comes next
> Is a lacuna in the text.

In *An Exploded View* Longley moves about a world more apparently 'serious' — a world of bombs and murders — than that of his first collection. The difference is more of appearance than substance. The

political violence is a form of terror with its counterparts in private
risks and insecurities. The poems are constantly making such connections, while aware too of affection and communion. The poet's
commitment is to the words and the structures which will shape these
diversities into his 'secondary world':

> The accommodation of different weathers,
> Whirlwind tours around the scattered islands,
> Telephone calls from the guilty suburbs,
> From the back of the mind, a simple question
> Of being in two places at the one time;

finding the numbers which will answer between life and life-in-art,

> Siphoning through the ears
> Letters of the alphabet
> And, with the vowels and consonants,
> My life of make-believe.

Derek Mahon's 'As God is My Judge', in his first collection, *Night-
Crossing*, has Bruce Ismay, President of the White Star Line and a
Titanic survivor, as its speaker:

> As I sat shivering on the dark water
> I turned to ice to hear my costly
> Life go thundering down in a pandemonium of
> Prams, pianos, sideboards, winches,
> Boilers bursting and shredded ragtime.

It is a powerfully compassionate apologia for a life saved by a night-
crossing into lifelong despair. Its feelings envelop the scenes whose sole
reference now is to the one calamitous event that left Ismay shamefully
alive:

> The showers of
> April, flowers of May mean nothing to me, nor the
> Late light of June, when my gardener
> Describes to strangers how the old man keeps his bed
> On seaward mornings after nights of
> Wind, and will see no one, repeat no one. Then it is
> I drown again with all those dim
> Lost faces I never understood. . .
> Include me
> Honoris causa in your lamentations.

The poem has in it a good deal of Mahon's sense of 'Lives in infinite
preparation', of the individual perpetually catechized by the transition
of his state, by 'each fragile, solving ambiguity' of circumstance:
crossing, stations, landings, departures, schedules of age and season.

The life of Mahon's poems is endlessly mobile, annexing *points
d'appui* from teasing essence into some endurable form: 'An eddy of
semantic scruple / In an unstructurable sea.' Water — the sea, rivers,
coastlines — the flight of birds, refractions of light, cities giving upon
country views: all represent the mutability which defies, yet with its

rhythmical patterns provokes, the human urge for an equilibrium disposable, like a climate, into unpredictable elements. Animal life is one focus of man's equivocations, wanting the best of two worlds. It has a victim's role, with man as predator, yet also in a way that of an innocent god, without evasion reproaching human destructiveness.

On his 'Day Trip to Donegal' Mahon sees the catch of fish landed on the pier. Despite their agony, realism insists,

> Their systematic genocide
> (Nothing remarkable that millions died)
> To us is a necessity
> For ours are land-minds, mindless in the sea.

Reparation is due. After his outing, the poet at home sleeps into nightmare, adrift at sea.

> Cursing my mindless failure to take due
> Forethought for this, contriving vain
> Overtures to the mindless wind and rain.

'Four Walks in the Country near Saint Bruic' puts him similarly at odds with the birds who watch 'The shadowy ingress of mankind'. His 'whistle-talk' does not disarm them, for, as he recognizes, good reason:

> So perhaps they have something after all —
> Either we shoot them out of hand
> Or parody them with a bird-call
> Neither of us can understand.

No resolution is possible; the two worlds are worlds apart. Man would be the victim if animals did not know, 'as I know, I am not alone'; yet in the final poem of the sequence, 'Exit Molloy', the birds have the last word: 'I am already dead, / But still I can hear the birds sing on over my head.'

The modern city is a counter-world to the one of 'primeval shapes'. 'Glengormley', an archetypal, as it happens Belfast, suburb invites an ironical acceptance of the apotheosis of twentieth-century man, 'Who has tamed the terrier, trimmed the hedge / And grasped the principle of the watering can.' The Irish gods have gone, their retreat bequeathing sombre burdens:

> The unreconciled, in their metaphysical pain,
> Strangle on lamp-posts in the dawn rain
>
> And much dies with them.

There is maybe something to be said for coddled suburbia, if only as a fact of life to be reckoned with. 'Gipsies Revisited' in *Lives*, Mahon's second volume, is more mordant about this particular kind of place. The slow reduction of the gypsies anticipates the ruin of their persecutors, buried in their own debris:

> our strong
> double glazing groans with

> foreknowledge of death,
> the fridge with a great wound. . .
> I listen to the wind
> and file receipts. The heap
> of scrap metal in my
> garden grows daily.

These poems appear at times to be dealing in plainspoken statement, the simplest words, sparing imagery. Mahon is a more adventurous speculator; words find offbeat, but as it turns out, compatible partners. For 'Dowson and Company', 'a dutiful spectrum of stars'; Marilyn Monroe, rescued from the trash and rubble of her slum, is a tragic Cinderella: 'Cinders swept to the palace from her shack' to an unhappy ending —

> Stars last so long before they go scattering ash
> Down the cold back-streets of the zodiac;

the funeral of the poet's 'Wicked Uncle' is 'absorbing' in more ways than the word's tone of offhand civility first suggests. We are to be on guard for innuendo that conjugates a meaning.

Mahon's wit can be purely light-hearted. 'The Poets Lie Where They Fall' is an engaging synopsis of poetry-reading odyssies. 'First Principles', having dismissed the elegant, earthy and innocent modellings of feminine ideals, confesses to the poem that is to the writer's fancy:

> No, it will so derange
> The poor bitches, that they
> Will come round on their knees
> At all hours of the day,
> Crippled with visceral rage
> And croaking please, please.

'Visceral rage', however it's treated here, has the vehemence of feeling that fastens human beings to their difficult contracts with sensuous life. 'An Unborn Child', in a poem that delicately scores its divinations of a mysterious future, answers to the amplifying signals of sensation: 'the rain / Wiping its wet wings on the window-pane':

> I slip the trappings of my harness
> To range these hollows in discreet rehearsal.
> And, battering at the concavity of my caul,
>
> Produce in mouth the words I WANT TO LIVE — . . .
> I want to see, hear, touch and taste,
> These things with which I am to be encumbered.

The child will enter a world like that of 'Grandfather' and 'My Wicked Uncle'. Scenes (the Ismay poem is similar) intrude into lives, as they do into the poems, with a suddenly defining force: 'Boiler rooms, row upon row of gantries rolled / Away to reveal the landscape of a childhood'; and in 'My Wicked Uncle',

> I saw sheep huddled in the long wet grass

> Of the golf course, and the empty freighters
> Sailing for ever down Belfast Lough
> In a fine rain, their sirens going,
> As the gradual graph of my uncle's life and
> Times dipped precipitately
> Into the bowels of Carnmoney Cemetery.

'Spring Letter in Winter', a beautiful love poem, brings to a distress articulated in wintry landscapes the relief of spring, the letter its swallow:

> Water is flowing where no river was or
> I have come early to the sea in spring.

These are some of the lives of Mahon's first collection. The *Lives* of his second are less likely to be those of actual acquaintances. The grandfathers and uncles have retired into more distant *personae*, though the same concerns are their escorts. When Mahon says, 'I am Raftery, hesitant and confused among the / cold-voiced graduate students and inter- / changeable instructors', he is looking amidst the unremitting confusions of life to one of many lives outside his own that may offer both a lodgement and a point of departure. Both conditions are necessary. Travel, real or metaphorical, is inescapable; to make any sense of it, 'One part of my mind must learn to know its place'. The sense of the poems in this volume is generally more of the dislocation of journeys than of settlement. 'Homecoming', crisply desperate about a flight from Boston to Dublin, ends up in a destination which is essentially no different from the derangements of jet travel: 'Skies change but not / souls change'.

In 'In the Aran Islands' the poet hears a pub singer, rapt in his own music, one hand 'earthed to his girl'. It is a moment suggestive of union, not only for the singer, but between the poet and an island tradition, harsh but striking a 'reverberation / Down light-years of the imagination'. The last voice of the poem, though, is that of the gull startled when the poet left the pub. Restless, nomadic, it pulls the poem away from its momentary dream:

> A crack-voiced rock-marauder, scavenger, fierce
> Friend to no slant fields or the sea either,
> Folds back over the forming waters.

The present seeks out its own features in the past, not only in personal history but in the far elsewhere of lives fossilized in legend, or literally in the earth. 'The Archaeologist', 'Lives', 'A Dark Country', 'What will Remain' sadly disinter the relics of an unrecognizable ancestry:

> So many lives,
> So many things to remember!
> I was a stone in Tibet,

> A tongue of bark
> At the heart of Africa
> Growing darker and darker. . .
>
> I know too much
> To be anything any more —
> And if in the distant
>
> Future someone
> Thinks he has once been me
> As I am today,
>
> Let him revise
> His insolent ontology
> Or teach himself to pray.

'Rage for Order' and 'As It Should Be' envisage similar fates for present lives in a society whose premises have no place for them: the poet looking 'beyond / The scorched gable-end / And the burnt-out / Buses'; 'the mad bastard' gunned down 'Between ten sleeping lorries / And an electricity generator'. 'Ecclesiastes' is a magnificent self-comminatory sermon on a similar theme.

The last poem, 'Beyond Howth Head', brings together the volume's themes in a brilliantly executed jaunt around ideas and disasters: 'Dover Beach' re-visited with all the aplomb of Auden's public manner. It is preserved from despair by its coolly reckoned balance-sheet of the light and darkness of its mid-twentieth-century ambience. As we see Mahon reaching honestly 'Into a dark country / Beyond appraisal or report', we may apply to him his own verdict on Beckett:

> The pros outweigh the cons that glow
> from Beckett's bleak *reductio*;
> and who would trade self-knowledge for
> a prelapsarian metaphor,
> love-play of the ironic conscience
> for a prescriptive innocence?

IV

New poets continue to appear, wholesomely unawed by their immediate predecessors. Frank Ormsby and Michael Foley, co-editors of *The Honest Ulsterman* with a good line in polemic, 'run a tough school', as Foley says in 'No Delicate Pose Poems'. Ormsby, in 'Manifesto', claims to 'eschew all statements of concern, all relevance, / All issues but those simple that accrue / To daily living.' The result can be strident. It can also pull aside sudden curtains on the uneasily steady state of lives mundanely dependent on each other, a marriage

> Not disenchantment, more a compromise
> Charged with affection.
> We settled to the limited surprise
>
> That day-to-day insists on.

There is not a composite poet, Formsbley, but the two men do share a healthy belief in the superiority of the old rag and bone shop to greenery-yallery.

Lists and capsule descriptions are odious but hard to avoid. A better introduction to the continuing Northern progress of poetry is *The Honest Ulsterman.* It has a gift of choice, in acceptance and dismissal, comparable to Geoffrey Grigson's in his 1930s *New Verse.* Among the poets it has published, in pamphlet form as well as periodically, are William Peskett, Anthony Weir, Tom Matthews and Tom McLaughlin. If the latter three share an aim, it is to make words the servants of experience, preferably the experience of everyman in his apparently unremarkable engagements. The poem is there to speak for the experience, the experience must not become a peg to hang words on. They would agree with James Simmons that technique has its 'temptations, and style can be something to hide behind':

> . . .the civil-servant, language, draws his ring
> Around experience. And every living thing
> Sits speechless in officialdom.

(McLaughlin)

William Peskett is more inward-looking, more disposed to indirection, elaboration, symbol. But it is the world of common observation which instructs his hauntingly uncommon observation of it; as, at its simplest, of a lake where

> on a still day
> there is twice as much of everything
> except ripples.

Selection from among these poets (who will make it to the home straight?) would be an offensive tombola. One other poet, though, Paul Muldoon, also published in *The Honest Ulsterman,* has singled himself out with the publication of his *New Weather.* 'The Upriver Incident' has a rather sinister ballad-like narrative of outcast lovers drowning, and a villanelle structure in which varying ballade-like refrains link the stanzas. Muldoon is fond of the infinitesimal verbal changes that can totally reverse a meaning, and they often become analogies of — a favourite theme — the shocking metamorphoses of love. In 'The Cure for Warts' — there is none — 'The pair of warts nippling your throat' images some erotic attraction which turns into the canker of the final, 'That pair of warts nibbling your throat.' Sensual pleasure is real, as in 'Leaving an Island' or 'Clonfeacle':

> You turn towards me,
> Coming round to my way
>
> Of thinking, holding
> Your tongue between your teeth.

> I turn my back on the river
> And Patrick, their sermons
>
> Ending in the air.

'Vespers', 'The Kissing Seat', 'Grass Widow' are concerned with its rapacities, one road from innocence to experience.

Muldoon's world is threatening and at times disheartening. 'The Electric Orchard' is an ironic fantasy on the progress of 'progress'. The suspicious, defensive 'Hedgehog' is witness to a condition where 'never again / Will a god trust in the world.' 'The Field Hospital' and 'Party Piece' are part-mythical representations of this 'world grown older'. In it, the loss of innocence is blood-letting and physical dismemberment; sexual encounters are party to the pornography of violence:

> Their heads,
> Lifted clean off by the blast,
> Lying here in the back seat
> Like something dirty, hold our
> Sadness in their eyes, who wished
> For the explosion's heart, not
> Pain's edge where we take shelter.

While Muldoon is a bit inclined to make a virtue of opacity, the statements of *New Weather* imperatively echo in the mind. He belongs, with his unique cadences, to what Michael Allen, reviewing *New Weather,* has called 'one of those cultural confluences which have often proved important in literary history.' 'Literary history' sounds like premature burial, but the poets withstand any last offices; they speak on within the tradition they perpetuate and should have the last word: from Michael Longley's poem about John Clare, 'Journey out of Essex':

> I am lying with my head
> Over the edge of the world,
> Unpicking my whereabouts
> Like the asylum's name
> That they stitch on the sheets.

The Prose of
Samuel Beckett:
Notes from the Terminal Ward
by James Atlas

1

THERE IS a moment in Proust's novel when Marcel hears a bird calling through the long afternoon:

> Somewhere in one of the tall trees, making a stage in its height, an invisible bird, desperately attempting to make the day seem shorter, was exploring with a long, continuous note the solitude that pressed it on every side, but it received at once so unanimous an answer, so powerful a repercussion of silence and of immobility that, one would have said, it had arrested for all eternity the moment which it had been trying to make pass more quickly.

This 'long, continuous note' of solitude resonates through Samuel Beckett's work since the publication of his trilogy, *Malloy, Malone Dies,* and *The Unnamable,* between 1951 and 1953. With increasing spareness and economy, he has reduced his prose to the point, in *Lessness,* where a few words are entered on the page, then repeated in various orders or identical phrases until their possible meanings have been exhausted. In his plays, we are asked to observe a stage littered with garbage, while an 'instant of recorded vagitus' (in the O.E.D., the word is obsolete, 'a cry, lamentation, or wail') punctuates the sound of breathing, or listen to a disembodied voice hectoring a hooded, silent auditor (*Not I,* 1973). What we are witnessing is the termination of an *œuvre* designed to die with its author; the trope of immortality, of a work surviving its creator, has been suspended. Beckett would rather dismantle his own fictions than claim their endurance through time.

And yet, despite this dwindling, the French editions of new texts appearing in their thin, white jackets, Beckett's impulse to make of his work an autonomous tradition resembles in its strategies no one more than Joyce and Proust. Nor is this really surprising, given Beckett's close personal relations with Joyce (some portions of *Finnegans Wake* were transcribed in his own hand, and he collaborated in the French translation of the Anna Livia Plurabelle chapter under Joyce's direction);

moreover, his first substantial work had been the monograph on Proust, published in 1930. A year earlier, he had contributed an essay, 'Dante. . . Bruno. Vico. . .Joyce', to the famous collaborative exegesis of *Finnegans Wake,* later collected in *Our Exagmination round His Factification for Incamination of Work in Progress.* In the light of his later decision to write in both English and French, composing two separate literatures, the convergence of Joyce and Proust becomes crucial.

With Joyce, Beckett's affinities are more obvious; Hugh Kenner has argued that 'Beckett is the heir of Joyce as Joyce is the heir of Flaubert, each Irishman having perceived a new beginning in the impasse to which his predecessor seemed to have brought the form of fiction'.* Flaubert once expressed the desire to write 'a book about nothing, a book without external support which would sustain itself by the internal power of its style as the earth is suspended in the air'. Beckett later detected the same ambition in Joyce, whose 'writing is not *about* something; *it is that something itself*. And Beckett's own writings in French after 1945 owe a great deal to this legacy of pure style. He once said that he wrote in French 'parce qu'en français c'est plus facile d'écrire sans style'. Such a remark would seem at first to counter the Flaubertian obsession with style, but what Beckett implies here is a writing in which all traces of 'literature' have disappeared, and been replaced with what has now come to be called *écriture;* so that when Roland Barthes draws attention to 'this precarious moment of History in which literary language persists only the better to sing the necessity of its own death', he intends *écriture*, a 'closed system' of discourse, to be its survivor. In this, Beckett resembles Ponge, whose 'texts' purport to be no more than explorations of the materiality, the viscous texture of language.

The place of Proust in Beckett's work becomes apparent when we look to the tradition he has appropriated and made his own, a tradition located in what, speaking of Proust, he names 'the necessity of art'. After the war, Beckett returned from the Unoccupied Zone to Paris (active in the Resistance, he had been forced to retreat there), and retired to his room to write the trilogy; for nearly four years, he lived in a manner that can't escape comparison with Proust, spinning a dense web of remembrance in the voices of several related characters, all sharing in the sickliness of Proust's narrator, and in his obsession with

---

* It's significant that Pound, writing in the *Mercure de France* as early as 1922, traced the sources of *Ulysses* to *Bouvard et Pécuchet*; after all, it had been Flaubert who first caricatured the requirements of realism in the novel, aspiring to produce an exhaustive inventory of *idées reçues*, and, more important, a satire on scientific method, with its claims to the verification of reality. In a novella, *The Expelled,* Beckett echoes the first incident in Flaubert's novel, where Bouvard and Pécuchet discover that both have their names inscribed inside their hats; Beckett's narrator refers to 'the metal initials in the lining of my hat'.

reconstructing past events in all their inexorable complexity. Moreover, despite their dereliction, these Molloys, Malones and Mahoods are no less literary than the Marcel of *A la Recherche du Temps Perdu*. In a reference to the trial of Madame Bovary, Molloy hears 'what the great Gustave heard, the benches cracking in the Court of Assizes', while in *Malone Dies*, the Lambert family (in the French version, Les Louis), recall Balzac's own autobiographical model, Louis Lambert. Nevertheless, Molloy insists, during a difficult moment in his narrative, 'It is not at this late stage of my relation that I intend to give way to literature', and Malone breaks off a lyrical passage to announce: 'To hell with all this fucking scenery'. This is Beckett's declaration that, like Proust, he will surrender to the necessity to write, but will abjure the writing of 'literature'.

There is another literary influence as well. Though Beckett refers to Baudelaire only once in all his work (in *Premier Amour*), the motif of illness, the temptation to 'enthrone my infirmities' is everywhere in evidence. Baudelaire's direct echo of Poe, 'anywhere out of this world', has its correlative in Beckett's figures, literary enough to long for burial in the *Père Lachaise*, yet suffering, in a variation of Proust's asthma, from the 'grand apnoea'; and Baudelaire's sense of isolation in the crowd, the world he fashioned on the boulevards, appears in Beckett's Malone, observing 'the people who throng the streets' toward evening: 'At this hour then erotic craving accounts for the majority of couples. But these are few compared to the solitaries pressing forward through the throng, obstructing the access to places of amusement, bowed over the parapets, propped against vacant walls.' Walter Benjamin, in his remarkable study of Baudelaire, *A Lyric Poet in the Era of High Capitalism,* noted that 'It takes a heroic constitution to live Modernism'. Beckett's characters inherit this resistance to the disease of the modern, which so disfigures human relationships. Their sturdiness and endurance belong more to Baudelaire's resourceful *flâneur* than to the later Symbolists, whose aesthetic depended on the exacerbation of nerves.

Beckett's early work, though, is intensely Joycean, consciously Irish. His first fictional work, *More Pricks than Kicks*, the distillation of an earlier, abandoned novel, *Dream of Fair to Middling Women,* reveals both the broad humour and geographical specificity of Joyce. The protagonist of these ten stories, Belacqua Shuah,* is a Trinity student, a wanderer through Dublin, and a sort of comic Stephen Dedalus. More than *Ulysses,* the resemblance here is to *Dubliners,* with its rehearsals of Irish dialect (Beckett has also acknowledged the influence of Synge). But there are scattered explicit imitations of the later Joyce: the in-

* Belacqua appears in the fourth canto of Dante's *Purgatorio*, idly waiting a second lifetime before he can enter Purgatory, while Shuah is taken from *Genesis*; his name in Hebrew means 'depression'.

clusion of invitations, dates, and letters; archaic or invented words (cenotheca, aliquots, ebriety); foreign languages; passages of music; borrowed names (Purefoy recalls Joyce's Wilhelmina Purefoy in *Ulysses*); deliberate echoes of Swift; and an immense word compounded of English and German that mimes Joyce's hundred-letter thunderclaps in *Finnegans Wake.*

Murphy, his first published novel (1938), was no less Joycean than the stories: landladies reading A. E.'s *Candle of Vision*; versions of the Ithaca chapter in *Ulysses,* where Joyce organized and parodied scientific knowledge in a manner reminiscent of *Bouvard et Pécuchet* (in *Murphy,* Beckett informs us that 'the moon, by a strange coincidence full and at perigee, was 29,000 miles nearer the earth than it had been for four years'); an extravagance of jokes and Irish banter. Beckett's apprenticeship to Joyce was calculated and intense, from 1929, when he came to Paris, until the publication of the trilogy, by which time he was writing exclusively in French. Even in *Watt* (1942-4), where the weird, repetitive mode that later came to dominate his work was first unveiled, there are obvious Joycean elements: disruption of the text by spaces and musical notations; the long, elaborate sentences incorporating all possible explanations of an event; Watt's odd internal monologues that echo Leopold Bloom's. The novel, set in the Ireland Beckett remembered from his childhood, is no less localized than Joyce's own Dublin, and his characters talk in loquacious Irish voices not heard again in Beckett's writing until the radio play, *All That Fall,* of 1957.

In these earlier works, Beckett's ambivalence toward Ireland, like Joyce's, was expressed in a close attention to detail, and in the portrait of Irish history as an experience rooted in oppressive politics and religion. Both Joyce and Beckett, in their Paris exile, devoted themselves to the reconstruction of their abandoned nation, the plotting of Dublin streets and landmarks, and both examined their own backgrounds in considerable depth. Beckett's Ireland is more opaque than Joyce's, his explicit references obviously fewer; nevertheless, the same events that excited Yeats and Joyce appear in *Murphy*, even if in a parodic rather than solemn manner. Where Yeats had applauded, with some reserve, the Easter Rebellion, and commemorated its heroes, and where Joyce had seen in Parnell Ireland's 'Uncrowned King', Beckett satirized the intensity of feeling generated by Ireland's embattled past; Neary, a character in *Murphy*, is observed 'in the General Post Office, contemplating from behind the statue of Cuchulain. . .Suddenly he flung aside his hat, sprang forward, seized the dying hero by the thighs and began to dash his head against his buttocks, such as they are.'*

---

* A. J. Leventhal, in the *Festschrift Beckett at Sixty*, has related how he received a postcard from Beckett requesting him to measure the statue in order to verify the plausibility of such an episode; this was the sort of meticulous research Joyce practised in the composition of *Ulysses*.

Joyce's hatred of what he has Simon Dedalus call 'an unfortunate priestridden race', and of Ireland, 'the sow that eats her own farrow', competed with his loyalties, just as Yeats both ranted against and celebrated his country, often in a single breath; Beckett, like Yeats a member, not of the Ascendancy, but of the Protestant middle class, noted once that Protestantism 'had no more depth than an old school tie'. Even so, the portrait of Father Ambrose in *Molloy* reveals a hostility toward those religious institutions (in this case, Catholic) which had made Ireland so moribund. Adaline Glasheen, in a fine essay on 'Joyce and the Three Ages of Parnell', suggested that Joyce, in his later work, 'had come to see that spiritual sickness is not localised or Irish, but common to all men everywhere'; and it was this insight, evident in the bleak landscape of the trilogy, that led Beckett to universalize the situations he treated, to withdraw from the later work all but a few traces of the more specific Ireland of *Murphy* and the earlier stories, leaving only the distillation of his own mental experience. Conor Cruise O'Brien has proposed that Irishness 'is not primarily a question of birth or blood or language. It is the condition of being involved in the Irish situation, and usually of being mauled by it.' In this sense, Beckett has drawn from Ireland a number of characteristics that he shares with Synge, the sprawl and wit of Irish speech, with Yeats, a story-telling ability, and with Joyce, among whose cherished traits were 'silence, exile, and cunning'.

When Beckett began writing in French, he continued to exploit some of the more conventional narrative elements of the novel. *Mercier et Camier* (the first work of Beckett's to be composed in French, with the exception of a few poems and the translation of *Murphy*) relates the journey of two characters through some indeterminate landscape. Their dialogues, like those of Bouvard and Pécuchet, are bewildered and abstract; every third chapter offers a 'résumé des deux chapitres précédents' not unlike Flaubert's abbreviated lists of adventures in his two protagonists' lives. Here, too, despite the absence of a specific plot or situation, an episodic development could be discerned, and there was a coherence to their comic meditations:

> What have we done to God? he said.
> We have denied him, said Camier.
> You will not make me believe that his rancour goes to these lengths, said Mercier.

And in *Premier Amour*, written the same year (1945; English translation 1971), Beckett produced a masterpiece of storytelling. This novella, the recollections of a wretched affair initiated on a park bench years before, belongs more among Beckett's novels in English; like the earliest stories, *Premier Amour* features a reclusive and somewhat distracted narrator who recalls his past without bitterness, divulging only that he had been evicted from his house following the death of his father and had then moved in with a woman, who supported them by prostitution. She became pregnant, upon which he abandoned her, having decided that 'l'amour, cela ne se commande pas' (in the English version, 'love doesn't depend upon our will').

Metaphorically, the direction of Beckett's own life can be detected here; well-educated and more urbane than the later protagonists, the dour speaker admits: 'J'avais lu des romans, en prose et en vers, sous la direction de mon tuteur, en anglais, en français, en italien, en allemand.' After resigning from Trinity, where he had been a lecturer, Beckett spent several years travelling through Europe; his self-imposed exile, like Joyce's, was a condition expressed in figures like Belacqua Shuah and the narrator of *Premier Amour*, who suggests, 'Bricoler, c'est encore une chose possible.' Lévi-Strauss, in *The Savage Mind*, describes the *bricoleur* as someone 'adept at performing a large number of diverse tasks', but whose 'universe of instruments is closed. . .the rules of his game are always to make do with "whatever is at hand", that is to say with a set of tools and materials which is always finite'. In Beckett's case, this finite set*is language, which articulates its own borders; it could be conjectured that Beckett had been oppressed by the virtual infinitude of English, with its excessive richness, its diversity of idioms, and so turned to French because it possessed such stringent limits. Joyce's solution, in *Finnegans Wake*, had been to exploit the resources Beckett rejected, invading other languages, inventing words, expanding ordinary grammar until it was capable of embracing several tenses at once. Beckett's, stated in *Premier Amour*, was to become a 'roi sans sujets': 'La chose qui m'intéressait moi. . .c'était la supination cérébrale, l'assoupissement de l'idée de moi et de l'idée de ce petit résidu de vétilles empoisonnantes qu'on appelle le non-moi, et même le monde, par paresse.'†

John Fletcher, in his book on *The Novels of Samuel Beckett*, has provided a close reading of Beckett's French style in its earliest stages, showing how gallicisms had begun to surface in his English prose, and how traces of awkwardness in the French of the *Nouvelles* (1946) were excised in later editions. What Fletcher's account reveals is the complexity of Beckett's transition from English to French, a transition which resulted in the location and refinement of a voice anxious to hear, 'beyond the fatuous clamour, the silence of which the universe is

---

* The mathematical term is relevant since, on several occasions, Beckett investigates the permutations of number; Pim's discourse on probability in *How It Is* becomes the model of a mathematics that could exhaust the possibilities of randomness.

†In Beckett's own translation: 'What mattered to me . . . was supineness in the mind, the dulling of the self and of that residue of execrable frippery known as the non-self and even the world, for short.'

made'. With the trilogy, Beckett turns to the first-person mode of narrative introduced in *Premier Amour,* and so enters the dense, reductionist world of the later prose. George Steiner has noted 'Beckett's thinness, his refusal to see in language and literary form adequate realisations of human feeling or society', and it is this conviction that inhabits all his work after 1945, when he wonders, 'What's the matter with my head, I must have left it in Ireland, in a saloon, it must be there still, lying on the bar'; having chosen to compose in French, Beckett abandoned the musical Irish lilt of Joyce and Synge. Nothing of Ireland would remain once the trilogy was complete, unless the 'desolate heaven' of Yeats.

II

Beckett's narrator in *The Calmative,* collected in *Stories and Texts for Nothing,* announces, 'we are in a skull'; it is from this hermetic chamber that all the later work issues. The characters in the trilogy share in a condition of impossible solitude, alone, like their author, in rooms where nothing reverberates except Memory, 'the sensation itself, annihilating every spatial and temporal restriction' (from the monograph on Proust). However opaque their situation, Molloy, Malone, Mahood, even the Unnamable, are storytellers, aware of each other and of their place in Beckett's *œuvre*: 'a gallery of moribunds. Murphy, Watt, Mercier, and all the others'. (Like Balzac's, Beckett's characters appear over and over in the novels, a troupe whose identities are assumed to be well known.) When Jacques Moran retires to his desk to write a report on Molloy, he begins: 'It is midnight. The rain is beating on the windows.' In the novel's last paragraph, Moran is referred to in the third person, while another voice concludes: 'Then I went back into the house and wrote, It is midnight. The rain is beating on the windows. It was not midnight. It was not raining.' This disclosure dissolves the fiction of the entire novel, just as the last pages of *Malone Dies,* where several inmates of a mental institution are murdered by a madman named Lemuel (Swift is a constant presence in Beckett's work), end in the breakdown of language:

> never there he will never
> never anything
> there
> any more

In the same way, Molloy finds it impossible to render his experience coherent: 'It seemed to me that all language was an excess of language.' Hesitant to elucidate what appears impenetrable, the *texture* of a world in which contingencies impose their will, Beckett verifies Wittgenstein's claim: '*Nothing* is lost if one does not seek to say the unsayable. Instead, that which cannot be spoken is – unspeakably – *contained* in that which is said!' The 'Unnamable' of Beckett's novel is a protagonist, but also a felt condition, the expression of necessity: 'Having nothing to say, no words but the words of others, I have to speak. No one compels me to, there is no one, it's an accident, a fact.' Inevitably, the identical nature of accident and fact is what determines Beckett's vantage, from which the violation of Wittgenstein's axiom would appear to be so dangerous; to state what is 'unsayable' is to invent reality rather than elicit its character.

There is a crucial passage in *Malone Dies* where Beckett notes the manner in which the Saposcats, a frail married couple, communicate: 'They had no conversation properly speaking. They made use of the spoken word in much the same way as the guard of a train makes use of his flags, or of his lantern.' Such a metaphor underlies the whole enterprise of structural linguistics and semiology, where meaning depends on the representation of signs; so that when Beckett complains there is 'nothing to signify', it should be clear that he will no longer operate within the realm of ordinary linguistic discourse. Inscribed in Beckett's trilogy is an obstinate refusal to mean; signs are to be self-referential, their employment no more ambiguous, no less arbitrary than a train-signal.

And yet, there still exist in these novels remnants of place and exact locale; Molloy's Bally is Beckett's Ireland, while Father Ambrose, who dispenses Communion to Moran, possesses the provincial temperament of Joyce's priests. The Unnamable's cadence of speech echoes the vehemence of Swift; on occasion traces of a baroque and formal prose remain, vestiges of Ruskin or Sir Thomas Browne left standing in the ruins of English literature. The *Textes pour rien* which follow the trilogy reveal Beckett's increased impatience with language, and his renunciation of those formal properties which once represented the novel. Writing has become, literally, 'wordshit' (in the French version, *fatras*, a somewhat milder epithet); the writer's apprenticeship to words is shown to be a chronicle of lost nerve: 'Words, mine was never more than that, than this pell-mell babel of silence and words, my viewless form described as ended, or to come, or still in progress, depending on the words, the moments, long may it last in that singular way.' What Beckett struggles to situate after the trilogy is 'a new no', since, 'were the voice to cease quite at last, the old ceasing voice, it would not be true'. Steiner has often contended that silence is the central motif of European Modernism, and will summon Webern, Hofmannsthal and Hermann Broch as witnesses to the devastation that has ended in what he calls 'post-culture': 'a strain of barbarism, of profound disillusion with literacy' ushered in by the spectacle of the Nazi Holocaust and hastened by mass culture. Beckett's disposition, despite the near-inarticulate, the diminished tonalities of his work over the last two decades, has been to counter this impulse toward silence.

The 'new no' that becomes clarified in the later texts corresponds to Adorno's gloss: 'To Beckett, as to the Gnostics, the created world is radically evil, and its negation is the chance of another world that is not yet' (*Negative Dialectics*). Ironically enough, then, it's possible to consider the shreds of discourse, the rude, unfinished soliloquys that are Beckett's tactic now, utopian, in that writing promises a way out of the impasse created by modern life, which is, after all, a 'concentration camp' (in Adorno's view). And this is what occupies the disembodied voices of *From an Abandoned Work, Enough, Ping, Imagination Dead Imagine, Lessness* and *The Lost Ones*: the activity of escape.

Even the thin appearance of these works implies the transience of a condition which poses no hope of respite in this world; there is nothing to be done except survive, always with Kafka's admonition in mind, that 'There is Infinite Hope, but not for us'. These texts disclose the dwindling store of experience that can still be validated and made other than random. Literature is discontinuous, a set of images that exist only to be repudiated. *From an Abandoned Work* (1958) illustrates this tendency: a figure wanders over some adumbrated landscape, falling, struggling up, then pushing on. During this ordeal, he recalls his parents, his education, his eventual dereliction, and a number of images which possess a stubborn importance: the colour white, a white horse, a synaesthetic white 'sound'; 'all has gone but mother in the window, the violence, rage and rain'. The voice still manages to achieve moments of lyrical utterance, though, before lapsing into repetition.

The thirteen pages of *From an Abandoned Work* are all that remain of a novel initiated in 1955 and, in a literal sense, abandoned later on. What Hugh Kenner calls the 'complex hermetic miseries' of this text elaborate a theme that has no resolution. Like *Ping*, a four-page fragment collected twelve years later in *No's Knife* (the title is drawn from the thirteenth 'text for nothing', where Beckett hears 'the screaming silence of no's knife in yes's wound'), *From an Abandoned Work* subscribes to Valéry's theory that a work is never completed, only abandoned in the midst of its composition. In a preface to the 1967 edition, the editors note: '*Ping* is all that is left of a novel that Mr. Beckett started on in late 1965.' It seems reasonable to say, then, that the texts after 1950 encounter a problem not entirely deliberate; since their development is entropic, tending toward a reduced state of consciousness, these works would appear to stipulate their own eventual disappearance. The dissolution of grammar, the reduction of language to mere sound notation, places Beckett's writing within the domain of contemporary criticism in France, where discussion no longer approaches an imaginative work as literature, but as *écriture*. The text has become an example, a literary artefact encircled by hermeneutics. Its intent is to provide a point of departure for speculation about linguistics, *critique de conscience* and phenomenology. The consequence of such practices is, of course, that literature forfeits its own interpretive capacities; where once it acted as a lens through which the social world could be magnified or distorted by the writer's own sensibility, now the work of art imitates theories of criticism, serving as a pretext for their otherwise unfocused energies. This explains why the progressive diminution of Beckett's work has been accompanied by the most elaborate criticism ever devoted to a contemporary (Kenner concludes his discussion of *Come and Go,* a miniature 'dramaticule', with the observation that he has written 'almost three times as many words as the text contains'), and why it requires the technical, immense apparatus of contemporary French criticism to support its lean structure.

Another feature of such enterprises is their claim to science; what are called in France *les sciences humaines* have increasingly taken over the procedures of science. Structuralism in linguistics, anthropology and psychoanalysis tends to construct exact and technical models, as if to refute any suspicion that such disciplines are still speculative or subjective. With science and its technological resources threatening to render imagination tautological (Adorno identifies in Beckett's *End Game* the notion that 'there really is not so much to be feared any more'), the only choice available to the writer who wishes to record this impingement of the actual upon the imagined is to appropriate science as a metaphor. So Beckett has erased from his texts those very features of literature which once made it capable of transcendence: fictions; imaginative re-creations of history; invented lives. His later texts plot a world circumscribed by mathematics. A remark he made once about the painter Jack Yeats informs his own work: 'He brings light, as only the great dare to bring light, to the issueless predicament of existence, reduces the dark where there might have been, mathematically at least, a door.' To locate this door demands the rigour of mathematics, and Beckett directs us, in *Imagination Dead Imagine,* to 'omit islands, waters, azure, verdure': in other words, all that represents the world in a figurative manner. Rather, we discover ourselves in a rotunda, 'Diameter three feet, three feet from ground to summit of the vault. Two diameters at right angles AB CD divide the white ground into two semicircles ACB BDA.' And *The Lost Ones (Le Dépeupleur,* 1970) inhabit a cylinder fifty metres round and eighteen high, from which escape seems possible, though none of the two hundred 'bodies' ever achieve it. *Enough* (1965) is Beckett's last attempt to report even the semblance of a story, though the discourse is entirely mathematical, expressed in what Kenner calls 'geometrical visualisations'; the narrative, told in the first person, relates the prolonged journey of a couple whose ages are unspecified, and the desertion of the other. Obsessive calculations of the distance travelled, 'Whole ternary numbers in this way to the third power sometimes in downpours of rain', dominate his recollections.

Lessness, Beckett's most recent published prose, announced a further diminution of landscape; the transition between 'subject object subject object' noted in *How It Is* has its counterpart in serial music, with its total organization of the tone row. In the twenty-four paragraphs of *Lessness*, each sentence is repeated once, and the sixty sentences that compose the work are divided in tens, within which each set features a recurrent word or phrase. There is no longer any question of episode or even voice; *Ping* has no verbs, and is orchestrated with an equivalent of rests: 'ping silence ping over'. Where, in *How It Is*, the absence of punctuation allows us to arrange the phrases to form variant readings, the later texts refuse even this modest anarchy, and insist on the suppression of randomness.

It could be said that Beckett has worked out the consequences of Modernism, producing the companion to Rauschenberg's white canvases. To wish that he had continued to write in the verbal, anecdotal tradition of Irish literature, or embroidered Proust, would be nostalgic; both *Finnegans Wake* and *A la Recherche du Temps Perdu* were the last comprehensive works in their respective literatures, when the totality of lived experience could be deposited in a book. Mallarmé had conceived a similar project, proposing that *Tout, au monde, existe pour aboutir à un livre.* Beckett's recent work constitutes the residuum of this *Livre*. There are moments, though, when I read these texts with the hope that, like Borges' Funes the Memorious, who devised a system in which all numbers were given special titles, he would provide us, not simply with ciphers, but with names to revive and enhance their value.

Flann O'Brien
by Lorna Sage

THAT THE past impoverishes the present is still, despite Yeats, the great burden of Irish writing. The windy, epic past, the oral culture, survives in tawdry rhetoric, evaporating events into talk, and suffering into a song, and dead people into a roll-call of heroes. Written things, made articles, the difficult word on the printed page, all have to compete with a readymade cadence, an easy accent, a continuous present tense that hasn't changed very much for centuries. Indeed, the complaint itself has long since become conventional, sucked into a sea of cant, so that one doubts at times whether there's anything in it.

Flann O'Brien, however, is an instance to dispel the doubts. Now that everything of importance has been published (eight years after his death — it seems symptomatic of his peculiarly marginal existence, on the boundaries of fiction, that it should have taken so long) the theme of poverty becomes inescapable. *The Poor Mouth,* written in Gaelic in 1941 (*An Béal Bocht*) and published in an English translation for the first time last year, proves ancient Ireland is dead-alive still. It is a wry, relentless anatomy of the Irish talent for suffering, glorifying suffering, and suffering more, and since it is built out of the very words and phrases and stock situations Gaelic writers employed to poeticize the hard life, makes its point twice over. Pastiche, of course, deliberately overbalances into parody — the endless rain becomes in O'Brien's hands a new deluge, with pigs and peasants and seals wallowing indistinguishably in a muddy soup; the self-inflicted misery is made to look like insane masochism; the isolation becomes a truly trance-like ignorance of even one's own extremities. The satire has a double target: not only the Gaelic writers whose lyrical clichés have turned squalid poverty into the poetry of suffering, but the 'poor Gael' himself, his own worst enemy. 'In Gaelic and in Anglo-Irish dialect', the translator says, ' "putting on the poor mouth" means making a pretence of being poor or in bad circumstances in order to gain advantage from creditors or prospective creditors' — in other words, real poverty is compounded by faking, and O'Brien's awful hero, Bonaparte O'Coonassa, assists at his own destruction.

Ignorance and the fine phrase ('I do not think that my like will ever be there again!') conspire to deny the possibility of change, of imaginative exploration of the world outside. It all recalls Joyce's nightmare perception in *Stephen Hero* (though with this significant difference, that O'Brien is writing in Gaelic, he stayed in Ireland):

> ...the old man blinked his red eyes at the fire and went on smoking evenly and talking to himself:
> – I've heerd tell them elephants is most natural things, that they has the notions of a Christian...I wanse seen meself a picture of niggers riding on wan of 'em – aye and beating blazes out of 'im with a stick. Begorra ye'd have more trouble with the children is in it now than with one of thim big fellows.
> The young lady who was much amused began to tell the peasant about the animals of prehistoric times. The old man heard her out in silence and then said slowly:
> – Aw, there must be terrible quare craythurs at the latther ind of the world.

History and geography, time and space, dwindle to a dim speculation. And Stephen's godfather stills the laughter the anecdote raises by saying, as if by rote, 'But we mustn't forget at the same time...that the peasant stands perhaps nearer to the true ideal of a Christian life than many of us who condemn him'. The automatic, mealy-mouthed piety and the absurd, red-eyed old man encapsulate the stupefying inertia that stands so menacingly between Stephen and imaginative freedom. In *A Portrait of the Artist,* this vignette, reduced to stereotype and without the comic elephants, is one of Stephen's final footnotes to his departure. And for all the similarities, you can see in this one of the contrasts between Joyce's measure of Ireland and O'Brien's: O'Brien would always, so to speak, leave the elephants in, he finds the old man and his like horribly funny, irresistible, he can't tear his attention away. *An Béal Bocht* was published under his other pseudonym, Myles na Gopaleen, the name he used for his regular satirical column in the *Irish Times*; he was, whether as Flann O'Brien, or Myles na Gopaleen, or Brian O'Nolan, a Dublin institution until he died there in the spring of 1966. The pull of inertia kept him home, his only distance was satiric, and he understood the red-eyed old man from the inside, perhaps better than Joyce ever did.

The action of *The Poor Mouth* is a black farce, so agonizingly slow-running that it seems almost static. O'Coonassa's mindless, sodden career follows all the conventions. When, for example, he returns from his first day at school, and tells his mother that the master beat him and told him his name was Jams O'Donnell, she explains the painful, inevitable decorum of it all:

> It was always said and written that every Gaelic youngster is hit on his first school day because he doesn't understand English, and the foreign form of his name, and that no one has any respect for him because he's Gaelic to the marrow...Alas! I don't think that there'll ever be any good settlement for the

Gaels but only hardship for them always. The Old-Grey-Fellow was also hit one day of his life and called *Jams O'Donnell* as well.
– Woman, said I, what you say is amazing and I don't think I'll ever go back to that school but it's now the end of my learning!
– You're shrewd, said she, in your early youth.

Equipped with this brand of changeless wisdom (none of the Jams O'Donnells has ever gone back to school), he shivers and scrapes and steals his way through life until, in the book's very last, extraordinary scene, he comes face to face with his destiny in a crowded station:

> I laid my eyes on one man, and, without any volition on my part, my gaze remained on him. It was apparent to me that there was something familiar about him. I had never seen him before but he was not a stranger in appearance. He was an old man, bent and broken and as thin as a stem of grass. He wore dirty rags, was bare-footed and his two eyes were burning in his withered skull. They stared at me.
>
> We approached timidly and slowly towards one another, filled with fear and welcome. I noticed that he was trembling, his lips were shaking and lightning shot from his eyes. I spoke to him quietly in English.
> – Phwat is yer nam?
> He spoke voice-brokenly and aimlessly.
> – Jams O'Donnell! said he.
> Wonder and joy swept over me as flashes of lightning out of the celestial sky. I lost my voice and I nearly lost my senses again.
> – My father!

Their ecstasy of tragic anagnorisis, however, is undercut by our cruel, comic suspicion that they're both mistaken. All Gaels are Jams O'Donnell, their fate is to be shapeless, nameless, aimless, with no memory and no future. What each recognizes in the other is the same old mess:

> – I'm told, said I, that I've earned twenty-nine years in the same jug.
>
> I wished that we had had conversation and that the eerie staring, which was confusing us both, should cease. I saw a softness creep into his eyes and settle over his limbs. He beckoned with his finger.
> – Twenty-nine years I've done in the jug, said he, and it's surely an unlovely place.
> – Tell my mother, said I, that I'll be back. . .

And so it goes, round again: nothing can change, nobody can learn anything.

The novel's imprisoning structure, returning on itself, is fairly clearly an emblem of the impoverished and impoverishing tradition. The plot is a treadmill parody of progress – there is no way of gathering experience into meaning, into a form that can be ingested and superseded; the past doesn't lend shape or dignity to the present, they confront each other helplessly, like two ragged Jams O'Donnells. Not that this is a judgement made from the outside, applying only to the mythical wisdom of the folk. *The Poor Mouth,* like each of his four English novels, is talking about O'Brien's own poverty too, though perhaps less elaborately than

they do. Its repetitious structure (promising an endless series of protagonists stretching, uncomprehending, back to infinity) is that which
lurks in the agile inventiveness of *At Swim-Two-Birds*, with its stories
inside stories, and its modern Dubliners rubbing shoulders with Finn
MacCool and Mad King Sweeney — just as wordy, just as violent, just as
blind. The past doesn't stay past in his books (in *The Dalkey Archive*
St Augustine gossips on in a Dublin accent) because it has not been
absorbed or transmuted. This was what John Wain was registering when
(in *Encounter* 28, 1967) after writing enthusiastically about O'Brien's
comic ingenuity, he recurred to the contrast with Joyce: 'Joyce's world
is bleak, but it is not elegiac. It affirms the stature of Man. . .O'Brien
remains a writer whose subject is not Man, but Irishman.' The Irish past
lives on, indestructibly, denying the present its uniqueness: new adventures don't merely recall, they *repeat* the old. And yet, with more of
this Irish O'Brien available now than Mr Wain had (apart from *The
Poor Mouth, The Third Policeman*, which was not published until 1967,
though it was written in 1940), his assumption that this paradoxical
trap doesn't concern the wider world — that Man is much wiser than
Irishman — looks less convincing. At least, it's clear that O'Brien was
thinking all along about the writer's role in a way that made Joyce's
self-exile seem redundant. In *The Third Policeman* it is revealed that
eternity is located 'up a lane that is found by looking at cracks in the
ceiling of a country policeman's bedroom'. Less startlingly, one can see
how the obsessive analysis of Ireland's past and present could itself
become the all-absorbing topic, a model for a universal human — or,
rather, inhuman — experience.

*

In fact, O'Brien argued a lot of this out with Joyce in the novels. *At
Swim-Two-Birds* borrows the great artificer's strategies, like encyclo-
paedism and parody, and turns them into a recipe for hilarious
imaginative squalor, with characters, incidents and phrases reasserting
their own stubborn, untidy identities against their creator's will. All the
joins show, the fragments remain separate, the bits and pieces of heroic
poetry, Dublin slang, popular science, skirmish uncontrollably with
each other, for ever unreconciled. And what this implies is not so much
that Joyce's grand synthesizing ambition has come to seem impossible
— as that it seems destructive and deluded. The would-be artists in *At
Swim-Two-Birds* are not to be trusted, their very urge to shape and
control and possess the world springs from murky depths of envy and
unreason. By the end they are being compared to those poor lunatics
who pursue through life a phantom of order:

One man will think he has a glass bottom and will fear to sit in case of breakage. In other respects he will be a man of great intellectual force and will accompany one in a mental ramble throughout the labyrinths of mathematics or philosophy so long as he is allowed to remain standing throughout the disputations. . .One man will rove the streets seeking motor cars with numbers that are divisible by seven. Well known, alas, is the case of the poor German who was very fond of three and who made each aspect of his life a thing of triads. He went home one evening and drank three cups of tea with three lumps of sugar in each, cut his jugular three times and scrawled with a dying hand on a picture of his wife, good-bye, good-bye, good-bye.

You are meant to feel a kind of comic awe in the face of such helpless unreason — and to conclude that, in such a world, what you need is not a distant writer of epics but a resident jester, a satirical voice at your ear to remind you of your infirmity.

Joyce's freedom, on this view, comes to seem false, and in *The Dalkey Archive* he makes a posthumous appearance to prove the point. He is discovered working incognito behind a nondescript bar in Skerries: he disclaims all responsibility for *Ulysses* (it was put together, he claims, by a gang of 'Muck-rakers, obscene poets, carnal pimps' for money) and he has never heard of *Finnegans Wake* (though he knows the song). Instead, he has devoted his creative energies to writing pamphlets for the Catholic Truth Society, bowdlerizing European literature, and disproving the existence (or at least the orthodoxy) of the Holy Ghost. 'The garrulous, the repatriate, the ingenuous' have displaced silence, exile, and cunning: the new James Joyce is all the Irish who banned his books could desire. It's a cruelly double-edged joke. On the one hand, the point is simply to show how monstrous Joyce would have been if he *had* been as good Catholics would like him. On the other hand, there is the insidious suggestion that one can detect, after all, something of the Jesuit aspirant, the misanthrope, the dogmatist in him — that his immersion in literary metaphysics insulated him from the processes of living, despite his escape from Ireland.

Or the man may not really be Joyce at all, but simply a madman with delusions of grandeur. The aim of these jokey manoeuvres is to map out where O'Brien stands himself. He distrusts absolutely the timid, prurient pieties of home, but he cannot believe in the literary orthodoxy (which says that the writer re-creates his world) either. Inertia is the answer. The changeless unreason in people seems to him awfully true, the truest thing about them; it infects all their enterprises, and turns their heroic gestures into sad comedy. And so, wryly, he accepts the readymade languages, the indigestible past — monstrous and absurd as they are, they are the pittance he has inherited. It makes a kind of sense; at least it's a very ingenious route for arriving back where you are. But where is that? Certainly not in the dour, disciplined world of Samuel Beckett, Joyce's other great fictional critic. Beckett's version of the Irish writer's poverty is one which has led him to empty out and re-invent his language — to banish old associations, to substitute grammar for rhetoric, to write in French. He is a tense, restless stylist, obsessively controlled, a world away from O'Brien's promiscuous pastiche. To find analogues for O'Brien one has to look in odder corners, where writing fiction has become a selfconsciously marginal business.

For example, in Jorge Luis Borges's philosophical fables, or in Vladimir Nabokov's explorations of imaginative imprisonment. They share O'Brien's scepticism about Joyce and all that Joyce stands for (except that for them, of course, he is more distant — the great modernist, not a treacherous compatriot). They take the same sort of perverse delight in the observation that art *cannot* rescue us from our limitations. Nabokov in his afterword to *Lolita* suggests mockingly that the book's first inspiration was 'a newspaper story about an ape in the Jardin des Plantes who, after months of coaxing by a scientist, produced the first drawing ever charcoaled by an animal: this sketch showed the bars of the poor creature's cage'. And what he implies is that we have not come very far from there: our fictional excursions are an immensely elaborate way of registering that dim, primitive perception (compare the Jams O'Donnells). Most telling, though, is the fact that all three writers are the hapless victims of a single structural idea — the demoralizing notion of infinite regress. That one banal, inexhaustible concept is all things to them, infuriating, depressing, amusing in turn. Each story they tell becomes a story within a story, and each character becomes a bamboozling series of selves.

Borges, in *Avatars of the Tortoise,* traced the history of this idea, and put a name to it — Zeno's paradox, first propounded by the Eleatic philosopher in the fifth century B.C., a dialectic which 'proves' that change is impossible, and motion an illusion. Zeno's paradox can be applied in many different ways, which is part of its dangerous attraction; O'Brien attributes this version of it to his demented man of science, De Selby, in *The Third Policeman:*

> If one is resting at A, he explains, and desires to rest in a distant place B, one can only do so by resting for infinitely brief intervals in innumerable intermediate places. . .points infinitely near each other yet sufficiently far apart to admit of the insertion between them of a series of other 'inter-intermediate' places, between each of which must be imagined a chain of other resting-places — not, of course, strictly adjacent but arranged so as to admit of the application of this principle indefinitely.

The argument that motion is a series of 'rests' fits in beautifully with O'Brien's vision of Irish inertia. You don't need, if you think about it, to move at all. Indeed you don't move. De Selby, we're told, makes an epic journey from Bath to Folkestone by shutting himself up in a room with lots of picture postcards of the countryside in between, 'together with an elaborate arrangement of clocks and barometric instruments and a device for regulating the gaslight'.

Apart from retailing such extraordinary experiments, *The Third Policeman* affords a great deal of evidence of the effects of Zeno's paradox on one's view of the world: actions are fragmented into parts until they arrive at near-stasis; the flow of time breaks apart into droplets, each of which contains within it further tiny bubbles; narrative is a series of stills. The materials of life are all there, but the dynamism has gone. The main character (who cannot remember his name) experiences things vividly, but as separate events, any of which may open out into a whole series of further events when he inspects it closely. Both his inner and outer lives are described so as to appear subtly discontinuous, lacking in fluidity and purpose. He has murdered an old man for a black box of money, but the box keeps receding from his consciousness; when he does remember it, he cannot remember what he wants it for. His adventures in search of it, or in search of the reason why he is searching for it, lead him to an extraordinary, two-dimensional police station where, through every device of vertigo, he is shown the nature of his brutal stupidity. He comes, painfully, to the terrifying conclusion that he found the black box long ago, that it was a bomb, and that he is dead. However, that is not the end of the book. In the final pages, we watch him beginning anew in the search, describing it in exactly the same words, with the same expressions of perplexity and wonder. What was in the black box was a black box. He has learned nothing. He has plumbed depths of greed, hate, remorse and tenderness, but they have nothing to do with each other, it is as if they belonged to different people. He is doomed to live his life in death over and over, an intermediate man.

The Third Policeman is perhaps O'Brien's best book: certainly it is a most impressive balancing-act on the edge of infinity, rivalling Nabokov's illusionist performance in his latest novel, *Transparent Things.* That too is about life in death and the nightmare of never being able to put anything right, or turn experience into wisdom. 'It is generally assumed' someone wearily notes in that book, 'that if man were to establish the fact of survival after death, he would also solve, or be on the way to solving, the riddle of Being. Alas, the two problems do not necessarily overlap or blend.'

*

For Nabokov, this tragi-comic reflection seems to be bound up with his own discontinuous *émigré* past, in which many lives and many selves have jostled without forming a unity. His pasts live on in the here and now, unmodified and restive: so that, for instance, in *Ada* (1969) he describes a hybrid, deliberately impossible country which is both Russia and America, and an equally impossible history which jumbles together the nineteenth and twentieth and twenty-first centuries.

Belonging to a tradition, and filling his mind with the words and images of the past, is supposed to help a writer transcend his individuality and acquire an authority not his own. However, when, as these writers do, you neutralize the mysterious mental acids that break down experiences, and enable them to be digested, then their accumulation becomes degrading and sickening. Borges's story *The Immortal* shows the piling-up of words over centuries into a Tower of Babel. An immortal bard, Homer, is imagined as having literally lived on, until he has become a naked, grey-skinned troglodyte, speechless through satiety and indifference, his identity dissipated in 'words, displaced and mutilated words, words of others'. The story (which was written in Spanish, and first translated into English in 1960) is itself a cento, a patchwork made up of scraps and fragments of other people's writings, and the narrator shifts disconcertingly from 'he' to 'I' to 'we'. It is more watertight and more obsessively literary than anything O'Brien wrote, but its central vision of the sub-human immortal is matched uncannily in *The Poor Mouth* where, in a cave on a barren, sodden mountain the hero finds an obscenely aged Gaelic bard, whom he takes at first for dead:

> A few unrecognisable rags were wrapped around him, the skin of his hand and face was like wrinkled brown leather and he had an appearance totally unnatural about him. His two eyes were closed, his black-toothed mouth was open and his head inclined feebly to one side. . .
> — He has nothing to say, said I, half to myself and half aloud.
> My heart faltered once more. I heard a sound coming from the corpse which resembled someone speaking from behind a heavy cloak, a sound that was hoarse and drowned and inhuman which took my bodily vigour from me for a little while.
> — *And what narrative might give thee pleasure?*

And he starts, like an automaton, on a windy fiction couched in the archaic language of centuries ago.

*

O'Brien's Irishness is also his claim to universality. Not that the native tradition is richer than it looked to Joyce — rather, the wide world seems poorer than it used to, and O'Brien is an expert in imaginative poverty. To say that he belongs with Borges and Nabokov is hardly to flatter him, since what they have in common is an elaborate futility, a shameless retreat from ambition. O'Brien is not unique, not an eccentric, but perhaps the most honest (certainly the funniest) exponent of this Tower of Babel theory of the novel. That we have failed to read his books (with the possible exception of *At Swim-Two-Birds*) in the right company was partly his fault. He seems to have distrusted readers: when the reissue of *At Swim* in 1960 received some of the attention it deserved, he published in 1961 *The Hard Life* and in 1964 *The Dalkey Archive*, both of which tone down the analysis of human stupidity and the dreadful comedy of infinite regress to the point where they could be mistaken for a more familiar mix of drabness and whimsy. *The Third Policeman* (written in 1940) and *An Béal Bocht* (1941) were the uncompromising originals.

However, there is none of his fiction one would willingly discard. The following quiet, pastoral passage (which appears more or less unchanged in both *The Third Policeman* and *The Dalkey Archive*) should show why. It is not exceptional, it simply reveals O'Brien's continuous, sceptical awareness of the implausibility of living:

> I looked carefully around me. Brown bogs and black bogs were arranged neatly on each side of the road with rectangular boxes carved out of them here and there, each with a filling of yellow-brown brown-yellow water. Far away near the sky tiny people were stooped at their turf-work, cutting out precisely shaped sods with their patent spades and building them into a tall memorial twice the height of a horse and cart. Sounds came from them to the Sergeant and myself, delivered to our ears without charge by the west wind, sounds of laughing and whistling and bits of verses from the old bog-songs. Nearer, a house stood attended by three trees and surrounded by the happiness of a coterie of fowls, all of them picking and rooting and disputating loudly in the unrelenting manufacture of their eggs. The house was quiet in itself and silent but a canopy of lazy smoke had been erected over the chimney to indicate that people were within engaged on tasks. Ahead of us went the road, running swiftly across the flat land and pausing slightly to climb slowly up a hill that was waiting for it in a place where there was tall grass, grey boulders and rank stunted trees. The whole overhead was occupied by the sky, serene, impenetrable, ineffable and incomparable, with a fine island of clouds anchored in the calm two yards to the right of Mr Jarvis's outhouse.

The elegant, geometrical layout of the opening, the ingratiating behaviour of the wind, the trees, the cloud-island, conspire to produce an air of unreality, as though the whole thing were as fragile as a masque. The illusionist perspectives are too well-done to deceive: in the two dimensions of this scene, the people *are* tiny, the island of clouds *is* 'two yards to the right of Mr Jarvis's outhouse'; and the smoke has been erected over the chimney to trick us into imagining people in the pasteboard house. And if human life is kept at a distance, the wind, the hens, and the road keeping its assignation with the hill advance into the foreground, so that there is no hierarchy, no great chain of being. Time, too, is flattened: the 'turf-work' is done with 'patent spades', the west wind 'delivered. . .free of charge', the courtly trees and the 'coterie of fowls' coexist with the 'unrelenting manufacture of. . .eggs'. In this landscape, nothing supersedes or overlaps anything else; or, in the terms of mad De Selby, this is a 'resting-place' which, if you inspect it care-

fully, is made up of other resting-places. You could find yourself staying
here for ever.

Constants in Contemporary
Irish Fiction
by Roger Garfitt

'The first constant was water' — John McGahern

Introduction

AT ONE point in his autobiographical novel *Black List, Section H,* (Southern Illinois University Press, 1971, Martin Brian & O'Keefe, 1975) when H is vainly searching for a kindred spirit among the writers of contemporary, (that is, prewar) English fiction, Francis Stuart remarks, 'What he'd yet no inkling of was that ninety-nine percent of seriously considered English novels were social commentaries of one kind or another without any pretensions to communication on the level where he was listening.' From that admittedly idiosyncratic dismissal of English fiction, let us turn to a summary of modern Irish fiction, in which Sean O'Faolain is being equally hard on his fellow countrymen. He is discussing the fact that,

> The greater number of all Irish writers in prose, verse or drama, deal with rural life . . . The main effect on our literature is that it is not, as yet, intellectually sophisticated. To take extreme examples, an Anouilh, a Sartre or a Montherlant would be unthinkable in Dublin. I feel certain that there is a close connexion between the two things: realism and thought are inseparable. No realistic writer can expand beyond a merely descriptive local naturalism, can universalize his subject until he knows it not merely with his senses but with his intellect. When the thing ceases to exist for him in impersonal isolation it becomes part of his whole life as a man passionately pondering on the entire human condition. He will not then pass cold judgements or moralize explicitly — either would be a great bore — but he will quietly, even imperceptibly provoke his readers towards that end. It is what all the greater novelists do. We Irish do not, so far, ponder deeply or write realistically.

> (*The Irish,* Penguin, 1969, pp. 130–1.)

Somewhere between these two statements, in their area of shared concern, the characteristic virtues of contemporary Irish fiction seem to lie. Sean O'Faolain, in fact, has been more prophetic than observant, in that he seems unaccountably blind to certain writers who come close to fulfilling the very requirements he laid down. His summary makes no mention of Francis Stuart, John McGahern, Aidan Higgins or Kevin Casey, all of whom had published significant work by the time at which he was writing. While making specific and intelligent use of Irish social conditions, the best of the new writing never rests at being a social commentary. Rather it is directed, with a clarity of aim and a quiet seriousness of purpose unusual in contemporary fiction, beyond the social framework, to the framework of birth and death, and what passes between them. It is here, surely, that we can perceive the quality of mind O'Faolain was asking for. The Irish have not developed an intellectual sophistication, although in a sense McGahern is perhaps the most truly Existentialist writer working in English today. What they have developed, and what gives their work its distinctive tension, is a passionate sense of the human condition.

Sophistication, indeed, may be the labyrinth they have refused to enter. At a time when fiction generally seems preoccupied with un-expected angles or multiple vision, their work possesses, by comparison, a simple but crucial perspective. Tradition and experiment spring from the same source, tradition from a framework that has been found to encompass basic questions, experiment from the need to rephrase those questions. Innovation then becomes a necessity, the imagination's hard-won expression. This does not seem to be the position in English and American fiction today. There is a great deal of innovation of a secondary sort. It is as if, in the absence of any ultimate, exterior frame of reference, attention is devoted increasingly to ingenious infra-structure. The writers I am examining are traditionalists, in terms of the modern novel – only early Stuart and early Higgins could possibly be called experimental, and then only to a limited extent – but they demonstrate just how much can be achieved by an intelligent renewal of traditional style. Their virtue is that they retain, not a sense of direction, which is tradition in full strength, but a sense of inquiry, a sense of concern. For them too, the social, moral and metaphysical nexus, the traditional framework of belief, has collapsed: but it has left a framework of questions in the air.

A number of reasons can be suggested why such questions have remained vividly apparent in Ireland, and not in England. One is that, as O'Faolain points out, most of the novels have a rural setting. In rural society, just as in urban, the articulate young grow up to find a vacuum: only there the outlines of the vacuum, as it were, remain clear. They can see around them the shape of a structure that once worked. The Big House in the last stages of decline has been the symbol for this in more than one Irish novel. Rural society preserves the question marks: at the same time it avoids the hectic trends, the improvisations on a

Lost Chord, of the urban middle classes. There is a strong theme of the loneliness and the pettiness of small town society, but only one or two writers, notably Mary Lavin, have become enmeshed to any limiting extent in provincial *mores*.

There is another aspect to this isolation, which Sean O'Faolain catches very well in 'Feed My Lambs', when he describes a car crossing the bogland 'as slowly as a dot of light emerging from one mirror and as slowly dwindling into another'. Inevitably, social history is one half geography. If one had to make one simple distinction, it might be that whereas English and American fiction seems to be written *puncto temporis,* out of the complexities of a moment of time, Irish fiction has a sense of the clouds flowing over the rim of the horizon, the days' procession towards World's End. Thus far, Chekhovian in temperament: but without Chekhov's deployment of the group, the full complement of the Ship of Fools. Recent Irish fiction has a distinctly individual focus, centring on a single articulate person, questioning existence among others who are less bothered, or too busy to care. This may well be the result of the first generation spread of higher education to the working population, the same phenomenon that gave England in the fifties a sudden rash of novels about the industrial Midlands. Only in England the novelists quickly became sidetracked into class distinctions, and the absorbing topic of social climbing. In Ireland, for the reasons suggested above, this mercifully hasn't happened, and we have a much clearer sense of the novelist writing from within a community from which he is separated by awareness, but to which in sympathy he still belongs.

The residual strength of the Catholic religion is undoubtedly another factor. Sean O'Faolain has suggested that the main importance of the priesthood in Irish life is now its political influence, in particular its conservative approach to all questions of thought and discussion. To say this already allows the Church a considerable role in public life: but in terms of Irish fiction, at least, the Church has an even more potent influence in private life, in the individual conscience. In McGahern's *The Dark* (Faber, 1965) the boy sees the priesthood as a taking of death into life, and thereby a conquering of the encompassing fear of death. This is very much the impression one has from a whole range of writing. The Catholic faith seems to act as a *memento mori,* in the widest sense. Even to those who no longer accept it, it presents a constant opposition, the challenge of values that make an ultimate claim. An engrained way of thought, it persistently enters the consciousness, no longer perhaps as light at the end of the tunnel, more often as darkness on either side of transition, but, in either case, establishing terminal points, a final frame of reference. Perhaps the most striking example is Sean O'Faolain's own short story 'Lovers of the Lake', where a middle-aged woman persuades her lover to take her to the pilgrimage at Lough Derg, the most rigorous and primitive of rituals, including three days' fast, a vigil and barefoot circuits of the rocky island. The situation is peculiarly Irish, as O'Faolain meant it to be. What is extraordinary, though, and crucial to the character of Irish writing today, is not the contradiction between their relationship and the act of penance — whether or not the affair will resume after the pilgrimage is a moot point, though on balance it seems likely it will — but the very fact that an affair between two such worldly people could be submitted to so unworldly a challenge. Nor is this simply a negative, puritan impulse: whether or not the lovemaking survives, their love has already grown, by an immeasurably deepened experience of each other. Whatever one thinks of the belief involved, it forces people to look at their lives *sub specie aeternitatis,* and that creates, at the very least, a more searching perspective. We are back to the distinction between *puncto temporis* and the sense of transience, and to the earlier distinction between infra-structure and a framework of questions. A number of different factors seem to have combined to keep perspectives wide, and the focus sharp. The distinctive feature of contemporary Irish fiction is a consequent concentration of the imagination on the enigma of existence, and on the individual's attempt to come to terms with it. There is a penetrating concern, a seriousness and a liveliness of the inquiring faculty, which is all too rare in writing today. Traditional structures have wavered or collapsed: but experience is still searched and tested against the background of a fairly rigid society, and in the shadow of absolute religious standards. For the writer, this situation balances freedom with astringency. Although the discovery of individual truth can be inhibited by such forces, it is more often, by their very pressure, forced into being.

There may be literary reasons too. One is the comparative health of the short story in Ireland. Free of the novel's commitment to reflect the complexities of its own time, the short story can go straight for the timeless issues, and so often turns out to be the more ambitious as well the more incisive form. Another reason may lie quite simply in the publishing situation of Irish writers. To make a living, and to enter the larger literary world, they have to aim beyond an Irish readership, at England and often at America. For frankly commercial reasons, they are committed to universality. They have, as it were, a modern Dr Johnson at their elbow, in the person of their agent, urging them to write for all mankind. All purely local, circumstantial detail must be made intelligible. And so the story is sifted out, and cast into an essential form. It is not by chance that the Irish, with the exception of Aidan Higgins, who has the indulgence of an avant-garde publisher, are among the most economical as well as the most plangent of modern writers. One can see the process at work most clearly, perhaps, in the novels of Jennifer Johnston, where specifically Irish situations are distanced, to achieve a spare, almost parable-like form, which is half their quality. There is still, of course, a certain market for Irishry, particularly in America: but even that, in its way, involves a selection from reality and towards the making of an artefact, an Arcadia in the west.

For once, commercial sense is a literary virtue. That does not explain literary merit, though, nor does any of the above social analysis. Of all literary forms, it is perhaps the novel which has the most delicate balance to hold, between reflecting the contemporary flux, the idiosyncrasies not even of an age but of a decade or of particular years, and confronting the common, unchanging mysteries of the human condition. In a society as fascinated by change as our own, and as uncertain of anything else, the balance tips more easily, it seems to me, towards the vivid and contemporary. It is the mark of the major writer to catch the immediate detail and extend its resonance, to set it echoing beyond its own time.

FRANCIS STUART

Perhaps the one aspect of Francis Stuart that is beyond argument is the consistency of his development over forty-five years of writing. *Black List, Section H,* the autobiographical novel in which he traces his actual progress along a path already foreshadowed in his instinct, is described as 'an imaginative fiction'. In that it includes a fair degree of self-justification, it could also have benefited from a measure of hindsight. Its testimony, however, is corroborated by the work itself. Stuart's remark in *The Pillar of Cloud* (Gollancz, 1948, republished Martin Brian & O'Keeffe, 1974) that 'one's own future is already contained within oneself, as the tree within the acorn' is true of himself to a striking extent. He deliberately sought out the future that he needed, and in this sense the key experiences of his own life, particularly the period in Germany during and just after the Second World War, should not be seen as formative but rather as confirmative of his own intuition.

Already in his second novel, *Pigeon Irish* (Gollancz, 1932) the themes are beginning to form which preoccupy him for the rest of his career. The novel ends with a man who has lost everything, wife, position, and the trust of his fellow men, keeping only the relationship with one woman, the girl Catherine who originally inspired him with her ideas. Attaining this condition of total loss, defined in *The Pillar of Cloud* as 'an inner stripping bare', is here the climax of the novel, the prelude to a new understanding that remains undefined. In later Stuart novels it becomes a prior condition, the matrix from which all his characters emerge.

The final isolation of Catherine and Frank comes after the failure of an attempt to establish small communities in which the Irish spirit can be preserved against the deadening influence of 'super-civilisation'. Almost all subsequent Stuart novels focus on the establishment of a small, informal community, disparate by every normal standard, but enshrining the understanding, more instinctive than intellectual, of a new way of life. The fundamental experience uniting the communities is, again, destitution, the necessity of which, as a prerequisite for any sort of understanding or communion, is already hinted at in *Pigeon Irish:* 'Suffering together brought people close, upsetting the formal mechanism that made intimacy difficult.' It is the sweeping away of these formal mechanisms, and the exploration of what can grow once they have been swept away, that preoccupy Stuart throughout his work. 'The Irish spirit' is seen as the only force that can resist 'super-civilisation' and the 'levelling of contrasts', later personified in Polensky in *The Pillar of Cloud,* that it brings: 'Contrast . . . that's what one doesn't get too much of outside Ireland. . . Life is not divided up into such watertight compartments in Ireland as it is almost everywhere else. Religion and sex and sport overlap. So that even a race meeting has its tragic side, and lovers disentangle their arms to cross themselves as the Angelus rings.' Religion and sex and sport are a recurring source of reference in Stuart's work: what unites them is that they are all in some sense anarchic and transcendent, a challenge to the 'formal mechanisms' that constitute the generally accepted notion of reality. It is in centring on these states of mind which are peripheral to the ordinary sequence of reality but central to any consideration of the meaning of human life that *Pigeon Irish* is finally most typical of Stuart's work. His whole canon can be seen as an attempt to displace formal mechanisms, and to create conditions in which such experiences are no longer anarchic or transcendent; conditions in which their creative energy is released, and in which there is a continuity of meaning between the smallest action and deepest impulse, so that transcendence can give way to immanence, to what Stuart later calls the 'fullness of measure', as Dominic and Halka experience it in *The Pillar of Cloud.*

> It was something which they could never touch or examine, but they were conscious of it. They felt themselves like the field in which it was hidden, this pearl. Or sometimes it was the room in which it was hidden; at least it was somewhere, in the air, in themselves, that they felt day by day, this hidden balm of life. It was in all that they did, under all that they did. Her body was luminous with this lambent glow to him; in her breasts and in her belly it burnt. But it passed from her body into a thought; what they read together sometimes was the vessel, the measure in which the balm was measured and poured out on them. Or in other ways, in other things. In a simple meal that they shared together, opening a tin, slicing the bread. All was a measure that held the balm, or the field in which the treasure lay buried. There was no division into sensual and spiritual. There was no division or weighing or measure. The measure in which life was given to them was running over, always full and overflowing so that they were filled and fulfilled.

The effect of these concerns is to give Stuart's novels a prophetic and

evangelistic function. In *Black List, Section H* he expresses his dismay
at finding literature treated as an activity separate from life. This attitude
he shared with D. H. Lawrence, and like Lawrence he has had to endure
a period of controversy and banned books. Unlike Lawrence, he has
also had to endure, over the last twenty years, a long period of neglect,
for the close association of literature with life has never been popular in
literary circles, and while Stuart's evangelistic concerns, are, if anything,
more fundamental than Lawrence's, they are less provocative of public
attention. It has undoubtedly been harmful to his prospects of serious
consideration that he is both more sensational than Lawrence, in the
major, or challenging sense of that word, and less sensational in the
lesser, or epidermal sense.

This neglect may well have had a deleterious effect on Stuart's later
work, causing him to overstate the revolutionary aspect of his insights,
and to exaggerate the perversity of the means by which they were
reached. The talk in *Black List* of 'extreme areas of consciousness' and
of 'lonely and dangerous paths' somewhat belies the deeply humane
and central concerns of his major novels (which I take to be those
written in the years immediately following the Second World War) as
well as giving no idea of their delicacy and restraint. For one action,
however, which has widely been considered perverse, and which has
certainly damaged Stuart's chances of recognition in his lifetime, *Black
List* does offer a complete, idiosyncratic, but most moderate explanation.
This is Stuart's residence in Berlin during the Second World War, and
his broadcasts to Ireland on behalf of the Germans. To put it at its
simplest, it was essential to the development of Stuart's psyche that he
put himself, at some point, beyond the pale, and this his association
with the Nazis effectively did. To assume from this, however, that he
had any sympathy for Nazi aims, or that he wished to see a Nazi
Europe, is to neglect the other half of this eccentric equation, for it
was equally necessary to the development of his psyche for him to place
himself on the losing side. It was in the desolation of postwar Germany,
among the starving population and the displaced persons, among the
hopeless, the criminal and the chronically sick, that he found the
experience of destitution he had instinctively sought, and out of which
his major works, with the excitement and certainty of a long-awaited,
logical development, were rapidly, even obsessively written. As Dominic
expresses it, in Stuart's first postwar novel, *The Pillar of Cloud* (completed in 1947, published in 1948): 'it was out of pain and suffering
that if there was to be a new peace, it would be shaped. . . I gradually
had a stronger and stronger desire to be among those who were suffering
most.'

The central impulse of the novels is towards establishing a small
community – Stuart explicitly compares it to the biblical 'where two or

three are gathered together. . .' — in which a new way of life grows out of a new understanding. From the rebel group in *Pigeon Irish* to the Provisionals' Community Centre in *Memorial* (Martin Brian & O'Keeffe, 1973), the novels remain autobiographical to the extent that there is always a recognizable Stuart figure, variously called Dominic, Ezra Arrigho, Louis, Fintan F. Sugrue etc. (as Mr Barkis would say, not a Christian name among the lot of 'em) who is usually either a writer or a sculptor, and a female figure clearly derived from the girl called Halka in *Black List*, who remains Halka in *The Pillar of Cloud*, becomes Margareta in *Redemption* (Gollancz, 1949, republished Martin Brian & O'Keeffe, 1975) and Alyse in *The Flowering Cross* (Gollancz, 1950). Only the Stuart figure, and sometimes the Halka figure and perhaps Father Mellows in *Redemption*, are able to be articulate about the community's changed awareness. Others belong to them or are drawn towards them out of a similar hardship, but have only an intuitive understanding of what their association means.

The value that Stuart assigns to the suffering and the deprived is that their experience has given them a more immediate perception of the central issues of existence. It is not that everyday things have been swept away, but that the everyday has been re-assessed in the light of mortality. It is not the suffering itself that is important, but the radical change that suffering brings about in one's perceptions and one's scale of values. Whether they are blind, crippled or simply destitute, whether they are men who have been imprisoned for an indefinite period without cause or women who have been compelled to prostitute themselves in order to survive, what unites all Stuart's protagonists is that all have had, in some way, an experience of radical shock.

For the men in particular the key experience is imprisonment. Stuart several times describes the moment when a prisoner's personal possessions are taken from his pockets and laid on the table in front of him for confiscation, and the sensation this gives almost of a private, inner skin being stripped away. He is equally quick to spot other moments when personality is threatened by the unthinking procedures of authority, witness Dominic watching a fellow-prisoner, 'The light in the pupils was as though shattered: it came to him at that moment how fear seemed to break up the light of the eye, which was the light of the heart, into an incoherence', or Father Thaddeus' concern, in *Good Friday's Daughter* (Gollancz, 1952), with the dehumanizing effect of an ordinary, civilian prison, 'the denial of the unique and concrete person'. The sexual abasement to which the woman figure has sometimes to submit is perhaps an equivalent experience, the loss of final modesty, the stripping-away of the last privacy.

It is important here to correct the impression given by Frank

Kermode — who has been, it should be said, virtually the only English critic of recent years to remind the world of Stuart's existence — that Stuart's work 'exhibits a sort of heterodox sex-laden Catholic mysticism'. 'Sex-laden' is a provocative epithet to apply. What matters to Stuart is not sexuality but tenderness. The most distinct quickening of excitement, which is very like a sexual quickening, is in the presence of pain, for it is the experience of pain, he believes, that unlocks the perception. It is almost as if sexuality belongs to the old way of feeling, and tenderness to the new. One only has to compare the weariness with which Ezra in *Redemption* takes Romilly's virginity, as a necessary step to rid her of her imprisoning purity, with the eagerness with which Dominic faces Halka 'in a new way'. Tenderness is both an act of appreciation, a celebration of the spirit liberated from complacency, and a carrying forward of the new experience into love-making: 'the tender damp flesh was like something newly opened, or newly broken out of its shell'. It is significant that the dominant emotion Dominic feels towards Halka is *fraternity* — the same emotion that he feels towards her young sister Lisette, and which equally governs the other small communities in Stuart's novels. In *Redemption* the love-making is put aside, as no longer of any account: it is physically possible for Ezra to make love to the crippled Margareta, for she had to submit to another man in the camp in order to secure her escape, but it no longer matters. The final act of tenderness is his sponging of her crippled body.

In fact, sexual desire, like other apparently normal drives, the desire for success or the desire for pleasure, belongs to a world of assumptions that Stuart's characters are no longer able to make. It is rather as Dominic reflects when his uncle goes off to play golf:

> In order to enjoy a good game of golf and come back to a glass or two of sherry in a well-appointed club-house, one must tacitly believe in the sacredness of property, in the sacredness of marriage, in the police force, in the established system of education. Dominic might once more play golf and even enjoy it, but it would always be with his tongue in his cheek, always with an amused wonder at there really being such things as golf links left in the world.

The essential quality of Stuart's central characters is that they have survived the collapse of all known forms of order, and that survival is the basic miracle of their new existence. On the other side of survival, tenderness replaces desire, just as gratitude replaces appetite. In this respect, Francis Stuart might seem eminently qualified to join Alvarez's 'select band of survivor-poets' — except that his response to destruction has been to face up, not to the violence it unleashes, but to the compassion.

The key experiences in Stuart's work have the quality of stillness after the storm. They begin with the interludes of silence in the Berlin blitz when 'a leaf falling and turning slowly in the still air was a peculiar balm' and recur as the sensation which informs the days that H and Halka spend in a German border town just before their joint arrest, when the simplest things, from H carrying their ration of a half-cabbage home through the snow to a piano recital in a wooden hall, 'echoed clearly and magically in this pure atmosphere'. This experience receives its definitive statement as that 'fullness of measure' which marks the closing pages of *The Pillar of Cloud,* quoted above. The quality of these days, the sense of a meaning uniting the simplest actions, even, somehow, in-dwelling the simplest objects, is fundamental to the conception of the communities in *Redemption* and *The Flowering Cross.* The attempt to live in the light of these moments of 'epiphany' is the central, uniting concern of Francis Stuart's work.

Such moments are symbolized, perhaps, by the story in the Gospels to which Stuart refers several times, of the disciples coming in from fishing on Lake Galilee and finding Christ grilling fish over a wood fire on the beach. That story has become a touchstone for Stuart because its mystery is contained in its naturalness, in the resurrected Christ performing a completely simple human act. For all Stuart's talk of 'defending extreme areas of consciousness', it is central, I think, to any understanding of his work to see that he is concerned, not with transcendence, but with immanence: so that although he sometimes describes himself in terms that might suggest a visionary of the other sort, concerned with glimpses of the unimaginable, the most important moments in his books always focus on the unextraordinary and the everyday. It is not that his characters pierce through to the Beyond, but that they suffer a shock which makes them notice the miraculous quality of the here and now.

This raises the whole question of Stuart's position as a Catholic writer. Though his handling of religious tradition may seem more Quaker at first, in that it is determinedly individual, the unorthodoxy springs from a concern to release the potency of what is believed in: hence the deliberate shock effect of statements like

> He [Christ] was the one prophet who did not promise peace on earth, but destruction and desolation. . . And He was the one prophet who has been right.   *(The Pillar of Cloud)*

> It's not the lesser sinner who's saved but the one whose despair is complete.
> *(Black List, Section H)*

Two of Stuart's guiding instincts come together here: one is his rejection of any compartmentalization, of belief being kept in one compartment and experience going into another, which is paralleled by his dismay at the thought of literature as an activity separate from life; the other is his opposition to any convention, on the grounds that convention leads to complacency which in turn leads to impercipience and inertia. Stuart's own conception of religious truth is consequently individual and intuitive, as expressed in this dialogue from *Black List:*

> I think that reality can express itself as well in fiction as in fact. Some fictions are completely true, and some facts are not true except on the most superficial level.
> That's beyond me.
> No, it isn't Maggie. Listen, let's take the Gospels. What we want to know is do they reflect reality, which is a better way of putting it than asking, are they true? Because the right question is the one that involves not just the upper mental surfaces in the answer. The worthwhile answers are in tune with the the deeper emotional and imaginative pulsations. Reasoning can't distinguish true from false except on fairly extraneous levels. Do you never feel inside you, Maggie, a series of nerve cells, some sort of fine chain, linking you with reality? I think, if we haven't broken it, we're aware of something like that, each link a little more substantial as it comes closer to consciousness, transforming the vibrations into what can just, as the last link, enter the mind as thought. What I'm getting at is that the Gospels, transmitted to us by this route, do have the impact of reality.

It is important to notice the direction of that last statement. It is not that the Gospels present a revealed truth, to which reality must match up, but that the Gospels have entered reality. In other words, religious truth is not an external frame of reference, but an energy felt within the current of the world. It is vital to see this in order to understand the character of Stuart's religious references. In *Memorial,* for instance, where they come thick and fast, linking the teenage Herra with the Magdalen, or the torn hare with the suffering Christ, if they are seen as ascriptions upwards, to a higher source of meaning, then they become absurd, giving the story a weight it will not bear: but if they are seen as marks of one and the same suffering, an anguish felt there and an anguish felt here, within a reality indissolubly one, then they return us to Stuart's characteristic emphasis on the simple and the everyday. In fact, the religious themes in Stuart's books are best understood in the light of the Catholic doctrine of Incarnation, which, as I understand it, teaches that with God's assumption of manhood in the person of Christ a divine factor has entered permanently into the affairs of men, or as Magnus puts it in George Mackay Brown's novel of that name, 'This crucifix is the forge and the threshing-floor and the shed of the net-makers, where God and man work out together a plan of utter necessity and of unimaginable beauty.' This seems to be the force, for instance, of Stuart's quotation from Julian of Norwich at the end of his first novel, *Women and God* (Cape, 1931) when, as the turmoil of the various couples' search for meaning settles into quietude, Colin has a memory of her description of Christ's passion:

> And in the coming-out the drops were brown-red, for the blood was thick; and in the spreading abroad they were light-red; and when they came to the

brows, then they vanished. . . The plenteousness is like the drops of water that fall off the eaves after a great shower of rain. . . and for roundness they were like the scale of herring, in the spreading on the forehead.

The effect of the quotation is not to exalt so much as to underline the seriousness of what has been undertaken. The light thrown upward onto the face of the dying Christ does not diminish the minor human uncertainties, the faintly ironic way, for example, that Frank's higher impulses dwindle to a cold, sober dawn on the long overnight train journey, nor does it magnify them: it simply includes them.

There is not space in this essay to detail Francis Stuart's limitations as a writer, but they can perhaps best be summarized by repeating that he is very much an evangelistic novelist, of the D. H. Lawrence type. In fact the most fruitful comparison seems to be with the work of Lawrence, whom Stuart admires but from whom he consciously diverges at a certain point. Thus, it is certainly a weakness that, with the occasional exception of the Halka figure, who never says much anyway, there is no one in the novels to challenge, or even to communicate, on an articulate level, with the Stuart figure. Woman may hold intuitive wisdom, and be moulded by suffering; but she is very much the mute companion of the man's researches, just as she is in Lawrence. A certain atmosphere of monologue results. Equally, like Lawrence, Stuart's work can seem repetitious, although, outside *Black List,* it never becomes as stridently insistent as Lawrence. Repetition, though, seems almost an irrelevant charge. Stuart's whole way of thought has led him to certain essentially simple but fundamental insights, which, in a sense, he can only repeat. It is perhaps a more serious limitation that his imagination carries him only to the perception of what a new way of life might be, and no further. Each of his communities was only at the foundation stage: its brief life might even be said to depend upon a sense of inevitable terminus, upon the suspension in crisis of the world outside. To ask more than this, though, is to ask literature to go beyond life, and at this point language ceases. By the end of *Women in Love* Birkin and Ursula are equally suspended in air; and Lawrence's subsequent ceaseless travelling, his quests to Mexico and Australia, were all part of the attempt to find a language in which to speak of anything other than the inherited cast of the western mind.

To go back, though, or even to stay where you are, is equally impossible, and this is made clear by the impassioned accuracy with which both Lawrence and Stuart demolish the society around them. Stuart is particularly good on the deadening influences that work against what he believes in, on what he calls 'the lack of contrasts' in modern life. In *The Flowering Cross* his study of the negative Polensky is quite as suggestive, perhaps finally more suggestive, than his study of the positive characters, Dominic and Alyse. Stuart is lucky, too, in that he has always had the differences of Ireland to return to, in a way that Lawrence could never return to the Nottinghamshire of the colliery towns, though they gave him his first touchstones of a way of life other than that proposed by the intellectual climate of his own day.

The comparisons end, though, on the important difference that Stuart has remained much more of a *maker* than Lawrence did. His themes are always intuitively felt and communicated. They grow from the structure and texture of the work itself. They include statement, but they do not resort to prolonged independent statement, as Lawrence's exposition does in his later work. On the other hand, there is nothing in Stuart to match the stylistic achievement of Lawrence's early work. Stuart's style has a rather orotund quality, a tendency to the sanctimonious. Within this, though, there is a consistent accuracy of expression, unobtrusive innovations of syntax and phrasing which show a careful control. At key moments, when accuracy at its most tense is married to the shaping cadence, the writing has a distinctive clarity and balance.

In *Black List, Section H,* his 'autobiographical fiction', the style is noticeably leaner, and better able to accommodate concrete detail. And as if to compensate for the rather grandiose, prophetic overtones, there is a delightful tongue-in-cheek humour, much of it directed at H himself, running through the narrative. As Frank Kermode pointed out in his review in the *Listener,* Stuart's method is to present H just as he was, with all his pretensions intact and unmitigated, but equally with all his fatuities evident and unobscured. This makes both for an unusual degree of honesty, and for an unusually subtle type of humour, a recurrent flicker of farce behind the poker-faced style.

In *Black List* Stuart rather gives the impression that the books he is aiming to write will be like nothing ever seen before: he subscribes to a 'subjective, imaginative style' and speaks of 'an all-obsessive and perilous inward journey'. In the event, in their formal aspects his books are markedly traditional. They *are* deeply original in thought: but even the more unusual of them, such as *Pigeon Irish,* do not desert the conventional narrative structure. The distinction is very relevant to Stuart's achievement, for what gives his novels their conviction is that, while they proceed from an idiosyncratic rationale, they are not in themselves idiosyncratic, or in any way bizarre.

Even the originality of their thought has to be carefully defined. One is left at the end of *Black List* uncertain whether or not H will find the insights he has been searching for, but expecting that if he does they will turn out to be something pretty odd. It is perhaps the most serious consequence of that long period of neglect that preceded *Black List* that Stuart dangerously misrepresents his own work. Essentially what he has done, in the major novels, is to take moments of perception that we all recognize as fundamental, but normally classify as subjective and un-assimilable, and assign to them an objective value. What is revolutionary is that his characters then attempt to live their lives in the light of such moments. There are insights which come to most of us at times of shock, particularly at confrontations with birth or death, which we respect, even cherish, but which we tend to lose sight of once routine is restored. Stuart has taken these deeper levels of experience and made them, rather than the interlocking reactions of normal social behaviour, the arbiters of future conduct. He is an innovator in this respect, that he has preserved narrative structure but discarded the social framework which that structure implies. He has built novels out of materials which are normally classified, and thereby dismissed, as the materials of lyric poetry.

Stuart is not able, any more than Lawrence was, to take his characters much beyond the threshold of a different consciousness: but, far more than Lawrence's evocation, first of otherness, then of a lost, primitive pulse, it is a consciousness of the here and now. Of all the writers who have made the extreme, rather than the norm, the basis of their work, Stuart seems to me the most central. The world of his imagination is one that restores meaning. In his work an insistent honesty, together with a quality that I can only call tenderness, combine to create a considered and moving re-assertion of human values. Not only does he manage, for instance, to be positive over very much the same ground over which Beckett is negative, but his vision seems to me at once more final in its courage, and more generous, more complete in its humanity, than Lawrence's, whose losing of the ego is essentially rather a private, even, paradoxically, rather a self-centred affair, aspiring to the impersonal rather than the selfless.

In *Black List, Section H* Stuart writes of the interludes of silence in the Berlin blitz as

> intimations of a reality that seemed to balance without annulling the one they were involved in. Looking up at the night sky above the park and gazing into the black depths in the pale shoal that ran across it, they glimpsed depths that weren't completely strange to them, and were conscious of contemplating reflections of abysses in themselves. The constellations were on the move, slowly spinning with a faint whirring that was the just audible beat of the silence they were in such need of.

I would like to set against this a passage from *The Pillar of Cloud,* in which Dominic makes love to Halka in an ancient, neglected graveyard, an area of peace in the destitute city: 'And there was Halka close to him, her breasts bare before him, the skin pale and almost luminous, not contradicting the tombstones, but completing them, both part of the one strange world, emblems of that called love and of that called death.' In this second passage, in which acceptance and abandonment become facets of one another, and the condition of mortality is equally the condition of life, Stuart seems to me to achieve exactly the quality that he found in that moment of the Berlin blitz, of being able to balance without annulling apparently opposing realities. It is in this quality that his work's distinctive achievement lies.

JOHN MCGAHERN

The work of John McGahern, though very different from Francis Stuart's in temperament, has this in common with it, that experience is lived, as it were, within sight of annihilation, and what values it can retain, it draws from this perspective. McGahern's settings are domestic, and precisely detailed. As Julian Jebb has written, he 'creates a small world indelibly' — but always with a distinct sense of terminus. Uncertainty has replaced the traditional destinations, and so the assumptions of transience are reversed: it is not that all things shall pass away, but that we travel towards emptiness.

This theme is reiterated, from the son in 'Wheels' watching 'my father come on the tractor, two creamery cans on the trailer, old felt hat on his head; I wondered if the sweat band stank as it used or if it was rotten now. I watched him take the cans off the trailer, then go inside, body that had started my journey to nowhere' to Sinclair's vision of mankind as, 'scratching our arses, refining our ignorance. Try to see some make or shape on the nothing we know', and the retired guests at 'Strandhill, The Sea' endlessly exchanging 'informations', 'always informations, informations about everythings, having come out of darkness now blinking with informations at all the things about them, before the soon when they'll have to leave'. It has its fullest expression in *The Barracks* (Faber, 1963), where Elizabeth Reegan, dying of cancer, faces 'the nowhere of herself': 'It seemed as a person grew older that the unknowable reality, God, was the one thing you could believe or disbelieve in with safety, it met you with imponderable silence. . .' Typically, Elizabeth is detached by this awareness from those about her, so that the awareness of loneliness only increases her isolation. There is a theme of 'internal exile', of an ordinary woman facing a world which stolidly refuses to let her call its bluff, that recalls the work of another Irish writer, George Buchanan's *Rose Forbes* (Faber, 1950). People move with dreamlike devotion about a clearly impermanent reality, almost as if there is a conspiracy of silence. Elizabeth reflects that

> she could run now, throw herself on the netting-wire, and call out across the lake to the woods where the saws still sung, 'Oh, answer me. Will Something answer me?' and she'd be met with echoes and real sounds of the saws and birds, cloud shadow on corrugations the wind had made on the water, and silence — the silence of the sky and lake and wood and people going about their lives.

It is characteristic of McGahern that the blankness should gather into

itself sights and sounds which might equally, at another time, seem
heartening, and that they should be evoked in precise detail, 'cloud
shadow on corrugations the wind had made on the water'. One aspect
of his impressive control is that his descriptive gift is used sparingly,
and detail is only brought into close-up at moments such as this, when
it creates an irony within the broader structure. The richness of the
world is made palpable at the point where it is clearly helpless to fill
the emptiness.

For instance, in 'Coming into His Kingdom', the boy suddenly learns
the facts of life, which he has seen, without knowing it, every day in the
country around him. He was expecting a mystery. Now 'the whole world
was changed, a covering torn away' and it is at this point, when it is
too late, that he sees the sensuous texture of everything around him,
'a delicate bloom on the clusters of blue sloes along the road, the
sudden gleam of the chestnut, or the woollen whiteness of the inside of
a burst pod in the dead leaves their shoes went rustling through'. In
'Korea'. where father and son are on the river, drawing up the nightlines
set for eels, the activity of the fishing is very simply but carefully
described to create a similar but more complex irony. It is the son's
last summer on the river. He will leave when his exam results come; and
so he sees everything with particular clarity. The father's livelihood is
shrinking: he tries to persuade the son to emigrate to America, with his
eye on the compensation he would get if he was drafted and killed in
Korea. The peaceful but essentially ruthless activity of the eel fishing
forms a counterpoint to the main story, both relaxing the tension and
providing an insidious parallel to it. The final and most subtle paradox
is that the son's sympathy with his father increases in proportion to the
wariness he must feel: 'I'd never felt so close to him before, not even
when he'd carried me on his shoulders above the laughing crowd to the
Final. Each move he made I watched as closely as if I too had to prepare
myself to murder.' One is reminded of another moment in 'Wheels'
when the father, who wants to give up the farm and come to live with
his son in Dublin, protests that the son has rejected him: 'There was
the treacherous drag to enter the emotion, and share and touch, the
white lengths of beechwood about his boots and the veins swollen dark
on the back of the old hands holding the sledge. With his sleeve he
wiped away tears, as a child.'

Emotional and sensuous responses go hand in hand with the 'careful
neutrality' McGahern writes about in 'Hearts of Oak and Bellies of
Brass', the determination 'to annul all the votes in myself'. It is this
ability to feel fully, and at the same time to withdraw from feeling, that
gives McGahern's objectivity its peculiar edge. It is central to his
achievement, the stylistic expression, carefully modulated, of his
underlying dilemma. One notices in The Dark (Faber, 1965) how word

order is slightly transposed to enact the sensation of transience, 'my life same as by the shops of the town had passed over these pages, it was over', and how it is this sensation that then becomes the basis of the novel's final resolution: 'no bitterness or anything else in some vision of this parting as both their lives passing utterly alone and lost in time, outside the accidental places and manners of their happening, and then one absolute compulsion to praise or bless'.

It is in *The Dark* that the boy sees the priesthood as a taking of death into life, and thereby a mastery of death: 'You'd be safe.' In 'The Recruiting Officer' an Irish Christian Brother visits a school to recruit for the order, and is quite explicit in using mortal fear as an enticement: 'For death comes as a thief in the night, the longest life is but a day. . . ' In these instances, as I remarked in my introduction, the *memento mori* is very Catholic in its roots, and would be as true of the Italian or Spanish countryside as of the Irish. The opposite impulse, the pull of life, naturally centres in *The Dark* on the boy's sexual imagination, for he is in the throes of adolescence. The horror of celibacy that he feels 'a priest all your days, hair coming away by its white roots on your comb till baldness and death, and never in all those days to have touched and entered the roused flesh of a woman in her heat' is again a specifically Catholic problem, and one echoed in much Irish writing.

Yet in his stress on the emptiness surrounding life, on the transparency of the world, McGahern sometimes seems more Buddhist than Catholic. His image of the wheel, several times repeated, may relate to this. In 'Wheels' it is, of course, primarily the 'ritual wheel' of family dependence, 'fathers become children to their sons who repay the care they got when they were young', and it may be used in this sense again in 'The Recruiting Officer', where the ex-Christian Brother thinks of his mother, and wonders why she pushed him into the order: 'but I don't ask, I walk by her side on the sand, and echo her life with "Yes and yes and yes", for it is all a wheel'. Yet the phrasing there, 'it is all a wheel', suggests a secondary meaning, the Buddhist symbol of the Wheel of Karma, or recurrent needs and desires, from which the soul must detach itself to become free. Certainly, McGahern's own detachment often seems rather Buddhist in character, and the conjunction of events in 'The Recruiting Officer', the CB interviewing his victim as the tinker buries the school shit and the infants chant their tables, seems to catch perfectly the ludicrous quality of *sangsara,* the sense in which our daily preoccupations are so unreal that they can only be seen as a game in which we all participate. The same awareness, perhaps, takes its most urgent and its most western form in Mahoney's anguished outburst in *The Dark:* 'This is my life, and this kitchen in the townland of Cloone is my stage, and I am playing my life out here on. . .

I went to school too.'

At the same time, McGahern's themes have not acquired an intellectual fixity: they reflect an open and developing concern. No dates are given for the individual stories that make up *Nightlines* (Faber, 1970), but whatever order they were written in, it is noticeable that, in the order in which they have been arranged, the anxious trading of 'informations' in 'Strandhill, The Sea' 'before the soon when they'll have to leave', is expanded into a coming-to-terms with anxiety, humorously expressed but intelligently conceived, in 'My Love, My Umbrella', 'Through my love it was the experience of my own future death I was passing through', and this in turn gives way to the wry, survivor's humour of 'The Recruiting Officer', with which the book ends: 'How, how, though, can a man be born again when he is old? Can he enter a second time his mother's bag of tricks?' In the novels there is an even clearer movement, not towards a resolution of the dilemma, for that's hardly possible on McGahern's terms, but towards a reconciliation with the facts. In *The Barracks* Elizabeth Reegan is finally able to make sense of 'the nowhere of herself': 'Nothing could be decided here. She was just passing through. She had come to life out of mystery and would return, it surrounded her life, it safely held it as by hands. . . she must surely grow into meaning as she grew to love, there was that or nothing and she couldn't lose.' In *The Dark* the son's increasing awareness of transience becomes a healing force. The antagonism between his father and himself fades before it: 'He watched him there old, and remembered. The looking moved from the cruelty of detachment out into the incomprehension, no one finally knew anything about himself or anybody, even moods of hatred or contempt were passing, were of no necessary consequence.' Death becomes finally 'the reality that set you free', and the knowledge of it 'an authority that was simply a state of mind, a calmness even in the face of the turmoil of your own passing. . . Nobody's life was more than a direction'. It is the possibility of a growth towards meaning, and the finding of a sense of freedom within what could easily have turned into a nihilist position, that makes McGahern's writing, while almost mercilessly clear-sighted, both positive and humane. McGahern is not a metaphysical writer as such. He is essentially a realist, with a shrewd understanding of what living in an apparently peaceable but deprived environment can do to people: but his realism is all the more effective because it takes its place within a central, metaphysical concern, and because that concern creates a perspective. Of all Irish writers McGahern seems to me to match up most closely to Sean O'Faolain's requirement, a realistic writer who knows his subject 'not merely with his senses but with his intellect', for whom it has become 'part of his whole life as a man passionately pondering on the entire human condition'.*

* For an extension to this essay, see my review of John McGahern's third novel, *The Leavetaking* in *The New Review*, I, 11 (February 1975).

AIDAN HIGGINS

Curiously, though Aidan Higgins is 'much possessed by death', and sees 'the skull beneath the skin', his work seems to suffer from the lack of any ultimate point of reference, which makes itself felt in the writing, I think, as a lack of perspective. In McGahern there is light at both ends of the tunnel, even if it is only the light of empty space, illuminating the bleakness between. In Higgins there is only the darkness pressing, and the shapes that darkness takes.

Higgins began, in *Felo de Se* (Calder, 1960), very much as a satirist of the original, or Juvenalian school, in whom the horror of death provokes a stream of vituperation, not at social vanity, but at the vanity of life itself. The condition of mortality into which man is born is so absurd as to dwarf all subsequent absurdities. In the English tradition it was the Jacobeans who rediscovered, in the tropes of classical rhetoric, the original horror of death. Thus Higgins not only quotes from classical philosophy, 'Thou art a little soul bearing a corpse, Epictetus said' but has an almost Jacobean vehemence of style, both in specific borrowings, 'Was there an unwritten law that Irish labourers are attracted to railways, as the ailing to lung charts, or gadflies to dung?' and in the characteristic weight of expression: 'this drear Heaven of abject claims'. At the same time this heaviness of language is indicative of a persistent tendency of his style, or rather, of its particular limitation, that he is altogether too writerly, too hedged with words. Just as the satirist's aggression is essentially a defensive mechanism, so in Higgins's writing the external world of experience is accurately perceived, but is rendered into a dense, highly subjective linguistic structure which becomes finally a bulwark against the experience itself. Reality is internalized, transmuted by Higgins's style into some sort of inner world, so that one could often be uncertain whether he is writing about a real or a dream world. It no longer matters, because by this internalizing process he is insulated. It is a means by which the writer has the last word. The procedure contrasts strongly with McGahern's deliberately bare style, which is a more courageous method, a means of allowing experience to have the last word. McGahern's clarity of focus comes from the admission of inner emptiness, so that what begins as something very like nihilism ends as an outgoing, inquiring impulse: whereas in Higgins the Gothick fogs, and at times in *Balcony of Europe* the roseate blur, come from an insistence, a pressure within.

Certain of the devices that we meet in *Felo de Se* recur throughout Higgins's work. In 'Asylum', for instance, Brazill is regaled by Boucher with the grotesque pageant of the past, for Boucher, like Higgins himself, is something of an antiquary of the human spirit. Boucher's monologues have a certain unity to them − one tirade is a dream of rare women, an account of those eighteenth-century women who managed to be both courtesan and bluestocking, another concerns the Great Fire and the Great Plague — and they are similarly orchestrated into the atmosphere of the story, into the threatening gloom of Stye, of Elizabeth's mother's house, and of Boucher's own accelerating breakdown. Later, in *Langrishe, Go Down,* when Otto Beck is the presiding antiquary, the oddities come staccato, as they cross Otto's mind, and they are themselves more eclectic and random. This, again, mirrors the character of Imogen's relationship with Otto, which keeps her in a constant state of surprise and annoyance: there is nothing of a piece, nothing she can make sense of. Returning to 'Asylum', the incredible list of props that Dr Vergiff uses for his performance is a variant of the same device, drawing on the comic detritus of the ages, and so, in effect, are the odd names and details picked out in 'Lebensraum', the bearded John Player sailor, the hooligans from Zoar Street etc.

From the same fascination with objects and people as expressions of each other comes Higgins's penchant, very marked in *Felo de Se,* for creating set-pieces of grotesquerie, of which perhaps the most remarkable are the pictures of Helen Kervick and Mother Richter in their respective lairs:

> Out of the depths of a tattered armchair Helen's pale features began to emerge, as Imogen went towards her, to the sound of defunct springs. A miscellaneous collection of fur and feathered life moved as she moved, flitting into obscure hiding-places. High above their strong but unnamable smell rose the fetid reek of old newspapers. In one corner a great pile had mounted until jammed between floor and ceiling, like clenched teeth.   ('Killachter Meadow')

> Mrs. Richter's bedroom was downstairs and sparsely furnished. A wardrobe rested there on the bare boards with a chest of drawers and the bed itself on a rectangle of faded blue carpet. A commodious chamber-pot was generally apparent under the sadly drooping edges of the bed coverings, almost magnetic in its importance to the general picture of Mother Richter abed, as though the parts of the iron bedstead and herself, covered in glad rags and a nightgown with a ruff, constituted the filings — the mesmeric field — which 'made' the whole happy unit.   ('Nightfall on Cape Piscator')

This is bravura comic writing, and the element of exaggeration is, of course, integral to the comic mode: but Higgins's attraction to this sort of effect results in character and plot being afflicted with a kind of literary dropsy, whereby they abandon linear progress, and are drawn down into providing one set-piece or another. Even the increased fluency and discipline of his later books are only really an advance in the fluency and discipline with which set-pieces are presented: the power of locomotion has never been recovered. Even what linear logic remains is severely stretched: Ned Brazill, having dominated the early part of 'Asylum' as 'a corpulent man with a walrus moustache', ages with suspicious suddenness, to reappear as a walking death's-head.

The tendency to visual fixation perhaps explains one of Higgins's minor quirks, that he must be almost the last writer in the western tradition to make serious use of the epic simile. His deployment of it can be delicate and precise, as in the image of a 'transfer' in 'Tower and Angels', but the two similes which conclude the brilliant description of Herr Bausch in 'Winter Offensive' are perhaps more typical, in the boldness of their incongruity:

> The pale stubble of a military haircut stood up, once free of fedora and feather, like aftergrass on his bullet head. Below it his features squeezed themselves together into a veritable snout, on each side of which were arranged little bloodshot eyes. . . As certain burrowing creatures, in order to gain their ends or to exist at all, are resolved down to one anxious or bitter form of themselves (the burrowing snout and its fellow darkness), so his features seemed to narrow down to one place and one gesture: his was a face falling back to a function. As winds in their persistence stretch and sharpen boulders, and as these in turn indicate free access to territory beyond, so the features of Herr Bausch spoke of only one preoccupation, and that preoccupation, venery.

Often Higgins seems a maker of verbal etchings, in the sense not only of the sharpness but of the density of an etching. This, though it has a subtle pattern of verbal association, from the opening 'lobeless ears. . . like a boar's' down to the final 'venery', is more of an Expressionist cartoon, a drawing by George Grosz. One needs to make the point, though, that the viciousness of Grosz's cartoon style arose from a consistent social concern, whereas in Higgins's use of German and South African settings, as indeed in his use of the Irish Big House setting in *Langrishe, Go Down,* there seems to be simply an attraction towards the grotesque in itself, with no attempt at a social perspective. With the exception of the early sections of 'Asylum', which have a real satiric bite, Higgins brings the voyeurism of the antiquary to time present as well as time past. In 'Tower and Angels' we are very close to the Francis Stuart territory, Germany in 1949, and briefly it looks as if Higgins is going to break out of the solipsistic caul: 'pain was a fact beyond justice, not to be calculated. . . he had seen hints of that desperation and encroachment which proclaims the breakdown of appearances. . . was cast back into the jungle where superstition — and religion — was born.' But there he stops: defeat, as in all his writing, is inherited, and 'Tower and Angels' returns with alacrity to Higgins's Unpromised Land, to alienatory sex and the frowziness of despair.

Over all, the structure of the short stories is that linear development is abandoned in favour of contrasting, densely-packed blocks, and, to a lesser degree, this is the structure of the novels too. *Felo de Se* presents a great range of talents, but, again, all massing in one direction. Eddy

Brazill's real working life in London, for instance, is presented with shrewd reportage, in which wit and imagination sharpen the documentary skill. This is then set against the dream-like eccentricity of Eddy's life with Boucher. Whilst it is possible to hold that the grotesquerie of the public world, of 'real life', is simply matched by the grotesquerie of the private world, typically it is the private world that gets all the attention, and furnishes the bulk of the story. It is difficult not to feel that there is an element of retreat here, from the vagaries of the real world into a private one that is more extreme but also more manageable. A similar resort, to the construction of parallel, private dilemmas rather than the confrontation of the actual and universal, seems to me to underlie both *Langrishe, Go Down* and *Balcony of Europe.*

On the other hand, there are many things in *Felo de Se* that one would not want to give up. It is often marvellously funny. There is a particular comic mastery in some of the more portly phrases — Mrs Boucher, for instance, who had 'departed to the Pale Kingdoms', or the girl in the picture who from the waist up 'was as unadorned as the town of Trim' — and an intense and consummate relish in some of the set-pieces, viz. the descriptions quoted above, of Helen Kervick and Mother Richter. The imagery, too, can be both ingenious and exact: as Mr Vaschel proceeds to the fulfilment of his wet dreams the stars appear to him as 'galactic spawn'; and as he stoops into the darkness of the African maid's hut he 'sensed his dog-rose sensing him'.

After *Felo de Se* Higgins must have faced a choice, between remaining in the fastnesses of his imagination and building his own *Gormenghast*, or moving on to common ground and confronting the everyday world. In the event, he seems to have hedged his bets. He has come a considerable way into the everyday world, but without accepting that world on its own terms, that is, without fully accepting the discipline involved. His imagination is so prolix, I suspect, because it retains a *pied-à-terre* in the catacombs of *Gormenghast*. The result is that, to date, *Felo de Se* remains his most eccentric book, and his most successful. The writing is taut, which in *Langrishe* it certainly is not, and effectively mixes different tones, an elementary refreshment that both *Langrishe* and *Balcony* leave one gasping for. The language, though dense, has an abrasive edge, which enters only towards the end of *Langrishe,* and at which *Balcony* aims, within a more contemporary and colloquial style, only to emollify it beyond recall by the lushness of expression elsewhere.

In *Langrishe, Go Down* (Calder and Boyars, 1966) Higgins returns to the territory that he first explored in 'Killachter Meadow': a decaying Anglo-Irish manor, peopled by spinster sisters, one of whom has had an affair with a German scholar. There is a marked difference in treatment between the short story and the novel. 'Killachter Meadow', in accordance with the general method of *Felo de Se,* approaches its subject from the outside, and sets its characters into a succession of grotesque, tragi-comic poses. In *Langrishe* Higgins works from the inside, through the thoughts first of Helen, then of Imogen, occasionally of Otto. The style has had to alter accordingly. It has lost its panache, and, apart from the closing stages of Imogen and Otto's affair, all its humour too: but it has not generated other qualities to replace them. The style falls somewhere between evocation and an impressionistic exactitude. It would be refreshed, I think, if it was more exact: but at key moments, particularly in the development of the emotions, it falls short of a final expression: 'Qualms of one's being there, a dread of falling, drowning, going under with that sound in one's ears; it makes your spine tingle, the hair of the head stiffen, quickens something inside you, sweet and secret, internal.' Those closing words, 'sweet and secret, internal', are no more than a gesture at meaning, and a pretty cliched one at that.

Structurally, the novel is equally inconclusive. True, on a formal analysis, the episodes seem quite tightly interlaced. Helen's visit to the graveyard, for instance, and her meditation on what it means to be interred, is proleptic of her own funeral; and it is while she is at the graveyard that Imogen goes through Helen's room, and comes upon a bundle of her own letters to Beck, which Helen had intercepted. What breaks the back of the novel, though, is the sudden switch of the attention from Helen to Imogen. Helen's character is consequently left unresolved, as it was in 'Killachter Meadow'. There is a clear antagonism between Helen and Imogen, but it is not developed into anything that might provide a structural tension. Thus the only tensile relationship in this long book is the central one, Imogen's belated affair with Otto, a late flowering set against the surrounding decline. Even this is given such a protracted and interminably inconsequential treatment that it becomes itself more like a feature of the general collapse. Though there is real wit, and many a curious gobbet of learning, to be found in the short passages, there is something rather arch and selfconscious behind their elisions, an insistent artiness, that makes them finally rather dampening, even sanctimonious in their effect. The abiding impression of this novel, for all its singular felicities, is one of monotony.

We come here to a central feature of Higgins's style, and one that is equally true of *Balcony of Europe* (Calder and Boyars, 1972), which I regard as another distinguished failure. He is clearly fascinated by, and very good at capturing what might be termed incidental cadences, the small, often ironic rhythms that run through a relationship. Thus in *Langrishe* many of the short scenes do not so much cut off as cut back in a characteristic manner, reflecting the oblique jumps of Otto's mind, and the sharp, rather snappish streak in Imogen. In *Balcony* there is a more open, reflective mood, and many of the passages seem designed to catch the enigma of being with this particular woman at this exact moment in this certain place. The endings of the passages, particularly, seem to strike this note: 'the three of them talking together. It was late October' or 'the dust of goats returning hanging on the evening sun'. The incidental cadences acquire a philosophical implication of their own, within a thematic organization that is considerably more interesting than anything attempted in *Langrishe,* and comes much closer to solving the problems of non-sequential structure. Within *Balcony*'s eighty-two short episodes there is a kind of concentric logic. A recurrent theme of vanished tribes and lost civilizations is focused into Charlotte's Jewishness, the fact that she, a second generation New York Jewess, could so easily have been one of the Polish Jews lost in the concentration camps: 'She is my opposite, yet part of me. She who appears so permanent, is transitory — a souvenir. Lost long ago. I can neither hold her nor let her go.' And so Ruttle's love for Charlotte ties into the novel's central theme, the transience and flux of all things. Charlotte is both herself, and the female principle of mutability, the enigma incarnate:

> Maud Gonne at Howth station waiting for a train. The sea-wall by the harbour, the tide coming in over the sandbar on Claremont beach. The English actress Lily Elsie standing on Windsor platform waiting for a train. To see the deeps, the aspirations and the vanity of civilisations lost in the wandering depths of an ageing and vain actress's eyes, an ageing ex-beauty waiting at Windsor for a slow local train.
>
> The human body made up of liquid, flesh, bones, humours, chemicals, puff-paste. Its bond, tie, kinship with inorganic matter, that slowly encroaching activity, the waste of the world; and how through the single loved body all that is most appealing in that other person is represented, continually fêted, yet continually being withdrawn. Love, that most despairing grip; the cruel fabled bird that pinches like a crab.
>
> She was all that for me.

His experience with Charlotte is finally reversed, or brought to rest, in the visit to Aran with Olivia that closes the book: 'A beautiful Aran day, a shameless colleen in the sea, old Nick Adams sunning himself on a rock. Aran, it is said, is the strangest place on earth. Sometimes for an hour you *are*, the rest is history; sometimes the two floods culminate in a dream.' His mother's death opened the book, and memories of his father's brief glory and long ruin: here their crossed lives, too, fall momentarily into place.

This outline should suggest the scale of Higgins's potential achievement here: the sad effect of his indiscipline is that the writing of *Balcony* quite simply lacks the passionate intelligence actually to achieve it. His presentation of Charlotte as Dan Ruttle's dream of truth is weakened by obvious borrowings from Nabokov, not only in the list of her avatars, but in the word play on her various names, Charlotte Bayless, Dolly Lipski, unmistakably reminiscent of 'Wanted, wanted: Dolores Haze'. His presentation of her as a physical woman veers continually between the accurate — 'a sharp, delicate, plant-like odour' — and the fatuous — 'herbal whiff of something wild'; between the humorous perception of her strutting walk, or her 'monkey paws', and a glutinous surrender to 'her famished tigress eyes', 'her ardent thighs' as they are both 'roused to a seismic pitch of excitement'. Ruttle's portentousness — 'I was soon to penetrate one of her disguises, in an atmosphere extraordinarily vivid and suggestive' — becomes as tiresome as the affair's ceaseless refrain of 'Take me, take me!'

The limitations of the book are finally rooted in the limitations of the relationship, and particularly perhaps in the limitations of Charlotte. And yet, while there is a deliberate irony in the gossamers of significance that Ruttle spins about her vigorous impercipience, Ruttle himself is too unperceptive of his own situation to develop it. Ruttle, in fact, has no real definition as a character at all, witness the way in which the realization of his middle age, which could have provided the basis for effective irony, only becomes suddenly, intermittently apparent towards the end of the affair. For most of the book, copulation simply alternates with cogitation: and so Higgins is once again the all-licensed scholiast, able to substitute by a range of allusion for his lack of controlled concern. Metaphysics in Higgins seems to reside in a kind of supernumerary ease, whereas in Stuart and McGahern it is born of simple pulmonary pressure, a dilation of the imagination essential to survival. It is noticeable that in Part 1 of *Balcony*, where Higgins is held down to a domestic Irish setting, and kept much closer to a narrative line, the writing is in a different class altogether, superior both in quality and in kind. It may simply be that Higgins has to write his *Portrait of the Artist* before proceeding to *Ulysses* and beyond.

*

It is significant that in the three writers I have examined so far three quite different social images of Ireland have emerged, and that those images have been put, in each case, to quite different uses. The Ireland of contrasts to which Francis Stuart subscribed in *Pigeon Irish* is the traditional image, which has always, for a small consideration, been readily convertible into Irishry, but which has, equally, been susceptible of more intelligent interpretations, to bring out certain qualities the writer perceived in the community, the unified sensibility, for instance, that Stuart emphasizes, or the instinctive dramatic sense that Synge and O'Casey were able to exploit. Not that all Irishry is necessarily unintelligent. The image it presents has certain values implicit within it, values considerably more humane, more perceptive in fact, than those implicit, say, in the Home Counties pastoral that still underwrites much English light entertainment. One has only to think back to some of C. E. Montague's stories to see what a subtle medium Irishry could become.

Among contemporary writers, Benedict Kiely has made the most unashamed use of Irishry, partly as a vehicle for his vigorous secularism — he never seems happier than when a student priest has mislaid his vocation under Rabelaisian circumstances — but more particularly, I think, because it is an ideal vehicle for his gift as a writer of farce. *Dogs Enjoy the Morning* (Gollancz, 1968, Penguin, 1971) is best seen as farce, though occasionally, as in the sketches of Christy and Cathy Hanafin, it touches a deeper level. A similar ribaldry animates his collection of short stories *A Ball of Malt and Madame Butterfly* (Gollancz, 1973). At the same time, this is entertainment with strong roots: 'Wild Rover No More' links back beyond Irishry into vanished folk customs; and 'An Old Friend' is gay as Yeats's old men were, with a gaiety that has taken account of tragedy, and is hard-won common sense. Kiely's earlier work is rather different in character: *Honey Seems Bitter* (Methuen, 1954) was a disturbing, imaginative thriller, which combined an effectively sardonic style with an altogether darker view of Irish rural life, while *Call for a Miracle* (Cape, 1950) used a Priestley-like popular format to create a moving and deeply serious novel, in which the modern city life of Dublin was set against traditional community values.

Mary Lavin has acquired a high reputation as a writer whose insights penetrate beneath the surface of the older type of settled community. Ever since Lord Dunsany started the ball rolling, in his preface to her first collection of short stories — a preface worth reading, incidentally, for its unrivalled fatuity of expression — it has been the custom to make complimentary comparison to the Russian short story tradition. I am not sure that a degree of illusion, beyond the fictional illusion, isn't operating here. In the small town settings, which are the territory of her best known work, many of her characters seem to me to be two-dimensional, to be types rather than characters, and the small towns to resemble mechanical universes, with Miss Lavin at the puppet strings, rather than accurately perceived communities. One formula common to a number of the early stories is the practical soul domineering over the dreamer: can people really be so simply defined? Aren't the important writers those who perceive the points at which everyone is, in Kevin Crossley-Holland's phrase, 'dream and bone'? The son in John McGahern's *The Dark* becomes estranged from his father, one might say, by the education of his awareness: but the book pivots on the fact that Mahoney has his own, imprisoned awareness. This theme, of the sensitive soul immured in isolation, produces different story patterns in Mary Lavin's later work, the bereaved woman facing life alone, or the spinster who has been trapped by having to look after her ageing father: but there is real improvement in the fact that now other people are seen to have their sensitive side too, Barney Crossen, for instance, in 'In the Middle of the Fields'.

The limitations of Miss Lavin's perception are evident in the curious moral balance of *The House in Clewe Street* (Michael Joseph, 1945, Penguin, 1949), the earlier of her two novels. The behaviour of the slavey Onny Soraghan is presented as regrettable immorality, without any sense of the pressures of social deprivation upon her, without the least hint that she might have been a vital individual in her own right, who was simply taking the only opportunities ever likely to come her way for discovery and growth. There is sympathy for Onny's death: but that, in literature as in life, is no substitute for the effort of under-standing. The fundamental condescension of the middle-class characters towards her goes unchallenged: the result is that Gabriel's sudden propulsion into maturity is left dangerously incomplete. He remains as subtly exploitive and as potentially destructive a prig as Michael Fane in Compton Mackenzie's *Sinister Street.* The limitations are still more apparent in the second novel, *Mary O'Grady* (Michael Joseph, 1950), which is sentimentality at its most vicious: there is a very real sense in which Mary Lavin is merely exploiting the emotional resources of Mary O'Grady.

One is left, finally, wondering to what extent the real world has penetrated Mary Lavin's imagination, whether she has not rather constructed another world of her own, anterior to it. The pettiness and boredom of her small towns seem real enough: but their unruffled calm, not to mention their customs and costumes, seem to hark back to an Edwardian stillness that must certainly ante-date her adult experience, and probably her childhood too. With the outstanding exception of 'The Patriot Son', her short stories present an Ireland in which the War of Independence and the Civil War might simply not have occurred. The consequent effects of muting and distance in her earlier work have led some critics to talk of her tact and eloquent reticence: to me they are characteristic of the manipulative illusion, essentially part of the same formal approach as the overt allegory of 'The Sand Castle'. The stylistic finish is the result, not of the shaping of the engaged imagination, but of an exclusively literary mode of vision: the world comes to resemble one of those glass domes inside which snow falls. The snow may have a surprising aesthetic sense, but it is important not to believe that it is real snow, as it settles with miniature precision upon the cut-out figures.

Her recent work has gained in conviction and dramatic power as it has become more immediate in style. The title story of *Happiness*

(Constable, 1969), for instance, uses a quite different fictional illusion, the impression of a close personal involvement, to create a story with an intense emotional charge. Another recent technique is not to bring a story to rest, but to end before the plot has quite concluded, at a point where the accumulating ironies re-ignite. 'One Summer', from *In the Middle of the Fields* (Constable, 1967), ends with the father's cry to the memory of his long-dead wife: 'Just to see her! Just to see her!' Those words, which mark the depth of his loss, mark also the emptiness of the bond for which his daughter has just renounced her own chance of love. On the other hand, the work remains curiously uneven: a story such as 'Villa Violetta' in *A Memory* (Constable, 1972) represents a considerable lapse from her own best standards.

Sean O'Faolain stands in a quite different relation to the traditional image of Ireland. His career as a man of letters could almost be seen as an extension of his early Republicanism, as an attempt to bring Ireland into the mainstream of contemporary culture. Certainly, no one has commented more acutely than Sean O'Faolain on the problems that face the contemporary Irish writer. He sees the Irish sensibility as split three ways, between the dewy-eyed vision the Irish have of their inner selves, the hard facts of how they actually make a living in the modern world, and the mythology they have invented to avoid confronting their real problems, so that, as he remarks in the introduction to his Penguin collection of stories (1970):

> for any kind of realist to write about people with romantic souls is a most difficult and tricky business. . . but when it comes to writing about people who, like the Irish of our day, combine beautiful, palpitating tea-rose souls with hard, coolly calculating heads, there does not seem to be any way at all of writing about them except satirically or angrily.

That said, it seems clear to me that Sean O'Faolain's own achievement lies in the degree to which he has not become satirical nor angry, but has allowed the conflicting sympathies to be held in balance. It is not simply a matter of material fairness, of the surprising equipoise with which Henn, for instance, the Anglo-Irish landlord in 'Midsummer Night Madness', is balanced against the Republican Stevey Long, but a basic tenet of his style. In 'Lovers of the Lake' the contradictions implicit between the fever of the religious experience at Lough Derg and the pull of the illicit love affair are left unresolved. They are poised against each other, just as the banality of the pilgrimage is set against the lovers' worldliness. To tip the scales would be to devalue one experience or the other, and thus destroy not only the story's structural tension but its credibility. Without the balance, there could be no story.

'A Broken World', set on a train journey, centres on Ireland's economic paralysis when the semi-feudal agricultural pattern broke up and was not replaced, as it was in England, by intensive mechanized farming. A priest raises the subject, and momentarily inspires the writer and a listening farmer with his vision of a lost 'moral unity': but he is a silenced Land Leaguer, and the marks of his long silencing show. He united his travelling companions, 'then scattered us and left us with his pox'. The writer turns to the farmer, but 'his stare was childish, and the eyes wavered, as if he was very tired. . . time and nature had engendered something no more human than a rock'. The writer is left with his yearning for an 'image of life that would fire and fuse us all', and with Ireland, under its snow, '. . . silent as a perpetual dawn'. Once again, the evenness of perspective here, what one might call 'the balance of deficiencies', seems the only possible mode.

Rather similar to the caution with which he treats his own visionary gleams is the caution with which he treats his characters. They are touched by moments of perception but not transformed by them: they sink back into their own selfishness, into the smell of rashers frying, as Phil does in 'Hymeneal'. Incidental details continually link us to the palpable world, and create an implicit history and geography, a shrewdly realized Ireland, in which the broken demesne walls and boarded granary windows along the Dublin-to-Cork road are set against 'the brittle sound of waves breaking in cold air', a sense of the weight and texture of the climate.

Where Sean O'Faolain does relate back to the older short story tradition is in the degree of fictional contrivance that he employs. Perceptive as the stories are, their limitation is that rather than being drawn from the daily process of living they tend to be set at chance cross-roads somewhere on the edges of experience. Against this, however, can be set an unusual lyric gift, often a matter of perfectly judged simplicity of expression, which in 'Thieves', for the final, crucial evocation, picks on the most natural detail – 'around the bend of the road, from maybe half a mile away they could barely hear it. It would be lighted, and empty. The first tram.' – and at the end of 'Brainsy' achieves an intensity of expression as traditional and as timeless as its imagery.

The social image that Aidan Higgins exploited in *Langrishe, Go Down,* the ruptured Eden of the Anglo-Irish, has been a favourite theme of Irish novelists, presenting them as it does with an in-built symbol of transience. The most intelligent use of it has been made by Jennifer Johnston. In her first two novels particularly she has created a double perspective, bringing the inherited life-style into contrast with the realities of modern Ireland, and yet handling the contrasts in such a way as to give them a lasting relevance beyond the Irish situation – the latter quality being a function, as I have already suggested, of her plangent economy of style, which gives the novels an almost parable-like form. To say this, though, should not be taken as implying that the novels are in any way schematic: the great difference between Jennifer Johnston's use of the framing effect and Mary Lavin's is that Jennifer Johnston's characters come alive, and retain a presence in the imagination, in a way that Mary Lavin's do not.

The Captains and the Kings (Hamish Hamilton, 1972) is an unsolemn but moving study of the recurrent bond between youth and old age: only in this case the old man, whose spirit was broken in childhood by his mother's possessive love for his elder brother, is unable to help the boy, whose spirit is in equal danger of being crushed by his parents' anxiety. Within this general irony is a specifically Irish one: what really oppresses the boy is the life of provincial dreariness that awaits him, and what draws him to the Big House is the ghost of a wider culture, now equally lapsed into tedium. *The Gates* (Hamish Hamilton, 1973) again brings youth into contact with old age, only in this case the young girl comes to understand, and even value, the compromises of the old. The second and sharper lesson she has to learn is the reality of class differences, or rather the way that different experiences of life create different expectations, and different values. Minnie, with middle-class crusading zeal, wants to start a market garden and get the estate back on its feet. She sells the Major's ornamental gates to get the money: but to Kevin, her accomplice, brought up in poverty and overcrowding, money means only one thing, the chance to escape to England, and he takes it.

How Many Miles to Babylon (Hamish Hamilton, 1974), which centres on the friendship between an Anglo-Irish heir and a village boy at the time of the First World War, subtly illuminates many aspects of class behaviour. Both young men, for instance, are sold to death by different class instincts, the son and heir by his mother's fiercely possessive love turning into a patriotic death-wish, the labourer by his mother's senseless but atavistically compelling command to find his father in France, when he is reported missing. The novel's curious blend of clarity and distance was best expressed by Ronald Blythe's remark in his *Listener* review, that it has all the poignancy of those fading photographs of First World War soldiers. One's only reservation might be that it is perhaps a shade too refined, the fear being that if Jennifer Johnston moves completely back into time past she may lessen the range of her considerable talent.

The deadliness of a class novel written completely without social perspective is exemplified by Helen Wykham's first novel, *Ribstone Pippins* (Calder & Boyars, 1974), which is set among the decadent survivals of Anglo-Irish society. In the first part the heroine's predicament as the gauche younger sister thrust into competitive society gives the satire real teeth and fingernails: then she makes the serious mistake of falling in love, and thereafter the author's indulgence to all her characters' pretensions has one wishing that the whole odious set would become involved in some sudden and conclusive accident.

James, latterly J. G. Farrell (who should perhaps be described as *émigré* Irish rather than Anglo-Irish: he was born in Liverpool of Irish parents, and spent much of his childhood in Ireland) set his fourth novel *Troubles* (Cape, 1970) in a dilapidated Anglo-Irish hotel at the time of the aforesaid disturbances, but once again failed, like Aidan Higgins, to reduce this fecund theme to manageable proportions. Despite some good comic touches, Farrell's treatment of it seems literally interminable. There was a similar weakness in the two engaging comic novels that preceded it, *The Lung* (Hutchinson, 1965) and *A Girl in the Head* (Cape, 1967), and in his first novel, *A Man from Elsewhere* (New Authors, 1963), a kind of moral thriller: Farrell seemed adept at setting up interesting situations, but unable subsequently to get anything really interesting out of them. With his fifth book, however, *The Siege of Krishnapur* (Weidenfeld & Nicolson, 1973), set in the Indian Mutiny, a number of themes that were inchoate in the earlier books have crystallized into a novel of real achievement. The pretensions of western civilization are brilliantly parodied as the ammunition runs out, and scientific gadgets from the Great Exhibition and the electroplated heads of famous men are fired at the advancing sepoys: Shakespeare proves to have excellent ballistic properties, on account of his baldness. At the same time, there is a deep and discriminating moral concern, expressed both through the community's formal debates on poetry and Progress, and in the reaction of individual characters to the breakdown of order. *The Siege of Krishnapur* achieves what many novels are said to achieve, but few actually do: it provokes thought.

On a particularly Irish subject, religious intolerance and sectarian violence, Thomas Kilroy has attempted an historical novel of similar range in *The Big Chapel* (Faber, 1971). It may be the documentary aspect, however, the fact that it is based on a famous controversy of the 1870s, that has caused a profound inconclusiveness in the novel's structure and development. Far more important than the reconstruction of external events, clerical intrigues and scenes of mob violence, are the reconstructions of the interior crises of those involved. These are convincing, as far as they go, but curiously incomplete. At one point, Nicolas Scully, who has been a staunch supporter of the deposed Father Lannigan, appears to lose all faith in the priest, and becomes a demented vagrant. The next thing we know, he is back looking after the priest. We do learn something of Nicolas's private torment, over his step-sister Emerine, but nothing of what went through his mind during his apparent madness, and nothing of the resolution that brought him back to the priest's side. Similarly, the promising alliance between Nicolas and Mr Butler, the eccentric rationalist landlord, and the immense potential of Mr Butler himself, are only sketchily exploited. The result is that though there are some shrewd hints, at the sexual repression that underlies the violence and some perceptive insights, Father Lannigan's remark, for instance, that 'Certainty is the end of growth', what may have been intended as an elliptical development ends up looking merely sporadic.

On the other hand, in his play *The Death and Resurrection of Mr. Roche* (Faber, 1969), characterized in Irving Wardle's *Times* review of the Hampstead Theatre Club production as 'a bleakly unforgiving study of that dismal Irish custom, the all-male drinking party', Kilroy's writing is entirely convincing. Here we come to the third social image of Ireland, the utterly unromantic, contemporary reality that underlies the work of John McGahern, compounded of economic struggle, provincial boredom and the increasingly problematical pressure of religious persuasion. Since the first two elements, at least, are never far away from any of us, and may well come a little closer in the near future, it is worth noticing that the younger Irish writers have proved themselves able to bring to unmalleable material the redeeming quality of the imagination. The courage and humanity of McGahern's writing is echoed, in a different medium, in *The Death and Resurrection of Mr. Roche*, so that, as J. W. Lambert wrote in his *Sunday Times* review of the original Dublin Festival production, the play 'transcends the Dublin which is its blood and bone; its melancholy theme... shot through with wild humour'.

There is another grim, yet finely balanced study of the results of social deprivation and limited opportunity in Kevin Casey's first novel, *The Sinners' Bell* (Faber, 1968). The account of Frank's two years in London as a labourer has the same harsh authenticity as McGahern's 'Hearts of Oak and Bellies of Brass'. This experience, coming on top of a childhood with an alcoholic father and humiliation at school, creates the disaster of his marriage to Helen: 'he could never forget the fear and violence he had felt when he first held her body to his own... his deep distaste and the automatic desire for violence he felt whenever he saw, touched or even heard her... He had convinced himself that he didn't need anybody and used people to prove it.' As with Graham Greene's delinquent in *Brighton Rock*, the engrained Catholicism turns to poison: in Frank's affair with an innocent skivvy, the motive that surfaces is that 'he could damn her soul for all eternity: the emotion was stronger and more violent than lust had ever been'. The only redeeming feature is the persistent courage of Helen: and yet perhaps the novel's one weakness is that both Helen and her father, a tenant farmer, seem altogether too nice, too middle-class in their outlook, to have come from the same world as Frank.

Kevin Casey's second novel, *A Sense of Survival* (Faber, 1974), is set in Tangier, and is, one hopes, a momentary lapse. Though it is skilfully constructed, and evinces genuine compassion for the boarding-house full of failures of whom it treats, there is a rather obvious debt to Greene in the smoothly sinister foreign policeman, and correspondingly a vicarious element in the writing: the sort of asides that in *The Sinners' Bell* provided real insights here come perilously close to platitude.

The one area of social concern where Irish fiction has drawn a blank so far is the conflict in Ulster. Literature has to defer to journalism in this one respect, that it is involuntary. To deal adequately with the roots of the situation would probably take a city-bred Ulsterman of the calibre of McGahern, and such writers are rare at the best of times.*

Contemporary Ireland has more than one face, however. If a significant proportion of the new Irish writing is concerned with the survival of human values under reductive economic pressure, Ireland also has, in Julia O'Faolain, an outstanding satirist of the affluent society. For a number of excellent reasons, her work is different in kind to that of other writers I have discussed in this essay. Born and brought up in Ireland, the daughter of Sean O'Faolain, she is married to an American Renaissance specialist, has lived in France and Italy, and now lives in the United States. Consequently, she is, along with Francis Stuart and Aidan Higgins, among the very few Irish writers who are truly international in range. Sean O'Faolain and Mary Lavin have both set stories in Italy: Julia O'Faolain has been able to write, as it were, from inside Italian life. Where she differs most sharply, however, from other Irish writers is in choosing to work from within the contemporary flux of modes and passions. Her characters generally have comparative economic freedom. Not being pinned down in one situation, they escape that terminal haunting that gives most Irish fiction its metaphysical unease. They do not escape, though, essentially the same challenges: only in their case the pressure comes from within, generally as a conflict between the direction of their own vitality and the assumptions of the way they have been brought up. Sally Tyndal, in *Godded and Codded*, is as much an explorer after the true nature of herself as McGahern's Elizabeth Reegan: only where Elizabeth, dying of cancer in her mid-forties, searches for meaning through reflection, Sally, in her twenties and hungry for experience, searches through action. To call Julia O'Faolain a satirist, as I did a few lines back, is to do her work only partial justice: it suggests the incisiveness of her talent — for wit and verbal devastation she has few equals among her contemporaries —

* Approaches have been made via the thriller by Shaun Herron in *Through the Dark and Hairy Wood* (1973) and *The Whore Mother* (1973) (see below pp. 000–00), and in a more conventional form by Terence de Vere White in *The Distance and the Dark* (1973). Ed.

but not the strength nor the subtlety of her concern. There is a power of mind behind her work, as well as an irreverently perceptive eye, that catches the intensity of human drives, the essential seriousness of the effort to live, without swallowing any of the trends in self-deception. She is an acute observer, who is involved at a level of concern deeper than the substance or sum of her observations.

Immediately striking in Julia O'Faolain's first collection of short stories, *We Might See Sights!* (Faber, 1968), is the use of surreal imagery, particularly of expressions: 'the wrinkles in her face moved in the sun like the long-jointed legs of agonizing insects'. Agonizing can have a transitive, as well as an intransitive use. Age, disappointment or lust, like medieval vices, become monsters that take over the flesh: 'multimouthed animalities stirred beneath her skin'. Particularly effective is the way the imagery is orchestrated into associative series: when Aunt Adie forced Gwennie, in 'Melancholy Baby', to abstract her employer's best blouse for her to wear, 'pale hair, pale lace confronted her in the glass, cold as spray and remote as an old snap'; as her covetousness struggled with her guilt,

> In her blurred vision the lace thickened consistency, became a caul of lard on the sloping shoulder of a leg of lamb.
> 'So what?' asked the lump of cold grey meat in the mirror, 'so what?'

This allusive technique can be subtle as well as startling: we are never told, though it becomes clear, that Aunt Adie is exploiting Gwennie for her own emotional ends; there is only the hint, early on in the story, that her affective energies were in suspense, 'like the poised claw of a crane'.

In her first novel, *Godded and Codded* (Faber, 1970) this verbal skill is employed to show the contradictions involved in being young, awake and Irish. The first contradiction is that in Ireland it is the old who seem young: they had enough excitement in the Troubles to give them a perpetual lien on romance, despite the decades of stolid respectability since. The young are up-staged, and yet still bereft of advice, for an unspoken double-standard operates. In England or France Sally's mother would be an easy-going, frivolous woman: in Ireland she is corseted by the harsh standards of her generation, so that 'conversations with her were tricky. You never knew which of her would answer you'. In any real crisis, the older generation were a positive danger: when Sally returns from Paris with a dark secret, and won't tell, 'Her mother looked hurt, excited, loving, ravenous. She too liked — and lacked — a bit of a stir. "Can't I help?" she begged.' Fortunately, no confusion seem to have befogged Julia O'Faolain herself, who not only makes whoopee with her Irish background,

The cabbage-cooked-green of the walls remained Fintan of a lavatory in some London underground station where he had once sat, studying the symptoms of gonorrhoea pinned reproachfully on the door above his knees, and fallen into a mood so reminiscent of the confessional that when he rose to flush the water he inadvertently genuflected. . .

but neatly defuses overbearing mothers and aunts alike, with character-istically shrewd compassion: 'all loosely applied powder, semi-grey hair, and a miscellany of clashing scents suggesting a listless drift into fragrant and flocculent decomposition'. That last passage shows her increased stylistic maturity, which has carried the energy of the surreal imagery over into a less obtrusive, more realist manner. It also focuses on an important sub-theme of *Godded and Codded*, the extreme difficulty with which a woman preserves her identity under social and biological pressures, and avoids simply ending up 'on the dull domestic shore, reduced to animality, at best a housing project for some future cocky male. . . '

Julia O'Faolain, in conjunction with Lauro Martines, has contributed an historical study to the feminist debate, *Not in God's Image* (Temple Smith, 1973, Fontana, 1974). The balance that she brings to such questions is best illustrated by two stories from her second collection, *Man in the Cellar* (Faber, 1974); both of them are outstandingly well written as short stories, and quite definitive as reflections of a con-temporary dilemma. In the title story an English wife actually chains up her Italian husband in the cellar, to teach him what being kept in dependence actually feels like. If this seems extreme, it is made to seem in the story simply the logical result of a legitimate and intelligent anger. Against this can be set 'I Want Us to be in Love', in which a sixteen-year-old girl, perfunctorily seduced by Mark, a French-American radical student, finds herself fêted in Paris by Michel, Mark's aged father, and the even more decrepit Jorge. Mark dismisses them as decadent old *roués*, but she finds them irresistibly alive, 'in their memories and yearning for youth. . . younger than she'. She ends up tearfully begging, ' "Mark, listen, please. I know it sounds. . . but, I'm serious. Mark, I. . .   I want us", she burst out "to be in love." ' The unexpectedness, and yet the rightness of this, is typical of Julia O'Faolain's writing.

A Necessary Provincialism:
Brian Moore, Maurice Leitch,
Florence Mary McDowell
by Tom Paulin

BRIAN MOORE is a skilled and highly professional novelist. His first novel, *The Lonely Passion of Judith Hearne* (1955), has been read as a character study of a frustrated spinster, but is really a semi-satirical analysis of an area of Belfast and its Catholic society. Moore's point of view is narrow and his technique is too schematic — Irish (or Ulster) attitudes to sex, the mother and drink are examined, and the inadequacies of the middle class, the priesthood and finally God are all neatly shown up. At rare moments Moore captures both a sense of place and a character living there:

> The rain began to patter again on the windows, growing heavier, soft persistent Irish rain coming up Belfast Lough, caught in the shadow of Cave Hill. It settled on the city, a night blanket of wetness. Miss Hearne ate her biscuits, cheese and apple, found her spectacles and opened a library book by Mazo de la Roche. She toasted her bare toes at the gas fire and leaned back in the armchair, waiting like a prisoner for the long night hours.

However, Moore's opinions are too near the surface and dictate his characterization and the shape of his story too visibly. His description of the centre of Belfast is just a piece of familiar name-calling:

> The newsvendors calling out the great events of the world in flat, uninterested Ulster voices; the drab façades of the buildings grouped around the Square, proclaiming the virtues of trade, hard dealing and Presbyterian righteousness. The order, the neatness, the floodlit cenotaph, a white respectable phallus planted in sinking Irish bog. The Protestant dearth of gaiety, the Protestant surfeit of order, the dour Ulster burghers walking proudly among these monuments to their mediocrity.

Next to *I am Mary Dunne, The Feast of Lupercal* (1958; reprinted by Panther as *A Moment of Love,* 1965) is Moore's best work. In it he manages to combine a related series of acute insights into the nature of

Ulster society — its attitudes to sex and authority — with the creation of a convincing central character, Diarmuid Devine, a schoolteacher in his middle-thirties, whose obvious decency and sensitivity amount to feckless diffidence and doom him to failure. He is too soft to succeed and ruefully admits that he never has 'much luck with the girls'. When his chance presents herself and he meets Una, the Protestant neice of one of his colleagues, he fails sexually and — much more importantly — fails to salvage her already compromised reputation by sacrificing his own and pretending that he had made her drunk in order to seduce her. Ironically, both are virgins and remain so though fearfully suspecting the other is experienced. When Devine acts to save Una — possibly to win her — he is too late and her enraged uncle beats him savagely, like one of their pupils, in the school playground: 'What if the boys see?' a priest asks, parting them.

Devine's job and public reputation are saved when his headmaster reveals an unexpected shrewdness and apparent sympathy, but privately he has failed. 'This is my private life you are discussing', he shouts at the dean of discipline and headmaster, in a belated understanding of that English value. He is defeated by his fear of what Lawrence, in his *Study of Thomas Hardy*, terms 'the mere judgement of man' — the socio-religious code of the community.

Moore's insights into the sometimes machiavellian workings of his Ulster community are extremely sharp and anyone from Ulster must recognize how brilliantly he captures many of the negative, claustro-phobic aspects of its provincialism. The fear of being seen and judged, the continual sense of being watched, the slavish attitudes to authority, the male attitude to women — a mixture of fear, hatred and desire — the guilt about sex, the passionate and destructive angers — Moore is acutely aware of all these characteristics. Mostly he presents them imaginatively: for example when Una starts to sob in a café, Devine, though he loves her, is divided between his sympathy for her and his fear that the waitress will see them. She does so, barges into their fragile privacy and interferingly and mistakenly sends Una off in a taxi. At the school where he teaches Devine is in constant fear that his pupils will learn about his romance (places of education being the most claustrophobic societies possible). They do find out and they write a coarse rhyme on the subject in the school lavatories which, in this novel, are a microcosm of provincialism. Devine and another master have to scrub the rhyme off while at the same time comically keeping a lookout for the other masters. The plot, a system of devious manipulation which in itself is typical and credible, is reasonably complicated. One of the many strengths of this novel is the way Moore makes the plot work largely through Devine's timidly decent character and not externally and mechanically. The burden of choice and responsibility is placed on Devine's shoulders and we wait anxiously to see if he will win or lose his opportunity.

Devine's botched affair with Una is often moving but Moore uses her too frequently as a mouthpiece for his own opinions. She says her ex-lover is 'just like a lot of Irishmen I know. He pretends to be a wild Celt but he's frightened to do anything his neighbours wouldn't approve of.' Undoubtedly a truth, but there are better ways of presenting it. Again, Una rebukes Devine for his humility: 'Priest-ridden?' he replies. Devine's character is certainly recognizable but Moore is wrong, both socially and artistically, to define it simply as Catholic and then blame the priests. Una's description of Devine as the type of man who is 'all things to all men', who would betray his mother to avoid a row, is shrewd on Moore's part rather than on her's. She ceases here, as too often elsewhere, to retain any independence or autonomy of character. And yet to read this novel is to read with that rare sense of forcefully receiving and actively recognizing certain significant truths about Ulster society and human character. There are some sharply powerful, poetic moments, especially when, knowing that Una 'still, behind it all . . . felt there was something to love in this pathetic figure, holding his hat above his head in farewell', we watch Devine fail. (He has of course already assured her that he's 'not any great catch'.)

> He put his hat back on his head as she reached the Herons' front door. It was not locked and she went in without looking back. He felt his hair wet, under the hat. He waited, as though he expected her to come out again. The rain stopped. It was getting dark. After a while, he went away.

In the scene near the end of the novel where Devine's headmaster becomes unexpectedly accommodating, there is a fascinating but difficult insight into the nature of authority in Ulster. Devine angrily asserts that he is not a schoolboy and has a right to privacy, but instead of sacking him instantly Dr Keogh gently asks him to sit down and rather too neatly solves the public difficulties that have resulted from Devine's personal life. We are told:

> Mr. Devine groped for the chair behind him and sat down once more. He had thrown himself off the cliff; but by some miracle, he was still hanging to a rock on the cliff face. The President was that rock. He had ignored the insults. You could not very well strike an old man who turned the other cheek.

Instead of resigning, Devine allows Dr Keogh to persuade him to remain and so avoid scandal to the school and himself. This is a victory for the community and Moore is pointing to the fact that while it takes some courage to rebel against authority, it takes a true maturity to be indifferent to it and resist its blandishments as well as its severities. Moore is showing how we can allow ourselves to be seduced by the human face that authority sometimes presents for its own ends. This sense of collusion, the glow when the statue winks, the lobby correspondent's delight in his privileged confidentiality, is something which Devine is finally unable to resist. He does not resign and stays to serve for the remainder of his life.

The trouble here is that Moore has ruined his interesting perception because we, too, are delighted to see the principal behave in this way as he humiliates the cruel and devious dean of discipline who has appeared earlier to be more powerful than him and who is an enemy of Devine. We applaud Dr Keogh's exercise of power and his greater deviousness, and so we participate in that fatal collusive glow which is the privilege of service.

The same is true of an episode in *The Luck of Ginger Coffey* (1960) where Coffey rejects an easy, servile job as a personal assistant and elects to decide his own destiny. Unfortunately Moore does not leave it here, because when Coffey later appears in court on a false charge of indecently exposing himself (he had been urinating in the doorway of 'The Royal Family Hotel') the judge, having threatened him with a seven-year sentence, suddenly reveals a humorous sympathy and dismisses the case as a joke. ('Twenty years on the Force . . . And I never saw a judge give a guy a break like you got', comments one of Coffey's captors in best Hollywood manner.)

If Moore is undecided about authority, he is apparently certain that, as Coffey's wife says in their sentimental moment of reconciliation, 'Home is here, we're better off here.' Freedom and exile in Canada are preferable to provincial servitude in Ireland. The effect of such a facile rejection on Moore's art in this novel is unfortunate. *The Luck of Ginger Coffey* is a superficial book about a superficial, Parolles-like character bouncing back from failure.

Moore's other Canadian novel, *The Revolution Script* (1971), is a piece of documentary journalism about the Cross and Laporte kidnappings by the Quebec Liberation Front in 1970. Ironically, as Moore implies, the position of the French Catholics in Quebec is a virtual carbon-copy of that of the Catholics in Ulster. However, Moore's style and treatment are inadequate to his subject: 'The coffin slid on to the support rails of the big Cadillac hearse and was locked into position. The hearse moved off on Pierre Laporte's last automobile ride, the journey to the grave.'

As so often in his work the slick, professional style crudely oversimplifies, reducing itself to a series of short, staccato sentences that have the air of having been rapped out tersely on a typewriter with an eye on the film rights, though as in two of the passages quoted from *Judith Hearne* and *Lupercal,* its spareness is sometimes capable of a poetic clarity. One of Moore's achievements is to resist the traditional temptations of the Irish writer — the urge to con his English and

American readers with winsome rhetoric and purple passages, or to waste his talents, as W. R. Rodgers did his, on adolescent puns and flatulent phrases. But too often Moore never tries to write with any distinction or to be anything other than merely competent. His style finds and fixes itself with his first novel and shows almost no development.

Near the beginning of Moore's *bildungsroman, An Answer from Limbo* (1962), Brendan Tierney tells us that he has

> escaped from the provincial mediocrity of my native land and now live, in exile, in the Rome of our day. Yet my employment in New York is as an editorial slave on a publication so banal in title and content that I cannot bear to reveal its name, and if asked why I do it I must talk of bills . . .

Only a deeper irony against the central character than Moore is prepared to allow can salvage this. It is a statement in line with the presentation of the similarly named Bernard Rice in *Judith Hearne*. He is a mother's boy who boasts of writing a great poem but who will, we know, never write it because he can never leave Ireland and his mother – the two seem always to be inseparable. However, the mother can be useful and Brendan imports his from Belfast as a nanny so that his wife can go out to work and he can apparently commute to Greenwich Village each day in order to finish the novel he has always boasted of writing. Moore handles his unpromising, first-novel subject with more authority than that subject might seem to possess, partly because this was his fourth novel and partly because we never learn what Tierney's novel is about as Moore never shows him labouring alone – not even as a ghostly double – in that not very credible garret in Greenwich Village. The real limbo that the writer exists in – that utterly asocial isolation Derek Mahon expresses in 'The Prisoner' – is never felt in the novel. In order to solve a technical problem that is the inevitable disadvantage of his subject, Moore has sacrificed something vital which he himself obviously knows.

The best moments in the novel are generated when Tierney's mother arrives in New York and reacts to her new surroundings. Until this novel Moore has been saying with Ginger Coffey that exile and freedom are preferable to staying home in Ireland. Judith Hearne's photograph of her aunt and picture of the Sacred Heart which made each successive rented room, each 'new place', seem like home and which, like Devine's two religious pictures, are shown to be false and frustrating idols, now modulate into something more subtle. When Mrs Tierney baptizes her pagan grandchildren in the bathroom of her son's New York apartment and when she puts a crucifix on the wall of the bedroom her daughter-in-law has trendily decorated for her, sympathy is enlisted for those 'mumbo jumbo' attitudes and superstitions which Brendan, his wife and part of Moore's mind have rejected. It is also enlisted for those who hold such beliefs, and Moore achieves a genuinely moving and authentic series of recognizable human statements in the following passages where Mrs Tierney appraises her new environment.

> Books galore and magazines, ashtrays every place and three half-empty bottles of spirits on a side table. But for all the untidiness, all the objects strewn about, the room made her think of a room on a stage: it was not real. There was not one thing in it from their family homes, not one thing which looked as though it had belonged to someone else before them. And yet she remembered sending them some silver as a wedding present; she remembered a silver christening mug she sent for the little boy, and a large Beleek vase Brendan's aunt had sent and surely Jane's family must have given her something, furniture or something? Where was it? Had they hidden it all or sold it? Were people in America ashamed of their past?
>
> *
>
> They were well named, she decided. The darlings. That was her private name for them, what with their darling this and darling that. Look at those back rests would you. Brendan not thirty and her even younger. Back rests, as if they had one foot in the grave! Bohemians my eye; they were as set in their ways – 'Is it drink time yet, darling?' 'Is it time to do the dishes, darling?' – as two old grannies. Bohemians, it's their children, not them, who are the Bohemians. Wild savages those children are, but whose fault is that when Jane treats them as equals.

Otherwise the novel is not a success. Tierney's personality is not sufficiently imaginative, witty or intelligent to capture us or make us believe that with what appears like amazing ease – not the intolerable wrestle with words and meanings that Moore wants us to believe in but cannot show – he can produce a novel which, his publishers say, promises to be both a bestseller and a critical success. When Mrs Tierney dies, partly as an accidental result of his single-minded artistic ruthlessness, there is a lack of conviction. Her son watches her burial and thinks: 'Remember, man, that thou art dust. And remember this. Some day you will write it.' The impression is one of banality and imaginative failure. As a study of solipsism this only grazes the shell.

In *The Emperor of Ice-Cream* (1965), an attempt at a mainly comic novel, either Moore or the hero, Gavin Burke, is given to quoting Yeats, Auden, MacNeice and Stevens, and when Gavin and his fellow ARP wardens welcome the start of the first German bombing raid on Belfast there is a profound application of the Irish truth in Yeats's prophecy: 'And what rough beast, its hour come round at last, / Slouches towards Bethlehem to be born?' In this novel 'The Second Coming' is quoted or referred to several times and the attitude which the poem dramatizes – a horrified revelling in the prospect of imminent violence, a welcoming of it – is given an all-too-recognizable expression: 'Tonight, history had conferred the drama of war on this dull, dead town'. Gavin and Frank watch the first bombs exploding and chant:

'Blow up City Hall.'
'And Queen's University.'
'And Harland and Wolff's.'
'Blow up the Orange Hall.'
'And the cathedral and the dean.'
'Jesus, what a show.'

However, the bombs start to fall closer and Moore then traces Gavin's and Frank's movement away from this typical playing-at-apocalypses to a truer realization of the realities of death and human suffering. In its powerful descriptions of the bombing of Belfast and Gavin's work in the mortuary helping to coffin innumerable mutilated corpses, the novel acquires real strength and authority. Like 'The Second Coming' it becomes prophetic.

Although Moore obviously understands the kind of temperament that can welcome the destruction of a society, or, to take a more recent example, deride a dying man, the difficulty is that he is unable or unwilling to follow his understanding through sufficiently. Frank is Protestant, Gavin is Catholic, yet this in no way impinges on their relationship simply because Moore, unlike Maurice Leitch, chooses to ignore the obvious fact that it would.

Moore's next work, *I am Mary Dunne* (1968), is a remarkable achievement, a lyric novel one of whose strengths is that it doesn't lend itself to the type of discussion which the other novels solicit. Moore is writing out of a single, deeply imagined character and not out of theme, idea, analysis or apparent self-justification. The famous couplet from 'Among School Children' which he prints as epigraph, gently insists both on the novel's passionate femininity and its lyric purity, its complete identification of dance and dancer. One of Moore's ambitions throughout his work has been the creation of female character — character defined in contradistinction to a crudely masculine view of women or 'dirty little sex fantasy' as Mary Dunne would term it. However, until this novel his success had been limited. His recognitions of a woman's equivalent centre of self had been mainly a matter of attributing to his female characters those very sexual fantasies (banal and cinematic) which his male characters so frequently indulge in. In *Limbo* Jane Tierney

dreamed of dark ravishers, young and fierce, who loomed in her thoughts like menacing yet exciting phalli, their silken white shirts disturbed at the openings by crisp black curls of body hair, who wore suits of impossible cut, gold watch bracelets and religious medals on silver chains, who used cheap cologne, whose olive-complected smiles revealed white predators' teeth. Men. With them, in fantasy, she performed unnamable acts and, willing yet afraid, was humiliated, robbed, degraded, defiled. Men who used their mouths as lyres of love, their tongues as navigators of every hidden orifice, their hands as cruel, yet gentle, tamers of flesh. Men who smoked dark cigars, men to whom desire came in improbable places, who performed the act of love with relish on tables, in trains, at high noon and in an open boat at dawn. Men. Not Brendan.

These cinematic fantasies — subtle as something by Bryan Forbes — as well as being direly imagined and expressed represent a short-cut to the creation of female character, a short-cut sanctioned by admirers of Molly Bloom rather than Lawrence's example. In *I am Mary Dunne* fantasy has been reduced to a single, naked-in-a-hotel-room, 'doom dream' which is, Mary recognizes, terrifyingly empty and banal. Her sexuality is given an altogether more convincing expression than Jane Tierney's.

The novel, which is a shimmering monologue occupying one day in her life in New York (here Joyce's influence is useful and controlled), exists in a kind of continuous present which melts her memories of her two previous marriages and life in Canada into her experiences during that day. The immigrant experience has been partly pushed back into the time of the potato famine and this means that it can more subtly shape Moore's convincing, often poetic presentation of a rootless, cosmopolitan world of New York apartments, fast jets and Mexican divorces. Interestingly, the story is structured in an extremely provincial fashion. In one day in New York Mary bumps into several people from her past, a series of accidental, sometimes surrealistic encounters which deepen her sense of panic and neurosis. These sudden, strange meetings are of the essence of any provincial society — Belfast or any village, for example — but they are naturally much less possible somewhere like New York or London. That Moore uses them, and uses them convincingly, shows that having written a series of novels which reject a narrow provincialism in favour of a cosmopolitan freedom he has now won through to a deeper understanding of its values. He has really brought Mrs Tierney to New York. Though Mary rejects Ginger Coffey's chosen land, Montreal, as boring and provincial, there is no simplistic affirmation of the virtues of the next stop, New York. Her cosmopolitan past-present life is symbolized by her father's death of a cerebral haemorrhage in a room in a now-defunct New York hotel. 'Daddy died screwing . . . some woman was in bed with him', she remembers. Her uncertain childhood memory of his military funeral in the Canadian rain is filtered through her subsequent discovery of the sordid nature of his death, so that both her provincial past and her cosmopolitan present have been defaced and made horrible. The harpies are everywhere.

Suddenly feeling a partly factitious, because partly selfish and guilty, anxiety about her mother back home in a place called Butchersville, Mary tries, unlike Brendan Tierney, to phone her:

your phone rang and rang there at letter's end, off that bleak highway eight miles out of town, down the rutted lane leading to your house, the shingles all crooked, the walls needing paint, rang in the kitchen (I see the wall phone near the scribbled grocery reminder notes under the calendar from Wilson Lumber Company), rang and rang and rang and where were you? Ill in bed, ill on the floor? I thought of Dick but (it's so long since I've written to him or spoken to him), I had to get his number from the long-distance operator and Dick's wife, Meg, answered and when I told her I'd rung you and was worried, she said she believed you'd gone to twelve o'clock Mass.

At last the style has broken out, achieving a fresh, tense spontaneity, a vividness absent from the rest of Moore's work. What also emerges for the first time — if we except Mrs Tierney's reactions to New York — is a fruitful dialectic between the opposing values of independence elsewhere and dependence at home. For this reason there is now a strong sense of place which is communicated by the many sharp, clear images that break across this fine novel's contrary sense of placeless desperation.

In *Fergus* (1970) the eponymous novelist-narrator (or Brian Moore) brings his whole family as a series of ghostly hallucinations all the way from Belfast Lough to the coast of the Pacific. The nicotine-stained father of *An Answer from Limbo* and *The Emperor of Ice-Cream* makes a further appearance and the attempt to come to terms with a provincial past in this novel is, unfortunately, a total failure. *Catholics* (1972), however, is a subtle and impressive novella. Its success is partly a result of an increased appreciation of the Irish Catholicism which Moore had earlier too easily rejected. He enlists our sympathy for the Abbot of a small monastery on an island off the coast of Kerry, the last place in a fashionably ecumenical future to celebrate the Latin Mass. There are a few moments in the story which have an almost religious texture, and this despite the fact that neither the Abbot nor Kinsella (a denim-clad radical priest) believes in God. The dialectic between old and new, Ireland and the wide world, succeeds here where it fails in *Fergus*.

*

Maurice Leitch's excellent first novel, *The Liberty Lad* (1963), touches on the theme of leaving home (the idea is surfacing in the mind of his engaging central character, Frank Glass), but the novel ends with the burial of his father, not the disposal of his mother. Leitch has a much firmer and more sympathetic sense of place than Moore and consequently a deeper understanding of his community and the nature of authority in that community. Essentially the two are inseparable, as Derek Mahon shows:

> One part of my mind must learn to know its place —
> The things that happen in the kitchen-houses

And echoing back-streets of this desperate city
Should engage more than my casual interest,
Exact more interest than my casual pity.

('In Belfast')

If one is to 'know one's place' in the local sense then one must also face
the problem of knowing it in the authoritarian-hierarchical sense of the
phrase. Though he is wittily glancing at the idea, Mahon does not
mean that we should finally settle for a submission to an external
authority, only that we should recognize the authority of Belfast's
permanent suffering — an authority which is not external but which
we are a part of and so owe a responsibility to and for. Brian Moore
is confused on this score and finally falls for authority, not locality,
coming to rest like Diarmuid Devine on the hard face of the Cavehill
with his back to the city below him.

The mill village of Kildargan in Co. Antrim where *The Liberty Lad*
is set is at once a recognizable community and a microcosm of Ulster
as it existed in the 1950s and 1960s. The province is represented
naturally as a row of terrace houses by a decaying linen mill faced
with imminent closure and employing a shrunken work-force of
ageing men all with 'a derelict air about them'.

Sam Bradley, a homosexual Unionist M.P., first tells Frank that
the linen mill where Frank's father has worked all his life is going to be
auctioned. Although Bradley has personally nothing to do with the
closure, Frank cannot 'dissociate him from the mill'. The political
analysis is neatly done here and it becomes acute when Frank seeks
Bradley's influence in securing the headmaster's job at the school
where he teaches. 'Canvassing', though ostensibly illegal as Frank
points out, used to be obligatory for all teaching jobs in Ulster.

The interest here is twofold: Frank discovers when Bradley tries to
seduce him how any of the girls he has tried, and failed, to seduce
must have felt. Leitch, like Moore, has great insight into misogyny and
its concomitant attitudes ('I HATE women', says Frank when he fails with
Mona). The other interest, again like Moore in *Lupercal*, is in the nature
of authority in Ulster. Frank's headmaster, like Devine's, reveals a hidden
sympathy and humanity and encourages Frank to apply for his job. In
order to become such an authority-figure Frank must literally 'court'
the influence of another powerful authority, Sam Bradley. Here again
is that curious sense of collusion, that seductive embrace of smiling
master and ambitious slave. Frank is relieved to fail with Bradley and
therefore lose the job, and so does not fall, in any sense, for authority.

In *Poor Lazarus* (1969) Leitch develops his profound understanding
of his country. Near the beginning, Yarr, a Protestant, is sitting with
Quigley, an Irish-Canadian and lapsed Catholic, in the centre of Slaney;
'It was one of those rare miraculous evenings when he felt that the true

sleeping heart of Ireland was not too far away. That if he travelled towards it there was a good chance of finding it — a wooded enclosed haven in the green green centre.'

Quigley's passage to Ireland is not to lead into this unrealistically innocent heart. Briefly, he and Yarr, like Aziz and Fielding, form a deep, quasi-homosexual relationship. The novel is set, physically and spiritually, in a border village in Co. Armagh and Leitch brilliantly uses both the setting and the relationship between these two misogynistic failures (though this doesn't do his sympathetic portrayal justice) to dramatize another sense of collusion which is deeply ingrained in Ulster — witness the excitement in the media when the I.R.A. and U.D.A. have one of their periodic confabulations. Leitch's insight into 'the dark uncivilized reaches' of his country's mind, as Frank Glass puts it, is terrifying. He captures unerringly the alcoholic misogyny and locker-room masculine togetherness, and he treats their attractions and shortcomings sympathetically. In a sudden moment of harmony in a bar-room Yarr loves Quigley, while all around them the other drinkers are singing happily. 'And not one woman in the place to spoil things.'

Returning to his detested, pregnant wife after a drunken night with Quigley during which he almost strangled an unexpectedly passionate village girl ('dirty wee bitch', he shouts impotently), Yarr flings an empty poteen bottle at the torturing 'fat white moon'. This is reminiscent specifically of the chapter in *Women in Love* where Birkin dashes stones against the white reflection of the moon in a pond, and generally of the several moonlight episodes in *The Rainbow* which also symbolize, much more successfully, masculine defeat. Like Yarr, Birkin wants a close relationship with a man which will be their mutual refuge from their failure with women. And in a most terrifying way Leitch relates his understanding of such relationships to the Irish environment. Through having Yarr assist Quigley by showing him, and sometimes staging for him, the sort of local sights and characters (Yarr is himself 'a character') that might make material for his documentary, Leitch is able, in just over two hundred pages, to give us a swift survey of the state of Ireland, North and South, just as the present situation was developing. As with Moore's novels the cinema has exerted a neat, stylizing influence, parcelling reality into a sequence of documentary 'fragments', as Quigley puts it in his own, doomed *cahier*. Yet as with Gavin Burke's initial welcoming of the publicity a German bombing raid would confer upon Belfast, there is a prophetic anticipation of the *esse est percipi* of incident and camera. Leitch's technique is too neat, but it was probably inevitable: instead of writing an old-fashioned, sprawling, three-decker novel, he has condensed his material into a series of significant scenes, just as Moore wrote *I am Mary Dunne* as an imagistic lyric.

Two scenes in *Poor Lazarus* stand out grotesquely and relate to each other. In the first Yarr arranges for Quigley to hear a pathetic, shell-shocked old soldier, Johnny Carbin, sing an Irish rebel song. Like another local character, Eoin Gallery, a passionately indignant, alcoholic Gaelic speaker, Carbin represents an influential area of Irish culture and politics. However, Leitch is too good a novelist to let this indirect comment rest as dramatic statement. In his analysis of Yarr's feelings towards Carbin whom he and the other men in the bar are tormenting, he finely captures a sense of cruelty, disgust, fear and alienation. Yarr is Protestant, Carbin and his other tormentors are Catholic, and Yarr suddenly realizes 'how apart he was from this mob. He didn't belong. He was, in fact, on a par with his victim.' Yarr knows how 'cruelly fast' the saloon bar mob might align themselves against him if the whim takes them. When he succeeds in utterly humiliating Carbin, who inadvertently exposes his penis, there is a demented cry of hatred against everyone, but especially against the 'British cunt' Yarr.

Sexual organs and politics — or, rather, the reality politics seek to express — are central to a horrific and related scene near the end of the novel. In the dead hours of the night Yarr drives Quigley to a main, an illegal cock-fighting match. They are unwelcome there and, significantly, the other men have tried to give Yarr the slip by telling him the wrong time and rendezvous. Again, Yarr has the sensation of not belonging, of being on the fringes of a hostile mob whose cruelty he shares but is still apart from. Here, 'in the most private place in the whole of Ireland' (an ironic variation of the earlier 'green green centre'), Yarr and Quigley watch both the fight and the mob:

> The feathers were stained as if by oil spots, a wing hanging useless. The men started mocking the dying cock. Once it was mounted and lay supine under the spurring, pecking frenzy. Ribald shouts rang out.
> On occasions, its owner went into the ring to retrieve his bird, the rules of the game allowed him this, and he massaged it, and holding it up, put its head in his own mouth. Its blood ran down his chin.

Leitch reaches and embodies a horrible truth here. In this heart of Irish darkness, this most 'private place', men derisively cheer a grotesque parody of a homosexual act, a fight to the death with which they are totally identified as both participants and spectators. The loser, who is also a torturer, masturbates (as Yarr does beside his wife), and finally sucks his own bleeding cock. The distinctions between victims and torturers, participants and spectators, winners and losers, all disappear. They merge into one — the ultimate, onanistic collusion.

Yarr finally goes completely mad on the day he learns, or thinks he learns, that Quigley is merely using him. Significantly, this is the same day that his wife gives birth to a son. When Yarr runs madly through the village men and children point imaginary guns at him (again Leitch embodies his prophetic understanding convincingly), and then Yarr races up a mountain road in his van so that his village, Ballyboe, is spread out innocently below him. A complex response to the positives and negatives of the entire Ulster community is implicit in this subtly familiar, synoptic view. Finally, as he wades into a lough, flapping his arms and calling like a bird:

> Three crows flap up clumsily from a rabbit carcase they've been feeding on by the lough's edge. He hears their cry and shouts in delight. As the water rises up his legs he echoes, 'Yarr. . . Yarr. . . Yarr. . . Yarr.' The brown obliterating depths rush to welcome him. Yarr yarr yarr. . .

Though the story ends ironically with Quigley's shooting-notes and his belated recognition of his and Yarr's dependence upon each other, Yarr's ending has something of the power of great tragedy. His name and his accent are stonily echoed by the cawing crows, their cold, mutually mocking laughter echoing the ribald laughter of the men at the cock-fight and Yarr's mad laughter there. Sounds like 'gurr' or 'yah-boo' are a long tame way from this sound which is the accent of that familiar name-calling which appears elsewhere in the story ('British cunt', 'fuckin' rebel kip', 'Prod', 'Fenian'). The sound is, to quote Frank Glass's comment on his initial reaction to a slum child's sad fantasy, 'the old deadly derision, the curse which we all are born with in this cold cynical northern province'. The accents of this derision represent what is really the final, terrible collusion: the sounds which men make and the sounds of their natural environment merge into one, there is a ghastly communion of men, crows and cocks, a reality where these distinctions have disappeared.

Like John McGahern's work, *Poor Lazarus* conveys a deep, dark sense of evil. This is something which most recent English fiction is incapable of — witness Angus Wilson's feeble attempt, in *Hemlock and After,* to represent a small *schadenfreude* in Piccadilly Circus as a significant example of evil. One has to turn to Patrick White, to Hawthorne and James, to Dostoyevsky, for types of a principle which rational humanism is inadequate to. Leitch's representation of this principle is disturbingly convincing.

*

If *Poor Lazarus* prophetically anatomizes the present and enduring condition of Ireland, Shaun Herron's *The Whore Mother* (1973) attempts more recently to diagnose the current 'troubles'. This taste-less and confused fantasy which, incredibly, received favourable reviews, seeks to apply to Ireland some of the insights which Moore and Leitch more profoundly explore. Following them Herron sees the great truth expressed in these lines from Yeats's 'Meditations in Time of Civil War': 'We had fed the heart on fantasies / The heart's grown brutal from the fare'. However, Herron's politico-sexual thriller is itself a brutalizing and simple-minded fantasy (' "I'm a country", she said, "feel my hills" '; ' "The name they call me," she said, "is Cathleen the Whore-Mother" '). Herron appears to believe he is lambasting the I.R.A. ('urbanized peasants'), but in fact the Provo killer, Powers, not his victim, emerges as the only figure in this story with anything that remotely resembles a 'character'.

*

Florence Mary McDowell's two volumes, *Other Days Around Me* (1966) and *Roses and Rainbows* (1972), which are her memories of growing up in Victorian Ulster and which are told, like O'Casey's autobiographies, in the third person, will probably never achieve the circulation of *The Whore Mother*, partly because they must largely interest Ulster readers and partly because they breathe and testify to an unfashionable wisdom and humanity, the product of an indigenous culture that once flourished and which still, more obscurely, exists. They are set in the same area of Co. Antrim as *The Liberty Lad* – a linen village at the height of the trade – and like Leitch's novel part of their distinction is the way that, in the cadences of their prose, they capture another of the accents of the country, a wry, soft, warm wisdom, a gentle humorousness.

> The master was a hard man. He drove everyone with little mercy. He drove himself with even less. His mainsprings of interest were his interpretation of Christ Crucified and his genuine love of music. To Mary he often showed kindness. Yet he found no difficulty in reconciling the love of God with soaking a bucketful of canes in cold water on Friday, ready for the slaughter of the innocents, dirty or stupid or both, on the coming Monday.
>
> Swish! Swish! Swish! went the wet canes on trembling bony fingers thrust out with pale-faced bravado. The water droplets flew in the sunshine in iridescent replicas of the promise of God's eternal love.
>
> *(Roses and Rainbows)*

As well as conveying a softer sound than 'yarr', this passage is one example of Florence McDowell's clear sense of life. Like Hardy she is rescuing and preserving the life of the folk, and like him she has a simultaneous responsiveness to beautiful perfections and human sufferings. This is true, for example, of her superb descriptions of Mary and her sister lying snug in their linen sheets and imagining a marvellous, village 'swarry' while hearing, in the dark early morning, the sound of the mill workers – some bare-foot children – tramping doggedly to work. It is also true of this passage which has something of the deftness and sense of human associations that there is in the best of Hardy's work:

the scutchers had a kind of pouce silicosis, which resulted in the racking coughs Mary heard. But she herself was too fascinated by the diaphanous rainbow arching the water-wheel in the sunshine to think about toil and disease.

The gracious pale beauty of the flax in bloom, waving in powder-blue and green swells, held no signification of the back-breaking labour that would be required before the splendour of a damask tablecloth would cover Victorian mahogany.

(Other Days Around Me)

Florence McDowell's two fine books, like Sam Hanna Bell's masterpiece, *December Bride,* are reminders that, as Hardy says, a 'certain provincialism of feeling' is invaluable in a writer, and it is their success in creating that feeling, that sense of place, which must be one of the standards by which we judge all these works.

Index